W9-API-327

201 crochet

motifs, blocks, projects, and ideas

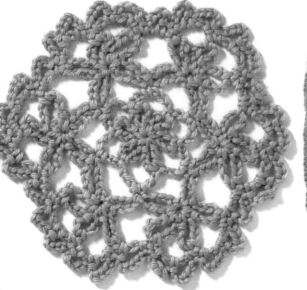

Melody Griffiths

CICO BOOKS
LONDON NEW YORK

First published in 2007 by CICO Books
an imprint of Ryland Peters & Small
519 Broadway, 5th Floor,
New York, NY 10012
www.cicobooks.com

10 9 8 7

Text copyright © Melody Griffiths 2007
Design, photography, and illustration
copyright © CICO Books 2007

The author's moral rights have been
asserted. All rights reserved. No part of
this publication may be reproduced,
stored in a retrieval system, or
transmitted in any form or by any
means, electronic, mechanical,
photocopying, or otherwise, without
the prior permission of the publisher.

A CIP catalog record for this book is
available from the Library of Congress.

ISBN: 978-1-904991-65-6

Printed in China

Editors: Kate Haxell, Katie Hardwicke
Design: Ian Midson
Design concept: Claire Legemah
Charts: Anthony Duke
Photography: Geoff Dann

For digital editions, visit
www.cicobooks.com/apps.php

contents

*Motifs marked with * have a chart.*

introduction

This book is an eclectic, hopefully exciting, mix of motifs inspired by some of my favorite things: fabric patchwork, ethnic carpets, vintage fabrics, and naive art. Although all designers owe a debt to the craftspeople who went before, as far as possible these motifs are original.

Sometimes I've taken a traditional motif and given it a little twist, so yes, there is a granny square, but it has a four-petal flower in the center. There are incredibly simple, beginner's-style motifs—just little shapes in the most obvious stitches—but these motifs are designed to unlock your creativity when you play with colors and assemble them to make pictures or patchwork designs. There are designs based on stitch patterns, but worked in the round or turned into a square, such as the shell-edged flower medallion (page 39) or the chevron pattern waves motif (page 74). There are motifs that play with different techniques —they are not difficult, but maybe have an unusual construction, such as the Celtic knot and bow designs (pages 63, 84). There are animal picture designs, all in easy-to-work stitches but again, totally original, along with flowers, too—it seemed that every time I played around with yarn and a hook, another flower grew to create a whole garden of crocheted blooms (pages 6–23). Oh, and

there's an alphabet (pages 42–53)
—crochet letters for you to
appliqué on fabric, or on
plain crochet squares to
add initials or names to
garments, or to make
banners or blankets.

Finally, there's a collection of 50 projects and
ideas for fun items to make with the motifs (see
pages 106–135). Some are quick to make, whereas
others are slower but satisfying. You can work them as
shown, or use the ideas as a springboard for developing and creating your
own designs. I've also included a quick reminder of all the techniques
you'll need to work basic crochet stitches and join the motifs—see the
instructions on pages 136–143.

Whatever your level of abililty, I hope these motifs, blocks, projects, and
ideas fire your imagination. And most of all, I hope you enjoy sharing this
exploration with me.

Melody

flowers

The flower designs vary from tiny motifs to composite blocks. Some are stylized, others use popcorns and raised stitches to create a naturalistic effect, enhanced by well-chosen colors.

millefiore

This versatile little six-petal flower motif is shown joined in a hexagon shape, but can also be arranged in rows or in a wave pattern. Each petal has a center stitch that's longer than the chain around it, giving a natural, slightly curved effect; the longer stitch is also the secret of the almost invisible join. You can easily adapt the motif by working more or less petals before fastening off to make individual flowers to use as a decoration or a corsage.

instructions

Center flower Wind yarn around finger to form a ring.

1st round [3ch, 1tr, 3ch, ss in ring] 6 times.

Fasten off and darn in ends.

1st ring of flowers Work 1st flower in same way as center flower until five petals have been completed.

Joining petal 3ch, keeping yarn to left of hook, slip hook through top of tr on underside of one center petal, then work tr in ring but pulling through 2 loops and strand of center petal to complete the st, 3ch, ss in ring. Fasten off and darn in ends.

Work 2nd flower until 4 petals have been completed, then join 5th petal into next petal of the center flower and 6th petal in the adjacent petal of the 1st flower. Join 3rd, 4th, and 5th flowers in the same way. Work 6th flower until 3 petals have been completed, join 4th petal in adjacent petal of first flower, 5th in last petal of center flower and 6th in adjacent petal of 5th flower. Fasten off and darn in ends.

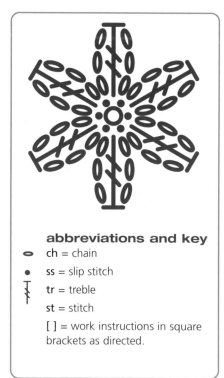

2nd ring of flowers Placing motifs so that 5th and 6th petals join in adjacent flowers, join 6 motifs around 1st ring of flowers.

abbreviations and key

- ch = chain
- ss = slip stitch
- tr = treble
- st = stitch
- [ ] = work instructions in square brackets as directed.

violet

This tiny three-round motif can be made very quickly. Scatter them on a scarf or join with triangles for a patterned fabric.

instructions

Colors: Yellow (A), lilac (B), and purple (C).

Using A, wind yarn around finger to form a ring.

1st round 1ch, 6sc in ring, ss in first sc. 6 sts. Fasten off.

Join B in same place as ss at end of last round.

2nd round 1ch, [1sc, 1hdc, 1sc] in same place as join, ss in next sc, [1sc, 1hdc, 1sc all in next sc, ss in foll sc] twice, ss in first sc. Fasten off.

Join C in same place as ss at end of last round.

3rd round 1ch, [1sc, 1hdc] in first sc, [1hdc, 2dc] in first hdc, [1hdc, 1sc] in next sc, ss in next ss, [1sc, 1hdc] in next sc, [2dc, 1hdc] in next hdc, [1hdc, 1sc in foll sc, ss in next ss, [1sc, 1hdc] in next sc, 3dc in next hdc, [1hdc, 1sc] in foll sc, ss in next ss, ss in first sc.

Fasten off.

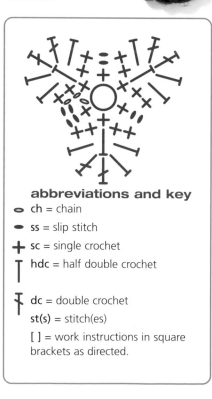

abbreviations and key

- ch = chain
- ss = slip stitch
- sc = single crochet
- hdc = half double crochet
- dc = double crochet
- st(s) = stitch(es)
- [ ] = work instructions in square brackets as directed.

irish rose

The stitch diagram for this raised flower on a picot background is expanded to show the chain loops that are hidden when the petals are worked. You could work it all in one shade in fine yarn for an Irish lace effect. Follow the first four, six, or eight rounds for flower motifs to use as a trim.

instructions

Colors: Lime green (A), pale pink (B), pink (C), and magenta (D).

Using A, make 7ch, ss in first ch to form a ring.

1st round 1ch, 16sc in ring, ss in first sc. 16 sts.

2nd round 1ch, 1sc in first sc, [* 1sc in next sc, 4ch, ss in 4th ch *, 1sc in foll sc] 7 times, rep from * to *, ss in first sc.

3rd round 1ch, taking hook behind, work 1sc around stem of first sc, [3ch. miss 1sc, 1sc around stem of next sc] 7 times, 3ch, ss in first sc. Fasten off.

Join B in next 3ch sp.

4th round 1ch, [1sc, 5hdc, 1sc] in each 3ch sp, ss in first sc.

5th round 1ch, taking hook behind, work 1sc around stem of first sc of 3rd round, [4ch, 1sc around stem of next sc of 3rd round] 7 times, 4ch, ss in first sc. Fasten off.

Join C in next 4ch sp.

6th round 1ch, [1sc, 1hdc, 4dc, 1hdc, 1sc] in each 4ch sp, ss in first sc.

7th round 1ch, taking hook behind, work 1sc around stem of first sc of 5th round, [6ch, 1sc around stem of next sc of 5th round] 7 times, 6ch, ss in first sc. Fasten off.

Join D in next 6ch sp.

8th round 1ch, [1sc, 1hdc, 7dc, 1hdc, 1sc] in each 6ch sp, ss in first sc. Fasten off.

Join A with an sc around stem of first sc of 7th round.

9th round [* 7ch, ss in 4th ch, 6ch, ss in 4th ch, 3ch *, 1sc around stem of next sc of 7th round] 7 times, rep from * to *, ss in first sc.

10th round [* 8ch, ss in 4th ch, 4ch, 1sc between picots in next sp, 8ch, ss in 4th ch, 4ch *, ss in next sc] 7 times, rep from * to *, ss in first ch.

Fasten off.

abbreviations and key

- ○ **ch** = chain
- + **sc** = single crochet
- T **hdc** = half double crochet
- **rep** = repeat
- ● **ss** = slip stitch
- **st(s)** = stitch(es)
- ⊤ **dc** = double crochet
- [ ] – work instructions in square brackets as directed.

sunwheel

This charming motif is so quick and easy to work. Despite the size, there are just two rounds and you're done. After you've worked one motif, you'll see how you could adapt the number of spokes in the wheel by working more or less pairs of double crochet stitches on the first round. To make the motif more flowery, change to a petal color for the second round.

instructions

Make 8ch, ss in first ch to form a ring.

1st round 1ch, 1sc in ring, 2ch, 23dc in ring, ss in 2nd ch.

2nd round 8ch, 1sc in 2nd ch from hook, 1dc in each of next 4ch, miss 1dc of 1st round, 1dc in next dc, [5ch, 1sc in 2nd ch from hook, 1dc in each of next 3ch, 1dc in top of dc, miss 1dc of 1st round, 1dc in next dc] 11 times omitting last dc, ss in 3rd ch.

Fasten off.

primrose posy

Three little primroses are worked separately, then linked together, surrounded by leaves and finished with a chain edging. If you want to make separate flowers to trim a hat or a jacket, fasten off after the third round.

instructions

Colors: Light green (A), dark yellow (B), pale yellow (C), and mid-green (D).

First flower Using A, wind yarn around finger to form a ring.

1st round 1ch, 5sc in ring, ss in first sc. Fasten off.

Join B in a sc.

2nd round 1ch, 2sc in same sc as join, 2ch, [2sc in next sc, 2ch] 4 times, ss in first sc. Fasten off.

Join C in a 2ch sp.

3rd round [3ch, 1dc, 1tr] in same 2ch sp as join, * miss 1sc, 1dc in next sc, [1tr, 1dc, 2ch, ss, 2ch, 1dc, 1tr] in next 2ch sp, rep from * 3 more times, miss 1sc, 1dc in next sc, [1tr, 1dc, 2ch] in first 2ch sp, ss in first ch.

4th round Taking hook behind, 1ch, 1sc around same ch as join, 4ch, [1sc around next ss, 4ch] 4 times, ss in first sc. Fasten off.

Make 2 more primroses.

Join flowers Using A, wind yarn around finger to form a ring.

abbreviations and key

- **ch** = chain
- **sc** = single crochet
- **ss** = slip st
- **dc** = double crochet
- [ ] = work instructions in square brackets as directed.

forget-me-not square

The center block is made from tiny flowers in different shades of blue, joined so closely that the petals overlap; the yellow bullion knots are embroidered afterward to give the impression of a carpet of blooms. The leafy shapes around the edge are just simple clusters with convenient spaces between for joining the squares. You could also use separate flowers as scattered decoration: Join them in a length for a trimming or join as many flowers as you want to make a larger square or oblong for a coverlet or cushion cover.

Center. 1st round 1ch, *1sc in ring, 1ch, 1sc in a 4ch sp of 4th round of first flower, 1ch, 1sc in ring, 1ch, 1sc in next 4ch sp of same flower, 1ch, 1sc in ring, 6ch, rep from * to join 2nd and 3rd flowers omitting last 6ch and ending 3ch, 1dc in first sc.

Leaves. 2nd round 1ch, 1sc in dc sp, 1ch, *[1sc, 1dc, 2tr, 1ch, 2tr, 1dc, 1sc] in each of 3 free 4ch sps of next flower, 1ch, 1sc in next 6ch sp, 1ch, rep from * two more times omitting last sc and ch, ss in first sc. Fasten off.

Join D in 1ch sp of a center leaf.

Edging. 3rd round 1ch, 1sc in same sp as join, [9ch, 1sc in 1ch sp at center of next leaf] 8 times, 9ch, ss in first sc.

Fasten off.

abbreviations

ch = chain

sc = single crochet

tr = treble

rep = repeat

sp(s) = space(s)

ss = slip stitch

dc = double crochet

[ ] = work instructions in square brackets as directed.

instructions

Colors: Four shades of blue (A), green (B), and yellow (C).

Center. 1st flower Using A, wind yarn around finger to form a ring.

1st round [3ch, 1dc in ring, 1ch, 1dc in ring, 3ch, ss in ring] 4 times.

Fasten off.

2nd flower Using second shade of A, work as 1st flower until two petals have been completed.

3rd petal 3ch, 1dc in ring, lengthen loop slightly, remove hook, insert hook from the front into a 1ch sp of 1st flower, catch loop and pull through 1st flower, then complete petal. Join 4th petal to next petal of 1st flower.

Varying shades of A, make and join flowers to 2 or 3 petals as necessary to make a square of 9 flowers.

Darn in ends.

Border Join B in a 1ch sp of a corner petal.

1st round 1ch, 1sc in same place as join, 3ch, 1sc in same place as sc, * [4ch, 1sc in sp between joined petals] twice, 4ch **, [1sc, 3ch, 1sc] in corner sp, rep from * two more times, then rep from * to **, ss in first sc.

2nd round Ss in first 3ch sp, [3ch, 2dctog, 3ch, 3dctog] in first 3ch sp, * [3ch, 3dctog in next 4ch sp] 3 times, 3ch **, [3dctog, 3ch, 3dctog] in 3ch sp, rep from * two more times, then rep from * to **, ss in 2dctog.

Fasten off.

Using C, embroider a bullion knot in the center of each flower.

abbreviations

ch = chain

sc = single crochet

rep = repeat

sp = space

ss = slip stitch

dc = double crochet

2dctog = leaving last loop of each stitch on hook, work 2dc, yo and pull through 3 loops on hook

3dctog = leaving last loop of each stitch on hook, work 3dc, yo and pull through 4 loops on hook

yo = yarn over hook

[ ] = work instructions in square brackets as directed.

3rd round, 3ch] 11 times, ss in first sc. Fasten off. Join C in a 3ch sp.

6th round 1ch, [1sc, 1dc, 4ch, ss in 4th ch from hook, 1dc, 1sc] in each 3ch sp, join in first sc in same way as 4th round.

7th round Taking hook behind 6th round, 1sc around the stem of first sc of 5th round, 4ch, [1sc around stem of next sc of 5th round, 4ch] 11 times, ss in first sc. Fasten off. Join D in a 4ch sp.

8th round 1ch, [1sc, 2dc, 4ch, ss in first ch, 2dc, 1sc] in each 4ch sp, ss in first sc. Fasten off. Taking hook behind, join E around the stem of an sc of 7th round.

9th round 1sc around stem of same sc as join, 6ch, [1tr around stem of next sc of 7th round, 3ch] 11 times, ss in 3rd ch.

10th round 1ch, 1sc in same place as ss, 4ch, [1dc in next 3ch sp, 2ch, 1dc in next tr, 2ch] 11 times, 1dc in last 3ch sp, 2ch, ss in 2nd ch.

Fasten off.

victorian aster

This magnificent flower would make a lovely corsage. Working into the back of the second-round stitches turns a simple start into a deep center and shading the layers of petals embellished with picots adds to the effect. The ninth and tenth rounds add a mesh edging to the flower so you can join motifs or integrate it with other blocks for an unusual afghan.

instructions

Colors: Yellow (A), damson (B), dark pink (C), light pink (D), and black (E).

Using A, wind yarn around finger to form a ring.

1st round 1ch, 12sc in ring, ss in first sc.

2nd round 1sc in same place as ss, 2ch, [1dc in next sc] 11 times, ss in 2nd ch. Fasten off. Taking hook behind, join B in back loop of 2nd ch.

3rd round 1ch, 1sc in same place as join, [2ch, 1sc in back loop of next dc] 11 times, 2ch, ss in first sc.

4th round Ss in first 2ch sp, 1ch, 1sc in same sp, 3ch, 1sc in same sp, [1sc in next sp, 3ch, 1sc in same sp] 11 times, remove hook, insert hook from back in first sc, catch loop and pull through.

5th round Taking hook behind 4th round, 1sc around the stem of first sc of 3rd round, 3ch, [1sc around stem of next sc of

abbreviations and key

○ ch = chain
+ sc = single crochet
tr = treble
sp = space

● ss = slip stitch
dc = double crochet
[ ] = work instructions in square brackets as directed.

granny flower square

This version of a granny square has raised petals for the center flower surrounded by leafy clusters. The last round picks up the traditional rhythm of stitches and spaces so you can easily mix it with other squares.

instructions

Colors: Yellow (A), pink (B), bright green (C), and bronze green (D).

Using A, wind yarn around finger to form a ring.

1st round 1ch, 1sc in ring, [3ch, 3sc in ring] 3 times, 3ch, 2sc in ring, ss in first sc. Fasten off. Join B in a 3ch sp.

2nd round 1ch, [1sc, 1hdc, 3dc, 1hdc, 1sc] in each 3ch sp, ss in first sc. Fasten off. Join C between 2sc.

3rd round 1ch, 1sc in same place as join, [5ch, 1sc between next 2sc] 3 times, 5ch, ss in first sc.

4th round Ss in first 5ch sp, 1ch, [1sc, 2ch, 2dctog, 3ch, 3dctog, 2ch, 3dctog] in same 5ch sp, * [2ch, 3dctog] twice in next 5ch sp, 3ch, [3dctog, 2ch, 3dctog] in same 5ch sp, rep from * two more times, 2ch, 3dctog in first 5ch sp, 2ch, ss in 2dctog. Fasten off. Join D in a 3ch sp.

5th round 1ch, 1sc in same 3ch sp as join, 5ch, 2dc in same 3ch sp as join, * [1ch, 2dc in next 2ch sp] 3 times, 1ch, [2dc, 3ch, 2dc] in next 3ch sp, rep from * two more times, [1ch, 2dc in next 2ch sp] 3 times, 1ch, 1dc in first 3ch sp, ss in 2nd ch. Fasten off.

abbreviations

ch = chain

sc = single crochet

hdc = half double crochet

rep = repeat

sp = space

ss = slip st

st = stitch

dc – double crochet

2dctog = leaving last loop of each st on hook, work 2dc, yo and pull through 3 loops on hook

3dctog = leaving last loop of each st on hook, work 3dc, yo and pull through 4 loops on hoo

yo = yarn over hook

[ ] = work instructions in square brackets as directed.

flower and leaves hexagon

This simple two-round hexagon motif with a stylized center flower surrounded by pairs of leaf shapes, is worked entirely with just chain and three double crochet clusters.

instructions

Colors: Lilac (A) and green (B).

Using A, wind yarn around finger to form a ring.

1st round 3ch, 2dctog in ring, 2ch, [3dctog in ring, 2ch] 5 times, ss in 2dctog. Fasten off. Join B in a 2ch sp.

2nd round [3ch, 2dctog, 2ch, 3dctog] in same 2ch sp as join, 4ch, * [3dctog, 2ch, 3dctog] in next 2ch sp, 4ch, rep from * 4 more times, ss in 2dctog.

Fasten off.

abbreviations and key

○ ch = chain

rep = repeat

sp = space

● ss = slip stitch

⊤ dc = double crochet

2dctog = leaving last loop of each stitch on hook work 2dc, yarn over hook and pull through 3 loops on hook

3dctog = leaving last loop of each stitch on hook work 3dc, yarn over hook and pull through 4 loops on hook

[ ] = work instructions in square brackets as directed.

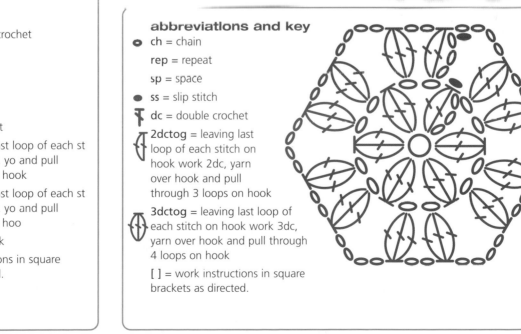

daffodil

The trumpet of this daffodil is a raised tube of firm single crochet, while the petals are worked by changing colors with clusters on the last round to shape them. The flower makes a versatile six-sided shape that could be repeated or combined with other hexagons to make a stunning host of daffodils coverlet.

instructions

Colors: Yellow (A), orange (B), and green (C). Remember when changing colors, pull last loop of last st of each color area with the next color.

1st round Using A, [make 4ch, ss in 3rd ch from hook] 3 times, ss in first ch to form a ring.

2nd round Hold picots toward center, 1ch, [2sc between picots] 3 times, leave A yarn, using B, ss in first sc.

Continue in B.

3rd round 1ch, 2sc in each sc, ss in first sc. 12 sts.

4th and 5th rounds 1ch, 1sc in each sc, ss in first sc.

6th round 1ch, 1sc in first sc, 2ch, ss in 2nd ch from hook, [1sc in next sc, 2ch, ss in 2nd ch from hook] 11 times, ss in first sc. Fasten off.

Return to A yarn.

7th round 1ch, inserting hook between sts of 3rd round each time, work 1sc between each st of 3rd round, ss in first sc. 12 sts.

8th round 1ch, 1sc in first sc, 2ch, 1dc in same place as sc, 2dc in next sc, 3ch, [2dc in each of next 2sc, 3ch] 5 times, ss in 2nd ch.

9th round 1ch, 1sc in same place as ss, 2ch, 1dc in same place as sc, 1dc in each of next 2dc, 2dc in foll dc, * change to C and work over A, [1dc, 2ch, 1dc] in 3ch sp, change to A and work over C, 2dc in next dc, 1dc in each of foll 2dc, 2dc in next dc, rep from * 4 more times, change to C and work over A, [1dc, 2ch, 1dc] in last 3ch sp, change to A, ss in 2nd ch.

10th round Using A and working over C, 1sc in same place as ss, 2ch, 5dctog, *

change to C and work over A, 1ch, 2dc in next dc, [2dc, 2ch, 2dc] in 2ch sp, 2dc in next dc **, change to A and work over C, 6dctog, rep from * 4 more times, then work from * to **, ss in ch at top of first cluster.

Fasten off.

abbreviations

ch = chain

sc = single crochet

foll = following

sp = space

ss = slip stitch

st = stitch

dc = double crochet

5dctog = leaving last loop of each st on hook, work 5dc, yo and pull through 6 loops on hook

6dctog = leaving last loop of each st on hook, work 6dc, yo and pull through 7 loops on hook

yo = yarn over hook

[ ] = work instructions in square brackets as directed.

buttercup

This simple two-round flower is really quick to make. Use it as a trimming or see the ideas section for how to combine four motifs to make a square.

instructions

Colors: Green (A) and yellow (B).

Using A, make 8ch, ss in first ch to form a ring.

1st round 1ch, 15sc in ring, ss in first sc. Fasten off.

Join B in same place as ss.

2nd round 3ch, 3dc in same place as ss, ss in each of next 2sc, [7dc in next sc, ss in each of foll 2sc] 4 times, 3dc in same place as 3dc, ss in 3rd ch.

Fasten off.

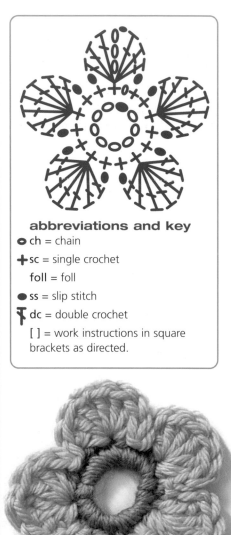

abbreviations and key

o **ch** = chain

+ **sc** = single crochet

foll = foll

● **ss** = slip stitch

Ŧ **dc** = double crochet

[ ] = work instructions in square brackets as directed.

little flower

This tiny two-round motif has six points so it can be joined in a line to make a trimming, joined hexagon-style to make a fabric, or individual motifs can be joined along an edge to make a border.

instructions

Wind yarn around finger to form a ring.

1st round 1ch, [1sc in ring, 4ch] 6 times, ss in first sc.

2nd round Ss in first 4ch sp, 1ch, [1sc, 1hdc, 2ch, 1hdc, 1sc] in each 4ch sp, ss in first sc.

Fasten off.

narcissus

Cramming the stitches together in the first round and working around the stem of the stitches for the second round gives a raised center without working as many rounds as for the daffodil motif (opposite). This motif can be used as a trim or an appliqué. If you want to join narcissus flowers to make a fabric, turn to the millefiore flower motif (page 6) for a way of joining the petals invisibly.

instructions

Colors: Orange (A), yellow (B), and warm white (C).

Using A, wind yarn around finger to form a ring.

1st round 1ch, 18sc in ring, leaving an end, cut yarn, thread it under top loops of first sc and down through last sc, fasten off.

Taking hook to back, join B around the stem of an sc.

2nd round 1ch, 1dc around stem of same sc as join, [1dc around stem of next sc] 17 times, leaving an end about 3ft long, fasten off in same way as first round and continue with B.

3rd round 1ch, ss around stem of first dc, [3ch, miss 2dc, ss around stem of next dc] 5 times, 3ch, ss in first ss. Fasten off. Join C in a 3ch sp.

4th round 1ch, [1sc, 4ch, 1tr, 3dtr, 1tr, 4ch, 1sc] in each 3ch sp, ss in first sc. Fasten off.

abbreviations and key

- **ch** = chain
- **sc** = single crochet
- **tr** = treble
- **sp** = space
- **ss** = slip stitch
- **dc** = double crochet
- **dtr** = double treble
- **[ ]** = work instructions in square brackets as directed.

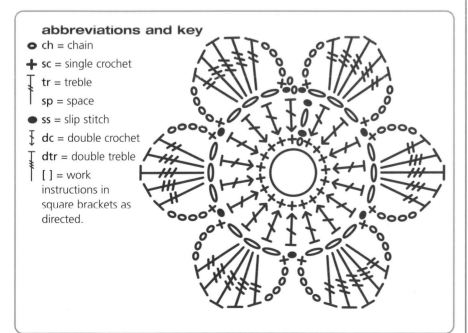

abbreviations and key

- **ch** = chain
- **sc** = single crochet
- **hdc** = half double crochet
- **ss** = slip stitch
- **[ ]** = work instructions in square brackets as directed.

sunburst flower

This large hexagonal motif looks complex, but the elements are very simple. There's a quick-to-work double crochet center surrounded by a ring of double crochet clusters, then radiating petals of double crochet fabric alternating with chain mesh. Worked in yellow, it looks like rays of sunshine but you could change colors within the motif for a more flowery effect.

instructions

Wind yarn around finger to form a ring.

1st round 1ch, 1sc in ring, 2ch, 11dc in ring, ss in 2nd ch.

2nd round 1sc in same place as ss, 3ch, [2dc in next dc, 1ch] 11 times, 1dc in same place as sc, ss in 2nd ch.

3rd round Ss in first 1ch sp, 1sc in same sp, [5ch, 1sc in next 1ch sp] 11 times, 2ch, 1dc in first sc.

4th round 3ch, 2dctog in dc sp, [5ch, 3dctog in next 5ch sp] 11 times, 2ch, 1dc in 2dctog.

5th round 1sc in dc sp, 2ch, 2dc in dc sp, 3dc in next 5ch sp, [5ch, 3dc in each of next two 5ch sps] 5 times, 5ch, ss in 3rd ch.

6th round 1sc in same place as ss, 2ch, 1dc in same place as ss,

abbreviations and key

- **ch** = chain
- **sc** = single crochet
- **foll** = following
- **rep** = repeat
- **ss** = slip stitch
- **st** = stitch
- **dc** = double crochet
- **2dctog** = leaving last loop of each st on hook, work 2dc, yo and pull through 3 loops on hook
- **3dctog** = leaving last loop of each st on hook, work 3dc, yo and pull through 4 loops on hook
- **yo** = yarn over hook
- **[ ]** = work instructions in square brackets as directed.

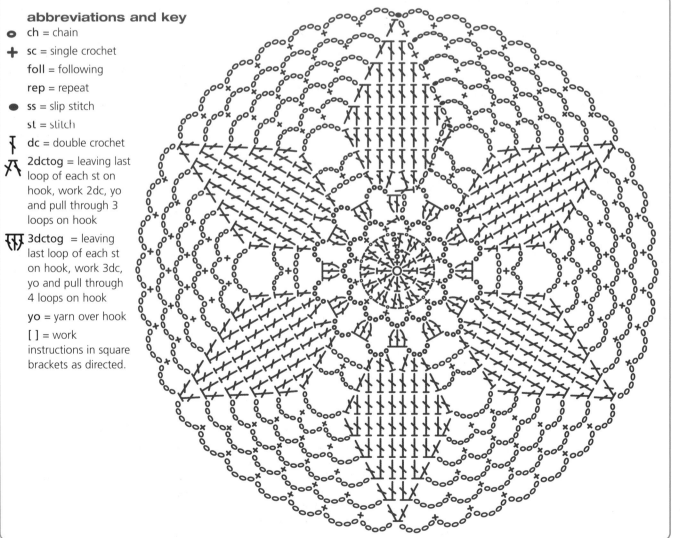

1dc in each of next 4dc, 2dc in foll dc, [4ch, 1sc in 5ch sp, 4ch, 2dc in next dc, 1dc in each of foll 4dc, 2dc in next dc] 5 times, 4ch, 1sc in 5ch sp, 4ch, ss in 2nd ch.

7th round 1sc in same place as ss, 2ch, 1dc in each of next 7dc, [1dc in next 4ch sp, 8ch, 1dc in foll 4ch sp, 1dc in each of next 8dc] 5 times, 1dc in next 4ch sp, 8ch, 1dc in last 4ch sp, ss in 2nd ch.

8th round 1sc in last dc of 7th round, 1ch, 1dc in 2nd ch, * 1dc in each of next 6dc, 2dctog, [5ch, 1sc in next 8ch sp] twice, 5ch, 2dctog, rep from * 5 more times omitting last 2dctog, ss in first dc.

9th round 1sc in same place as ss, 1ch, 1dc in each of next 5dc, 2dctog, * [5ch, 1sc in next 5ch sp] 3 times, 5ch **, 2dctog, 1dc in each of next 4dc, 2dctog, rep from * 4 more times, then rep from * to **, ss in first dc.

10th round 1sc in same place as ss, 1ch, 1dc in each of next 3dc, 2dctog, * [5ch, 1sc in next 5ch sp] 4 times, 5ch **, 2dctog, 1dc in each of next 2dc, 2dctog, rep from * 4 more times, then rep from * to **, ss in first dc.

11th round 1sc in same place as ss, 1ch, 1dc in next dc, 2dctog, * [5ch, 1sc in next 5ch sp] 5 times, 5ch **, [2dctog] twice, rep from * 4 more times, then rep from * to **, ss in first dc.

12th round 1sc in same place as ss, 1ch, 1dc in 2dctog, * [5ch, 1sc in next 5ch sp] 6 times, 5ch **, 2dctog, rep from * 4 more times, then rep from * to **, ss in first dc.

Fasten off.

sunflower square

This magnificent square is made up from very simple elements. The textured center is just single crochet and chain loops, then the flower grows quickly as each petal is made by working single crochet into a length of chain. Alternating petals are worked on separate rounds to vary the shades of yellow. The flower is finished into a square with simple double crochet groups and spaces to make it easy to join the motifs.

instructions

Colors: Brown (A), yellow (B), ocher (C), bright green (D), and olive green (E).

Center Using A, wind yarn around finger to form a ring

1st round 1ch, [1sc in ring, 3ch, ss in side of same sc] 6 times, ss in first dc. 6 sts.

2nd round 1ch, 2sc in same place as ss, [2sc in each sc] to end, ss in first sc. 12 sts.

3rd round 1ch, 1sc in same place as ss, 3ch, ss in side of same sc, [1sc in next sc, 3ch, ss in side of same sc] 11 times, ss in first sc.

4th round 1ch, 2sc in same place as ss, [2sc in each sc] to end, ss in first sc. 24 sts.

5th round 1ch, 1sc in same place as ss, 3ch, ss in side of same sc, [1sc in next sc, 3ch, ss in side of same sc] 23 times, ss in first sc. Fasten off.

1st ring of petals Join B in an sc of 5th round, [9ch, working into back loop of chain only, ss in 3rd ch from hook, 1sc in each of next 6ch, ss in same sc of 5th round, 2ch, miss 1sc, ss in next sc of 5th round] 12 times. Fasten off.

2nd ring of petals Join C in an sc of 5th round in front of 2ch between two petals of first ring of petals, work as given for 1st ring of petals, placing each ss into 5th round in front of 2ch sp and working each 2ch behind each B petal.

Edging Join D in sp at tip of a petal in B.

1st round 1ch, 1sc in same place as join, 6ch, * [1sc in next petal, 3ch] 5 times, 1sc in next petal, 6ch, rep from * 2 more times, [1sc in next petal, 3ch] 5 times, ss in first sc.

2nd round Ss in first 6ch sp, 1ch, [1sc, 5ch, 3dc] in same 6ch sp, * [1ch, 3dc in next 3ch sp] 5 times **, [1ch, 3dc, 3ch, 3dc] in next 6ch sp, rep from * two more times, then rep from * to **, 1ch, 2dc in first 6ch sp, ss in 2nd ch. Fasten off.

Join E in corner 3ch sp.

3rd round 1ch, [1sc, 5ch, 3dc] in same sp as join, * 1ch, [3dc in next 1ch sp, 1ch] 6 times **, [3dc, 3ch, 3dc] in next 3ch sp, rep from * two more times, then rep from * to **, 2dc in first 3ch sp, ss in 2nd ch. Fasten off.

abbreviations

ch = chain
dc = double crochet
rep = repeat
sp = space
ss = slip stitch
st(s) = stitch(es)
sc = single crochet
[ ] = work instructions in square brackets as directed.

poppy

The center of this poppy is worked in rounds with ridged stitches and chain picots. The four petals are worked one at a time, so they curl and overlap in a naturalistic way. For a throw, work the background and join medallions in the spaces at the leaf tips.

instructions

Colors: Yellow (A), black (B), red (C), and green (D).

Using A, wind yarn around finger to form a ring.

1st round 1ch, 8sc in ring, remove hook, insert from the back in first sc, catch loop and pull through.

2nd round 1ch, 1sc around the stem of same sc as join, [1sc around the stem of each sc] to end, ss in first sc. Fasten off.

Join B in first sc of 2nd round.

3rd round 1ch, [1sc, 3ch, ss in side of sc, 1sc] in each sc, join in first sc in same way as 1st round.

4th round 1ch, 1sc around the stem of first sc of 2nd round, 3ch, [1sc around the stem of next sc of 2nd round, 3ch] 7 times, ss in first sc.

5th round Ss in first 3ch sp, * [1ch, 1sc, 1ch, 2dc, 2tr] in same 3ch sp, [2tr, 2dc, 1ch, 1sc, 1ch, 1ss] in next 3ch sp, ss in foll 3ch sp, rep from * 3 more times omitting last ss. Fasten off.

Petals With RS facing, join C in first sc of 5th round.

1st row 1ch, 1sc in first sc, 1hdc in 1ch sp, 1dc in each of next 2dc, 2dc in each of next 4tr, 1dc in each of next 2dc, 1hdc in 1ch sp, 1sc in last sc, turn. 16 sts.

2nd row 1sc in first sc, 1hdc in hdc, 1dc in each of next 12dc, 1hdc in hdc, 1sc in last sc, turn.

3rd row Work as given for 2nd row.

Fasten off. Work 3 more petals in the same way.

Background With RS facing and taking hook behind petals, join B at end of a petal in a 1ch sp in B of 5th round.

1st round 1ch, 1sc in same place as join, [1sc in 1ch sp at beg of next petal, 6ch, 1sc in 1ch sp at end of same petal] 4 times omitting last sc, ss in first sc. Fasten off. With RS facing, join D in a 6ch sp.

2nd round 1ch, 1sc in same sp as join, * 6ch, [6sc, 6ch, 6sc] in next 6ch sp, rep from * two more times, 6ch, [6sc, 6ch, 5sc] in first 6ch sp, ss in first sc.

3rd round Ss in first 6ch sp, [1ch, 1sc, 3ch] in same 6ch sp, [1dc, 1ch] 4 times in same 6ch sp, [1dc, 1ch] 5 times in each 6ch sp, ss in 2nd ch.

4th round 1sc in last 1ch sp of 3rd round, * 1ch, [1dc in next 1ch sp, 2ch] 3 times, 1dc in foll 1ch sp, 1ch, 1sc in next 1ch sp, rep from * 7 more times omitting last sc, ss in first sc.

5th round Ss in first 1ch sp, 1ch, 1sc in same sp, * 1ch, 1dc in next 2ch sp, 2ch, [1dc, 2ch, 1dc] in foll 2ch sp, 2ch, 1dc in next 2ch sp, 1ch, 1sc in each of next two 1ch sps, rep from * 7 more times omitting last sc, ss in first sc.

Fasten off.

abbreviations

ch = chain
dc = double crochet
tr = treble
foll = following
hdc = half double crochet
rep = repeat
RS = right side
sp(s) = space(s)
ss = slip st
sc = single crochet
[ ] = work instructions in square brackets as directed.

daisy

Although this is another simple two-round flower, the construction is quite different to the buttercup on page 12. Link the flowers in a line for a daisy-chain trimming, or group them to make a square and combine them in a buttercups and daisies afghan.

instructions

Colors: Yellow (A) and warm white (B).

Using A, wind yarn around finger to form a ring.

1st round 1ch, 12sc in ring, ss in first sc. Fasten off.

Join B in same place as ss.

2nd round 1ch, 1sc in same place as ss, [4ch, 1sc in 2nd ch from hook, 1sc in each of next 2ch, 1sc in next sc of 1st round] 12 times, omitting last sc, ss in first sc. Fasten off.

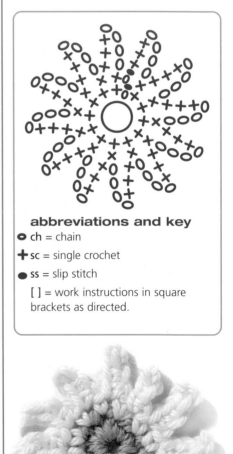

abbreviations and key

● **ch** = chain
✚ **sc** = single crochet
● **ss** = slip stitch
[ ] = work instructions in square brackets as directed.

frost flower

This pretty, stylized six-petal flower is a hexagonal shape just like a snowflake. Although it looks elaborate, it's quick to make because of the openwork rounds.

instructions

Wind yarn around finger to form a ring.

1st round (RS) 1ch, 18sc in ring, ss in first sc.

2nd round 1ch, 1sc in same place as ss, [13ch, ss in 11th ch from hook, 2ch, miss 2sc, 1sc in next sc] 5 times, 13ch, ss in 11th ch from hook, 1dc in first sc, turn.

3rd round * [1sc, 1hdc, 2dc, 3tr, 1dtr, 3tr, 2dc, 1hdc, 1sc] in 10ch sp, ss around base of loop **, 5ch, ss in same ch as ss at base of next loop, rep from * 4 more times, then rep from * to **, 2ch, 1dc in ss at base of first loop, turn.

4th round * 2ch, miss sc, [1dc in next st, 2ch] 13 times, miss sc, 1sc in 5ch sp, rep from * 5 more times omitting last sc, ss in last dc of 3rd round. Fasten off.

With RS facing, join yarn in 3rd sp back from end of 4th round.

5th round 1ch, 1sc in same sp as join, * 1sc in 3rd sp of next petal, [1sc in next sp, 5ch, 1sc in same sp] 8 times, 1sc in next sp, rep from * 5 more times omitting last sc, ss in first sc.

Fasten off.

abbreviations and key

- ○ **ch** = chain;
- ● **ss** = slip stitch
- ✛ **sc** = single crochet
- T **hdc** = half double crochet
- ⊤ **dc** = double crochet
- **tr** = treble
- **dtr** = double treble
- **RS** = right side
- **sp** = space
- **st** = stitch
- **[ ]** = work instructions in square brackets as directed.

twelve-point chain flower

This quick-to-work motif is made up of two design elements—a simple chain loops flower center surrounded by a chain and single crochet pointed edging.

instructions

Wind yarn around finger to form a ring.

1st round (RS) 1ch, [1sc in ring, 16ch] 12 times, ss in first sc. Fasten off.

With RS facing, join yarn in a 16ch sp.

2nd round 1ch, 1sc in same sp as join, 6ch, [1sc in next 16ch sp, 6ch] 11 times, ss in first sc.

3rd round Ss in first 6ch sp, 1ch, [3sc, 5ch, 3sc] in each 6ch sp, ss in first sc. Fasten off.

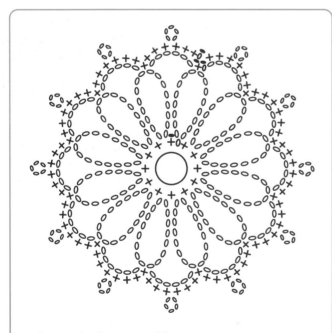

abbreviations and key

- **o ch** = chain
- **+ sc** = single crochet
- **RS** = right side
- **sp** = space
- **● ss** = slip stitch
- **[ ]** = work instructions in square brackets as directed.

raised rosette

Three alternately overlapping rings of petals, gradated in size, surround a simple, contrast-color center. By the time you've worked the three rings of petals you'll see how easy it could be to add more rings of petals to make a cabbage rose. Use a single motif as a corsage or join flowers at the tips of the petals on the last round to make a rosette ring or border.

instructions

Colors: Yellow (A) and red (B).

Using A, wind yarn around finger to form a ring.

1st round 1ch, 1sc in ring, 2ch, 11dc in ring, remove hook, insert from back in 2nd ch, catch loop and pull through.

2nd round 1ch, taking hook behind work 1sc around the 2ch, then around the stem of each dc, ss in first sc. 12 sts. Fasten off.

Join B in same sc as ss.

3rd round 1ch, 1sc in same place as join, 2ch, [miss 1sc, 1sc in next sc, 2ch] 5 times, ss in first sc.

4th round Ss in first 2ch sp, [1sc, 4dc, 1sc] in each 2ch sp, ss in first sc in same way as 1st round.

5th round 1ch, taking hook behind first ring of petals, ss in first missed sc of 2nd round, 1ch, 1sc in same place as ss, 3ch, [1sc in next missed sc of 2nd round, 3ch] 5 times, ss in first sc.

6th round Ss in first 3ch sp, 1ch, [1sc, 2dc, 2tr, 2dc, 1sc] in each 3ch sp, ss in first sc in same way as 1st round.

7th round 3ch, taking hook behind and under arch of next petal made on 5th and 6th rounds, work 1sc around next sc of 3rd round, 5ch] 6 times, ss in first sc.

8th round Ss in first 5ch sp, 1ch, [1sc, 3dc, 3tr, 3dc, 1sc] in each 5ch sp, ss in first sc in same way as 1st round.

Fasten off.

abbreviations

- **ch** = chain
- **dc** = double crochet
- **sc** = single crochet
- **sp** = space
- **ss** = slip stitch
- **tr** = treble
- **[ ]** = work instructions in square brackets as directed.

popcorn flower octagon

This motif starts with a round of double crochet, then a round with spaces for the center, which is surrounded by popcorn petals. The last round has groups of stitches with handy chain spaces for joining motifs.

instructions

Colors: Yellow (A), orange (B), purple (C), and green (D).

Using A, wind yarn around finger to form a ring.

1st round 1ch, 1sc in ring, 2ch, 15dc in ring, ss in 2nd ch. Fasten off.

Join B in same place as ss.

2nd round 1ch, 1sc in same place as join, 3ch, [1dc in next dc, 1ch] 15 times, ss in 2nd ch. Fasten off.

Join C in next 1ch sp.

3rd round 1ch, [1sc, 2ch, 3dc] in same sp, remove hook, insert in 2nd ch, catch loop and pull through to close 1st popcorn, 3ch, [4dcpc in next 1ch sp, 3ch] 15 times, ss in first popcorn. Fasten off. Join D in next 3ch sp.

4th round 1ch, [1sc, 2ch, 3dc] in same 3ch sp, 4dc in next 3ch sp, 3ch, [4dc in each of next two 3ch sps, 3ch] 7 times, ss in 2nd ch. Fasten off.

clematis

Four raised petals are created by working different-height stitches into chain loops that are clustered around a simple single crochet center. The edging looks like leaves, but has picots at the corners so it's easy to join motifs.

instructions

Colors: Yellow (A), pink (B), and green (C).

Using A make 5ch, ss in first ch to form a ring.

1st round 1ch, 8sc in ring, ss in first sc. Fasten off. Join B in first sc.

2nd round 1ch, 1sc in same sc as join, [6ch, 1sc in each of next 2sc] 4 times omitting last sc, ss in first sc.

3rd round Ss in first 6ch sp, 1ch, [1sc, 1dc, 5tr, 1dc, 1sc] in each 6ch sp, ss in first sc.

Fasten off. Join C between first and last sc of 2nd round.

4th round 1ch, 1sc between first and last sc of 2nd round, [8ch, 1sc between next 2sc of 2nd round] 3 times, 8ch, ss in first sc.

5th round Ss in first 8ch sp, taking hook behind petals, 1ch, [6sc, 3ch, 6sc] in each 8ch sp, ss in first sc. Fasten off.

abbreviations and key

- **o** ch = chain
- **+** sc = single crochet
- sp(s) = space(s)
- **⬥** ss = slip stitch
- **⊤** dc = double crochet
- **⬥ 4dcpc** = work 4dc, remove hook, insert hook in first dc, catch loop and pull through to close popcorn
- [ ] = work instructions in square brackets as directed

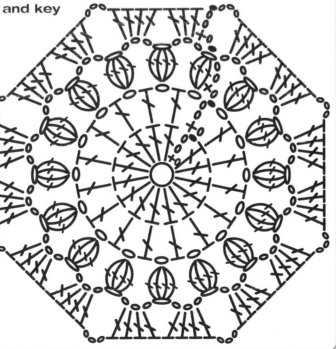

abbreviations

ch = chain

sc = single crochet

tr = treble

sp = space

ss = slip stitch

dc = double crochet

[ ] = work instructions in square brackets as directed.

dahlia hexagon

The raised petals that make this flower look like a pom-pom dahlia are made with popcorn stitches, and the three-chain spaces in the last round give an easy place to join the motifs. If you want to work the motif all in one color, don't fasten off and rejoin the yarn, simply slip stitch to the next space.

instructions

Colors: Green (A), pink (B), and red (C).

Using A, wind yarn around finger to form a ring.

1st round 1ch, 6sc in ring, ss in first sc. 6 sts.

2nd round 1ch, 1sc in same place as ss, [3ch, 1sc in next sc] 5 times, 3ch, ss in first sc. Fasten off.

Join B in next 3ch sp.

3rd round 1ch, 1sc in 3ch sp, 2ch, 4dc in same 3ch sp, remove hook and insert it in 2nd ch, catch loop and pull through to close first popcorn, [4ch, 5dc popcorn in next 3ch sp] 5 times, 4ch, ss in 2nd ch. Fasten off.

Join C in next 4ch sp.

4th round 1ch, 1sc in 4ch sp, 3ch, 5tr in same 4ch sp, remove hook and insert it in 3rd ch, catch loop and pull through to close first popcorn, [5ch, 6tr popcorn in next 4ch sp] 5 times, 5ch, ss in 3rd ch. Fasten off.

Join A in next 5ch sp.

5th round 1ch, [1sc, 4dc, 3ch, 4dc, 1sc in 5ch sp, ss in top of popcorn] 6 times, ss in first sc. Fasten off.

abbreviations and key

○ **ch** = chain

+ **sc** = single crochet

⌗ **tr** = treble

• **ss** = slip stitch

  st(s) = stitch(es)

Ɏ **dc** = double crochet

🕸 **5dc popcorn** = work 5dc, remove hook and insert hook in top of first st, catch loop and pull through to close popcorn

🕸 **6tr popcorn** = work 6tr and complete as 5dc popcorn

[ ] = work instructions in square brackets as directed.

pansy

Work this pretty pansy motif in shades of purple, black, and yellow. Different-height stitches make lifelike petals and the chain gaps in the last round offer convenient places to join the motifs. You can use the pansies separately, join them in rows, or make them into blocks.

instructions

Colors: Yellow (A), black (B), and purple (C).

Using A, make 4ch, ss in first ch to form a ring.

1st round 1ch, [1sc, 2ch] 6 times in ring, ss in first sc. Fasten off.

Join B in a 2ch sp.

2nd round 1ch, 1sc in same sp as join, [2ch, 2sc in next sp] 5 times, 2ch, 1sc in first sp, ss in first sc.

3rd round Ss in next sp, [1ch, 1dc, ss] in same sp as first ss, [ss, 3ch, 4dc, 3ch, ss] in each of next 2 sps, [ss, 1dc, ss] in foll sp, [ss, 1ch, 3sc, 1ch, ss] in each of next 2 sps, ss in first sp. Fasten off.

Join C to the right of the first large petal.

4th round 1ch, inserting hook in 2ch sp of 1st round below, work 1 long sc, continue working behind petals made on 2nd and 3rd rounds, [5ch, 1 long sc in next sp of 1st round] twice, 3ch, [1 long sc in next sp of 1st round, 4ch] twice, 1 long sc in last sp of 1st round, 3ch, ss in first sc.

5th round [1sc, 1hdc, 1dc, 1ch, 1dc, 3tr, 1ch, 3tr, 1dc, 1ch, 1dc, 1hdc, 1sc] in each 5ch sp, [1sc, 1dc, 1ch, 1dc, ss] in 3ch sp, [ss, 1hdc, 1dc, 1ch, 3dc, 1ch, 1dc, 1hdc, ss] in each 4ch sp, [ss, 1dc, 1ch, 1dc, 1sc] in 3ch sp, ss in first sc. Fasten off.

waterlily

Two-tone petals and raised stamens in the center give this flower character, but it's easy to make using just chain, single, and double crochet stitches. Leave off the background square if you want to use the flower as a corsage.

instructions

Colors: Yellow (A), cream (B), pink (C), and green (D).

Flower center Using A, wind yarn around finger to form a ring.

1st round (RS) 1ch, 8sc in ring, remove hook, insert from back in first sc, catch loop and pull through.

2nd round 1ch, taking hook behind, 1sc around the stem of same sc as join, [4ch, ss in 3rd ch from hook, 1ch, 1sc around the stem of next sc] 7 times, 4ch, ss in 3rd ch from hook, 1ch, ss in first sc.

3rd round 1ch, taking hook behind, 1sc around stem of same sc as join, [2ch, 1sc around the stem of next sc] 7 times, 2ch, ss in first sc. Fasten off.

Petals With RS facing, join B in a 2ch sp.

1st round [10ch, work into back strand of ch, 1dc in 4th ch from hook, 1dc in each of next 5ch, ss in same 2ch sp, 2ch, ss in next 2ch sp] 8 times omitting last ss.

Fasten off and darn end into first ch.

With RS facing, join C in sp between ss at base of a petal.

2nd round 1ch over ss at right of base of petal, [work in base of ch, 1sc in next ch, 1hdc in foll ch, 1dc in each of next 4ch, 3dc in sp at end of petal, 1dc in each of next 4dc, 1hdc in foll dc, 1sc in next dc, ss over ss and into sp at base of same petal, ss over ss in sp at base of next petal] 8 times omitting last ss

Fasten off and darn end in first ch.

Background With RS facing and taking hook behind petals, join D in a 2ch sp in B made on 1st round of petals.

abbreviations and key

- **o** ch = chain
- **+** sc = single crochet
- **⟊** tr = treble
- **T** hdc = half double crochet
- **•** ss = slip stitch
- sp(s) = space(s)
- **⟊** dc = double crochet

[ ] = work instructions in square brackets as directed.

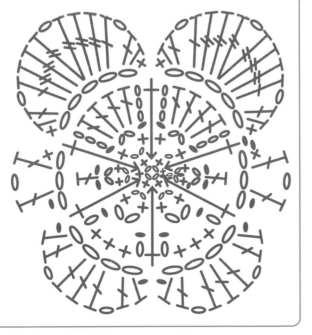

abbreviations

ch = chain

sc = single crochet

foll = following

hdc = half double crochet

rep = repeat

RS = right side

sp = space

ss = slip stitch

dc = double crochet

[ ] = work instructions in square brackets as directed.

1st round 1ch, [1sc, 3ch, 1sc] in same 2ch sp as join, * 1ch, 1sc in next 2ch sp, 1ch, [1sc, 3ch, 1sc] in foll 2ch sp, rep from * two more times, 1ch, 1sc in last 2ch sp, 1ch, ss in first sc.

2nd round Ss in first 3ch sp, 1ch, [1sc, 3ch, 1sc] in same 3ch sp, * [1sc in next sc, 2sc in foll 1ch sp] twice, 1sc in next sc, [1sc, 3ch, 1sc] in foll 3ch sp, rep from * two more times, [1sc in next sc, 2sc in next 1ch sp] twice, 1sc in last sc, ss in first sc.

3rd round Ss in first 3ch sp, 1ch, [1sc, 3ch, 1sc] in same 3ch sp, * 1sc in each of next 9sc, [1sc, 3ch, 1sc] in next 3ch sp, rep from * two more times, 1sc in each of next 9sc, ss in first sc.

4th round Ss in first 3ch sp, 1ch, [1sc, 3ch, 1sc] in same 3ch sp, * 1sc in each of next 11sc, [1sc, 3ch, 1sc] in next 3ch sp, rep from * two more times, 1sc in each of next 11sc, ss in first sc.

5th round Ss in first 3ch sp, 1ch, [1sc, 3ch, 1sc] in same 3ch sp, * 1sc in each of next 13sc, [1sc, 3ch, 1sc] in next 3ch sp, rep from * two more times, 1sc in each of next 13sc, ss in first sc.

6th round Ss in first 3ch sp, 1ch, [1sc, 3ch, 1sc] in same 3ch sp, * 1sc in each of next 15sc, [1sc, 3ch, 1sc] in next 3ch sp, rep from * two more times, 1sc in each of next 15sc, ss in first sc.

7th round Ss in first 3ch sp, 1ch, [1sc, 3ch, 1sc] in same 3ch sp, * 1sc in each of next 17sc, [1sc, 3ch, 1sc] in next 3ch sp, rep from * two more times, 1sc in each of next 17sc, ss in first sc.

8th round Ss in first 3ch sp, 1ch, [1sc, 5ch, 1dc] in same 3ch sp, * [1ch, miss next sc, 1dc in foll sc] 9 times, 1ch, miss next sc, [1dc, 3ch, 1dc] in next 3ch sp, rep from * two more times, [1ch, miss next sc, 1dc in foll sc] 9 times, 1ch, miss last sc, ss in 2nd ch.

Fasten off.

filet flower

A little grid of filet forms the center with groups of stitches worked into chain spaces for the petals, making a neat little squared-up flower.

instructions

Center Make 14ch.

1st row (RS) 1dc in 6th ch from hook, [1ch, miss 1ch, 1dc in next ch] 4 times.

2nd row 1sc in first tr, 3ch, [1dc in next dc, 1ch] 4 times, miss 1ch, 1dc in next ch.

2nd row forms filet mesh. Work 3 more rows filet mesh, do not turn after last row.

Petals. 1st round (RS) 1ch, 3sc in first corner sp, [2sc in each of next 3 sps, 5sc in foll corner sp] 3 times, 2sc in each of last 3 sps, 2sc in first sp, ss in first sc.

2nd round 1ch, 1sc in same sc as ss, [4ch, miss 3sc, 1sc in next sc, 4ch, miss 2sc, 1sc in foll sc, 4ch, miss 3sc, 1sc in next sc] 4 times omitting last sc, ss in first sc.

3rd round Ss in first 4ch sp, [1sc, 1hdc, 3dc, 1hdc, 1sc] in each 4ch sp, remove hook, insert hook from back in first sc, catch loop and pull through.

4th round 1ch, taking hook to back of work, 1sc around the stem of first sc of 2nd round, [9ch, 1sc around the stem of next sc of 2nd round] 12 times, ss in first sc, ss in each of next 4ch.

5th round 1ch, 1sc in first 9ch sp, * [7ch, 1sc in next 9ch sp] twice, 9ch, 1sc in foll 9ch sp, rep from * 3 more times omitting last sc, ss in first sc. Fasten off.

abbreviations and key

◯ ch = chain

+ sc = single crochet

foll = following

T hdc = half double crochet

rep = repeat

RS = right side

● ss = slip stitch

Ŧ dc = double crochet

sp = space

[ ] = work instructions in square brackets as directed.

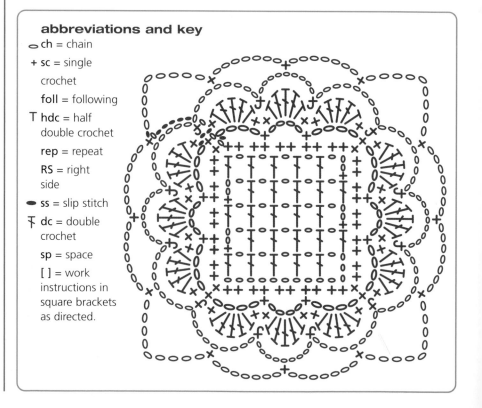

framed flower

You can change colors, as shown, or work this bold motif all in one shade. The open center gives you a quick start, the petals are made with different-height stitches, then a neat border holds the flower open.

instructions

Colors: Brown (A), orange (B), and lime green (C).

Using A, make 8ch, ss in first ch to form a ring.

1st round 1ch, 16sc in ring, ss in first sc.

2nd round 1ch, 1sc in same sc as ss, 7ch, [miss 1sc, 1dc in next sc, 5ch] 7 times, miss last sc, ss in 2nd ch.

Fasten off. Join B in a 5ch sp.

3rd round 1ch, [1sc, 1hdc, 1dc, 2tr, 1ch, 2tr, 1dc, 1hdc, sc] in each 5ch sp, ss in first sc.

Fasten off. Join C in a 1ch sp.

4th round 1ch, 1sc in same 1ch sp, [7ch, 1sc in next 1ch sp, 9ch, 1sc in foll 1ch sp] 4 times omitting last sc, ss in first sc.

5th round Ss in first 7ch sp, 1ch, * 7sc in 7ch sp, [6sc, 3ch, 6sc] in next 9ch sp, rep from * 3 more times, ss in first sc, turn.

6th round 1ch, 1sc in same sc as ss, 1sc in each of next 6sc, * [1sc, 3ch, 1sc] in next 3ch sp, 1sc in each of next 19sc, rep from * 2 more times, [1sc, 3ch, 1sc] in last 3ch sp, 1sc in each of last 12sc, ss in first sc, turn.

7th round 1ch, 1sc in same sc as ss, 3ch, [miss next sc, 1dc in foll sc, 1ch] 6 times, * miss next sc, [1dc, 3ch, 1dc] in next 3ch sp, 1ch, [miss next sc, 1dc in foll sc, 1ch] 10 times, rep from * 2 more times, miss next sc, [1dc, 3ch, 1dc] in last 3ch sp, 1ch, [miss next sc, 1dc in foll sc, 1ch] 3 times, ss in 2nd ch.

Fasten off.

abbreviations and key

- ○ **ch** = chain
- **+** **sc** = single crochet
- **ꓕ** **tr** = treble
- **T** **hdc** = half double crochet
- **rep** = repeat
- **sp** = space
- ● **ss** = slip stitch
- **ꓕ** **dc** = double crochet
- **[ ]** = work instructions in square brackets as directed.

lace

Create delicate lacework in a variety of stitch patterns including loops and clusters, openwork, chain, and picot mesh to make pretty floral and geometric shapes that will look stunning when joined together.

flower and mesh octagon

Double crochet and double crochet groups make an eight-petal, silhouette flower shape defined and surrounded by a simple chain mesh.

instructions

Wind yarn around finger to form a ring.

1st round 1ch, 1sc in ring, 2ch, 23dc in ring, ss in 2nd ch.

2nd round 1ch, 1sc in same place as ss, 2ch, 1dc in each of next 2dc, 3ch, [1dc in each of next 3dc, 3ch] 7 times, ss in 2nd ch.

3rd round 1ch, 1sc in same place as ss, 1ch, 2dctog, [4ch, 1sc in 3ch sp, 4ch, 3dctog] 7 times, 4ch, 1sc in 3ch sp, 2ch, 1dc in 2dctog.

4th round 1ch, 1sc in dc sp, 5ch, [1sc in next 4ch sp, 5ch] 15 times, ss in first sc. Fasten off.

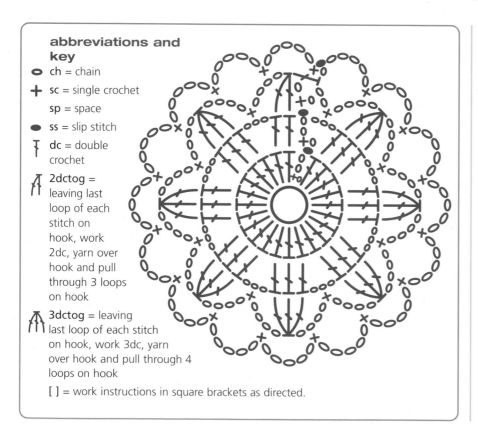

abbreviations and key

- ○ **ch** = chain
- + **sc** = single crochet
- **sp** = space
- ● **ss** = slip stitch
- ┬ **dc** = double crochet
- ⋀ **2dctog** = leaving last loop of each stitch on hook, work 2dc, yarn over hook and pull through 3 loops on hook
- ⋀ **3dctog** = leaving last loop of each stitch on hook, work 3dc, yarn over hook and pull through 4 loops on hook
- **[ ]** = work instructions in square brackets as directed

snowflake

This easy-to-work motif starts with a chain flower at the center with pairs of double crochet groups radiating out to make the points of the starlike snowflake. Using a double crochet in place of chain to join rounds in the center of an arch makes the joins almost invisible.

instructions

Wind yarn around finger to form a ring.

1st round 1ch, [1sc in ring, 6ch] 5 times, 1sc in ring, 3ch, 1dc in first sc.

2nd round 1ch, 1sc in dc sp, * 2ch, [1sc, 3ch, 1sc] in next sp, rep from * 4 more times, 2ch, 1sc in first sp, 1ch, 1dc in first sc.

3rd round 1ch, 1sc in dc sp, 2ch, 1dc in same sp, * 2ch, [2dc, 3ch, 2dc] in next 3ch sp, rep from * 4 more times, 2ch, 2dc in first sp, 1ch, 1dc in 2nd ch.

4th round 1ch, 1sc in dc sp, 2ch, 2dc in same sp, * 3ch, 1sc in 2ch sp, 3ch, [3dc, 3ch, 3dc] in next 3ch sp, rep from * 4 more times, 3ch, 1sc in last 2ch sp, 3ch,

3dc in first sp, 1ch, 1dc in 2nd ch.

5th round 1ch, 1sc in dc sp, 2ch, 2dc in same sp, * [3ch, 1sc in next 3ch sp] twice, 3ch, [3dc, 3ch, 3dc] in next 3ch sp, rep from * 4 more times, [3ch, 1sc in next 3ch sp] twice, 3ch, 3dc in first sp, 1ch, 1dc in 2nd ch.

6th round 1ch, 1sc in dc sp, 2ch, 2dc in same sp, * [3ch, 1sc in next 3ch sp] 3 times, 3ch, [3dc, 3ch, 3dc] in next 3ch sp, rep from * 4 more times, [3ch, 1sc in next 3ch sp] 3 times, 3ch, 3dc in first sp, 3ch, ss in 2nd ch.

Fasten off.

compass square

Double crochet and chain mesh create a stunning outlined compass points design.

instructions

Wind yarn around finger to form a ring.

1st round 1ch, 1sc in ring, 2ch, 19dc in ring, ss in 2nd ch.

2nd round 1ch, 1sc in same place as ss, 2ch, 1dc in each of next 3dc, 3ch, 1dc in next dc, 3ch, [1dc in each of next 4dc, 3ch, 1dc in next dc, 3ch] 3 times, ss in 2nd ch.

3rd round 1ch, 1sc in same place as ss, 2ch, 1dc in each of next 3dc, 3ch, 3dc in next dc, 3ch, [1dc in each of next 4dc, 3ch, 3dc in next dc, 3ch] 3 times, ss in 2nd ch.

4th round 1ch, 1sc in same place as ss, 1ch, 1dc in next dc, 2dctog, * 3ch, 2dc in next dc, 1dc in foll dc, 3ch, 1dc in same dc, 2dc in next dc, 3ch, [2dctog] twice, rep from * twice more, 3ch, 2dc in next dc, 1dc in foll dc, 3ch, 1dc in same dc, 2dc in next dc, 3ch, ss in first dc.

5th round 1ch, 1sc in same place as ss, 1ch, 1dc in 2dctog, 3ch, 2dc in next dc, 1dc in each of next 2dc, * 3ch, 1sc in next 3ch sp, 3ch, 1dc in each of next 2dc, 2dc in foll dc, 3ch, 2dctog, 3ch, 2dc in next dc, 1dc in each of next 2dc, rep from * two more times, 3ch, 1sc in next 3ch sp, 3ch, 1dc in each of next 2dc, 2dc in foll dc, 3ch, ss in first dc.

6th round 1ch, 1sc in same place as ss, 3ch, 2dc in next dc, 1dc in foll dc, 2dctog, * [4ch, 1sc in next 3ch sp] twice, 4ch, 2dctog, 1dc in next dc, 2dc in foll dc, 3ch, 1sc in 2dctog, 3ch, 2dc in next dc, 1dc in foll dc, 2dctog, rep from * two more times, [4ch, 1sc in next 3ch sp] twice, 4ch, 2dctog, 1dc in next dc, 2dc in foll dc, 3ch, ss in first sc.

7th round 1ch, 1sc in same place as ss, 2ch, 2dc in next dc, 1dc in foll dc, 2dctog, * [5ch, 1sc in next 4ch sp] 3 times, 5ch, 2dctog, 1dc in next dc, 2dc in foll dc, 1dc in sc, 2dc in next dc, 1dc in foll dc, 2dctog, rep from * two more times, [5ch, 1sc in next 4ch sp] 3 times, 5ch, 2dctog, 1dc in next dc, 2dc in foll dc, ss in 2nd ch.

8th round 1ch, 1sc in same place as ss, 2ch, 1dc in each of next 2dc, 2dctog, * [5ch, 1sc in next 5ch sp] 4 times, 5ch, 2dctog, 1dc in each of next 5dc, 2dctog, rep from * two more times, [5ch, 1sc in next 5ch sp] 4 times, 5ch, 2dctog, 1dc in each of next 2dc, ss in 2nd ch.

9th round 1ch, 1sc in same place as ss, 2ch, 1dc in next dc, 2dctog, * [5ch, 1sc in next 5ch sp] 5 times, 5ch, 2dctog, 1dc in each of next

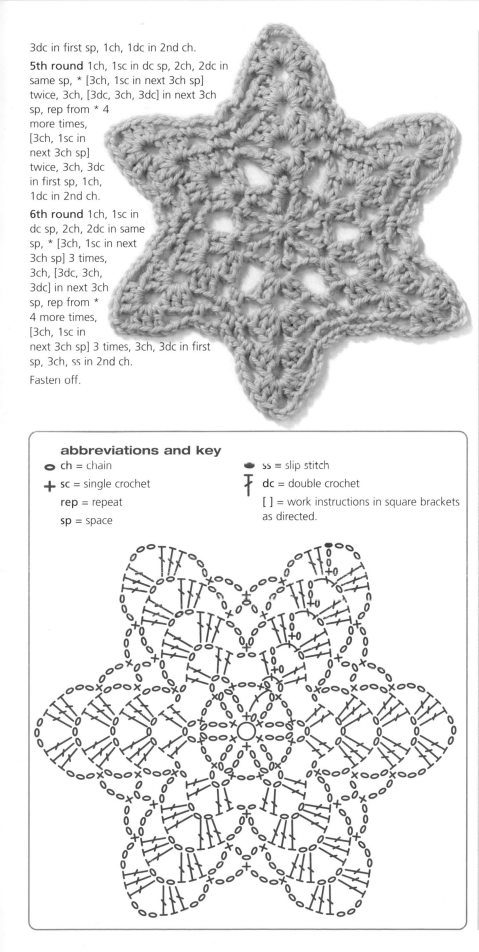

abbreviations and key

○ ch = chain

+ sc = single crochet

rep = repeat

sp = space

● ss = slip stitch

╪ dc = double crochet

[ ] = work instructions in square brackets as directed.

grand flower hexagon

Although this is a large motif it works up very quickly because there are just six rounds with treble stitches playing a major part in building the motif. You could join motifs on the last round by working a single crochet stitch in each adjacent chain space. For a more open effect, make separate motifs and join them with a zigzag of chain and single crochet.

instructions

Make 8ch, ss in first ch to form a ring.

1st round 4ch, 1tr in ring, 2ch, [2trtog in ring, 2ch] 11 times, ss in tr.

2nd round Ss in first 2ch sp, 1ch, 1sc in same sp, 5ch, [1sc in next sp, 5ch] 11 times, ss in first sc.

3rd round Ss in first 5ch sp, 1ch, 1sc in same sp, [* 12ch, 1sc in same 5ch sp, 5ch, 1sc in next 5ch sp *, 5ch, 1sc in foll 5ch sp] 5 times, rep from * to *, 2ch, 1dc in first sc.

3dc, 2dctog, rep from * two more times, [5ch, 1sc in next 5ch sp] 5 times, 5ch, 2dctog, 1dc in next dc, ss in 2nd ch.

10th round 1ch, 1sc in same place as ss, 2ch, 2dctog, * [5ch, 1sc in next 5ch sp] 6 times, 5ch, 2dctog, 1dc in next dc, 2dctog, rep from * twice more, [5ch, 1sc in next 5ch sp] 6 times, 5ch, 2dctog, ss in 2nd ch.

11th round 1ch, 1sc in same place as ss, 1ch, 1dc in 2dctog, * [5ch, 1sc in next 5ch sp] 7 times, 5ch, 3dctog, rep from * two more times, [5ch, 1sc in next 5ch sp] 7 times, 5ch, 1 dc in last 2dctog, ss in first dc. Fasten off.

abbreviations

ch = chain

sc = single crochet

foll = following

rep = repeat

sp = space

ss = slip stitch

dc = double crochet

2dctog = leaving last loop of each stitch on hook, work 2dc, yarn over hook and pull through 3 loops on hook

3dctog = leaving last loop of each stitch on hook, work 3dc, yarn over hook and pull through 4 loops on hook

[ ] = work instructions in square brackets as directed.

abbreviations and key

○ ch = chain

+ sc = single crochet

⊺ tr = treble

2trtog = leaving last loop of each stitch on hook work 2tr, yarn over hook and pull through 3 loops on hook

foll = following

rep = repeat

sp(s) = space(s)

● ss = slip stitch

⊺ dc = double crochet

[ ] = work instructions in square brackets as directed.

silhouette flower medallion

This easy-to-work motif has a six-petal flower shape made by alternating areas of closely worked double crochet and open filet-style mesh.

instructions

Wind yarn around finger to form a ring.

1st round 1ch, 12sc in ring, ss in first sc.

2nd round 1ch, [1sc, 2ch, 2dc] in same place as ss, 2ch, [miss 1sc, 3dc in next sc, 2ch] 5 times, ss in 2nd ch.

3rd round 1ch, [1sc, 2ch, 1dc] in same place as ss, 1dc in next dc, 2dc in foll dc, 2ch, [2dc in next dc, 1dc in foll dc, 2dc in next dc, 2ch] 5 times, ss in 2nd ch.

4th round 1ch, [1sc, 2ch, 1dc] in same place as ss, 1dc in each of next 3dc, 2dc in foll dc, 2ch, [2dc in next dc, 1dc in each of next 3dc, 2dc in foll dc, 2ch] 5 times, ss in 2nd ch

5th round 1ch, 1sc in same place as ss, 1ch, 1dc in each of next 4dc, 2dctog, 3ch, 1dc in 2ch sp, 3ch, [2dctog, 1dc in each of next 3dc, 2dctog, 3ch, 1dc in 2ch sp, 3ch] 5 times, ss in first dc.

6th round 1ch, 1sc in same place as ss, 1ch, 1dc in each of next 2dc, 2dctog, [3ch, 1dc in next 3ch sp] twice, 3ch, * [2dctog, 1dc] in next dc, 2dctog, [3ch, 1dc in next 3ch sp] twice, 3ch, rep from * 4 more times, ss in first dc.

7th round 1ch, 1sc in same place as ss, 1ch, 2dctog, [3ch, 1dc in next 3ch sp] 3 times, 3ch, * 3dctog, [3ch, 1dc in next 3ch sp] 3 times, 3ch, rep from * 4 more times, ss in 2dctog.

Fasten off.

4th round [6dc, 3ch, 6dc] in first 12ch sp, * 1sc in next 5ch sp, 5ch, 1sc in foll 5ch sp, [6dc, 3ch, 6dc] in next 12ch sp, rep from * 4 more times, 1sc in next 5ch sp, 2ch, 1dc in last dc of 3rd round.

5th round 8ch, 1tr in dc sp, [8ch, 1sc in next 3ch sp, 8ch, 1tr in next 5ch sp, 3ch, 1tr in same 5ch sp] 5 times, 8ch, 1sc in last 3ch sp, 8ch, ss in 5th ch.

6th round Ss in first 3ch sp, 1ch, 1sc in same sp, 3ch, 1dc, in same sp, 1ch, * [1dc, 1ch] 4 times in each of next two 8ch sps, [1dc, 1ch] twice in next 3ch sp, rep from * 4 more times, [1dc, 1ch] 4 times in each of next two 8ch sps, ss in 2nd ch. Fasten off.

abbreviations and key

o ch = chain

+ sc = single crochet

foll = following

rep = repeat

sp = space

● ss = slip stitch

dc = double crochet

2dctog = leaving last loop of each stitch on hook, work 2dc, yarn over hook and pull through 3 loops on hook

3dctog = leaving last loop of each stitch on hook, work 3dc, yarn over hook and pull through 4 loops on hook

[ ] = work instructions in square brackets as directed.

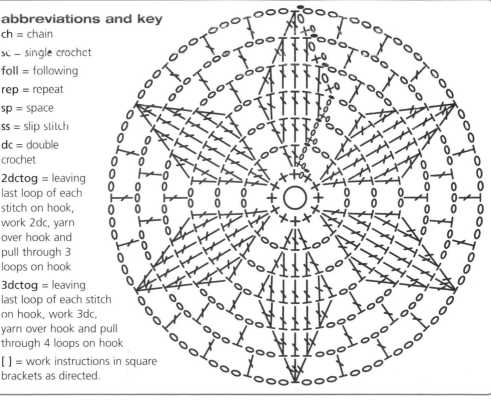

fan stitch octagon

This motif is based on the simplest of fan lace stitch patterns, but is given a new twist by being worked in the round instead of in rows. The result is a pretty, easy-to-work motif with an undulating edge.

instructions

Make 8ch, ss in first ch to form a ring.

1st round 4ch, [3dc in ring, 1ch] 7 times, 2dc in ring, ss in 3rd ch.

2nd round Ss in first sp, 4ch, 3dc in same sp, 1ch, [3dc, 1ch] twice in each of next 7 sps, 2dc in first sp, ss in 3rd ch.

3rd round Ss in first sp, 4ch, 3dc in same sp, * 1ch, 1dc in next sp, 1ch, [3dc, 1ch, 3dc] in foll sp, rep from * 6 more times, 1ch, 1dc in last sp, 1ch, 2dc in first sp, ss in 3rd ch.

4th round Ss in first sp, 4ch, 3dc in same sp, * [1ch, 1dc in next sp] twice, 1ch, [3dc, 1ch, 3dc] in foll sp, rep from * 6 more times, [1ch, 1dc in next sp] twice, 1ch, 2dc in first sp, ss in 3rd ch.

5th round Ss in first sp, 4ch, 3dc in same sp, * [1ch, 1dc in next sp] 3 times, 1ch, [3dc, 1ch, 3dc] in foll sp, rep from * 6 more times, [1ch, 1dc in next sp] 3 times, 1ch, 2dc in first sp, ss in 3rd ch. Fasten off.

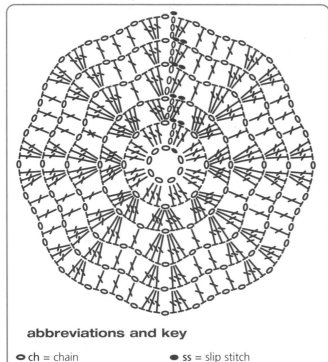

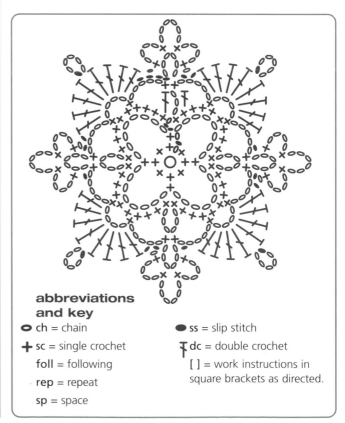

quatrefoil octagon

Four semicircles of chain worked around a small center and padded with single crochet make the quatrefoil motif, with the edging rounds developing the motif into eight points.

instructions

Wind yarn around finger to form a ring.

1st round 1ch, 8sc in ring, ss in first sc.

2nd round 1ch, 1sc in same place as ss, [8ch, miss 1sc, 1sc in next sc] 3 times, 8ch, miss 1sc, ss in first sc.

3rd round Ss in first sp, 1ch, 10sc in first 8ch sp, [6ch, 10sc in next 8ch sp] 3 times, 3ch, 1dc in first ch.

4th round 1sc in dc sp, [5ch, miss 3sc, 1sc in next sc, 4ch, miss 2sc, 1sc in next sc, 5ch, 1sc in 6ch sp, 6ch, 1sc in same 6ch sp] 3 times, 5ch, miss 3sc, 1sc in next sc, 4ch, miss 2sc, 1sc in next sc, 5ch, 1sc in first sp, 6ch, ss in first sc, ss in each of next 3ch.

5th round * [4dc, 5ch, ss in first ch, 4dc] in next 4ch sp, ss in next 5ch sp, ss in foll 6ch sp, [1ch, 1sc, 4ch, 1sc, 6ch, 1sc, 4ch, 1sc] in same 6ch sp, ss in next 5ch sp, rep from * 3 more times omitting last ss, ss in first dc. Fasten off.

abbreviations and key

○ ch = chain

foll = following

rep = repeat

sp = space

● ss = slip stitch

⊤ dc = double crochet

[ ] = work instructions in square brackets as directed.

abbreviations and key

○ ch = chain

✛ sc = single crochet

foll = following

rep = repeat

sp = space

● ss = slip stitch

⊤ dc = double crochet

[ ] = work instructions in square brackets as directed.

daisy chain medallion

Here, chain stitch with a few single crochet stitches linking the loops makes up the flowers and scalloped edging.

instructions

Wind yarn around finger to form a ring.

1st round 1ch, [1sc in ring, 6ch] 5 times, 1sc in ring, 3ch, 1dc in ring.

2nd round 1ch, 1sc in dc sp, [6ch, 1sc in next 6ch sp] 5 times, 3ch, 1dc in first sc.

3rd round 1ch, 1sc in dc sp, [8ch, ss in 4th ch from hook, 4ch, 1sc next 6ch sp] 6 times omitting last sc, ss in first sc.

4th round * 4ch, miss next 4ch sp, 1sc in foll 4ch sp, [8ch, 1sc in same 4ch sp] 3 times, 4ch, ss in next sc, * rep from * 5 more times. Fasten off. Join yarn in next 8ch sp.

5th round 1ch, 1sc in same 8ch sp, * [6ch, 1sc in next 8ch sp] twice, 3ch, 1sc in foll 8ch sp, rep from * 5 more times omitting last sc, ss in first sc.

6th round Ss in first 6ch sp, 1ch, 1sc in same 6ch sp, * [6ch, 1sc] twice in same 6ch sp, [1sc, 6ch] twice in next 6ch sp, 1sc in same 6ch sp, [1sc, 6ch, 1sc] in next 3ch sp, 1sc in next 6ch sp, rep from * 5 more times omitting last sc, ss in first sc. Fasten off.

abbreviations and key

o ch = chain
+ sc = single crochet
rep = repeat
sp = space
• ss = slip stitch
dc = double crochet
[ ] = work instructions in square brackets as directed.

chain flower square

This simple little square is worked mostly in chain and single crochet with a border of double crochet and chains. There's just one longer stitch, it's a treble at the end of the first round. All you have to do for this stitch is wrap the yarn twice around the hook, then work the wraps off in the usual way.

instructions

Make 8ch, ss in first ch to form a ring.

1st round 1ch, * [1sc in ring, 6ch] twice, 1sc in ring, 8ch, rep from * two more times, [1sc in ring, 6ch] twice, 4ch, 1tr in first sc.

2nd round 1ch, 1sc in tr sp, 3ch, 1sc in same sp, * [2ch, 1sc in next 6ch sp] twice, 2ch, [1sc, 3ch, 1sc] in 8ch sp, rep from * two more times, [2ch, 1sc in next 6ch sp] twice, 2ch, ss in first sc.

3rd round 1ch, [1sc in 3ch sp, 3ch, 1sc in same 3ch sp, 3sc in each of next three 2ch sps] 4 times, ss in first sc.

4th round Ss in 3ch sp, 1ch, 1sc in same 3ch sp, 5ch, 1dc in same 3ch sp, * [1ch, miss 1sc, 1dc in next sc] 5 times, 1ch **, [1dc, 3ch, 1dc] in next 3ch sp, rep from * two more times, then rep from * to **, ss in 2nd ch. Fasten off.

abbreviations and key

o ch = chain
+ sc = single crochet
tr = treble
rep = repeat
• ss = slip stitch
dc = double crochet
[ ] = work instructions in square brackets as directed.

squared circle

A simple openwork wheel is extended with pairs of treble clusters to build up four corners, with double crochet and chain edging.

instructions

Wind yarn twice around finger to form a ring. This ring will not pull up tight but makes a thicker center.

1st round 1ch, 16sc in ring, ss in first sc.

2nd round 1ch, 1sc in same place as ss, 3ch, [1dc in next sc, 1ch] 15 times, ss in 2nd ch.

3rd round Ss in first 1ch sp, 1ch, 1sc in same 1ch sp, [3ch, 2sc in next 1ch sp] 15 times, 3ch, 1sc in first 1ch sp, ss in first sc.

4th round Ss in first 3ch sp, 1ch, 1sc in same 3ch sp, 3ch, [1sc in next 3ch sp, 3ch] 15 times, ss in first sc.

5th round 1ch, 1sc in same place as ss, * 4ch, miss next 3ch sp, [3trtog, 5ch, 3trtog] in foll 3ch sp, 4ch, miss next 3ch sp, 1sc in next sc, 5ch, miss next 3ch sp, 1sc in foll sc, rep from * 3 more times, omitting last sc, ss in first sc.

6th round Ss in first 4ch sp, 1ch, 1sc in same sp, 3ch, 1dc in same sp, 1ch, * [1dc, 1ch, 1dc, 3ch, 1dc, 1ch, 1dc] in next 5ch sp **, 1ch, [1dc, 1ch] twice in each of next 3 sps, rep from * two more times, then rep from * to **, 1ch, [1dc, 1ch] twice in each of next 2 sps, ss in 2nd ch. Fasten off.

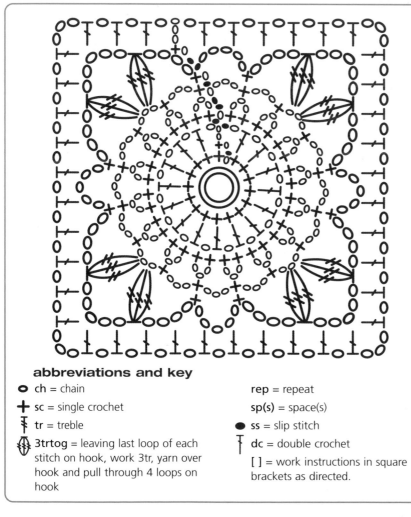

abbreviations and key

○ **ch** = chain

✛ **sc** = single crochet

⌶ **tr** = treble

3trtog = leaving last loop of each stitch on hook, work 3tr, yarn over hook and pull through 4 loops on hook

rep = repeat

sp(s) = space(s)

● **ss** = slip stitch

⊤ **dc** = double crochet

[ ] = work instructions in square brackets as directed.

pineapple square

Pineapple stitch is usually worked in rows of motifs arranged in a half-drop repeat. This square uses the same elements worked in rounds, radiating out from the center to make a block that's big and bold.

instructions

Wind yarn around finger to form a ring.

1st round 1ch, [1sc in ring, 4ch, 1sc in ring] 4 times, ss in first sc.

2nd round Ss in first 4ch sp, 1ch, 5sc in each 4ch sp, ss in first sc.

3rd round 1ch, [1sc, 2ch, 1dc] in same place as ss, * 1dc in each of next 3sc, 2dc in next sc, 3ch, 2dc in foll sc, rep from * two more times, 1dc in each of next 3sc, 2dc in foll sc, 3ch, ss in 2nd ch.

4th round 1ch, 1sc in same place as ss, 3ch, 1tr in each of next 6dc, [3ch, 1sc in 3ch sp, 3ch, 1tr in each of next 7dc] 3 times, 3ch, 1sc in last 3ch sp, 3ch, ss in 2nd ch.

5th round 1ch, 1sc in same place as ss, * [3ch, 1sc in next tr] 6 times, 5ch, 1sc in next tr, rep from * 3 more times omitting last sc, ss in first sc.

6th round Ss in first 3ch sp, 1ch, 1sc in same sp, * [3ch, 1sc in next 3ch sp] 5 times, 2ch, [2dc, 3ch, 2dc] in 5ch sp, 2ch, 1sc in next 3ch sp, rep from * 3 more times omitting last sc, ss in first sc.

7th round Ss in first 3ch sp, 1ch, 1sc in same sp, * [3ch, 1sc in next 3ch sp] 4 times, 4ch, [2dc, 3ch, 2dc] in foll 3ch sp, 4ch, 1sc in next 3ch sp, rep from * 3 more times omitting last sc, ss in first sc.

8th round Ss in first 3ch sp, 1ch, 1sc in same sp, * [3ch, 1sc in next 3ch sp] 3 times, 6ch, [2dc, 3ch, 2dc] in foll 3ch sp, 6ch, 1sc in next 3ch sp, rep from * 3 more times omitting last sc, ss in first sc.

9th round Ss in first 3ch sp, 1ch, 1sc in same sp, * [3ch, 1sc in next 3ch sp] twice, 8ch, [2dc, 3ch, 2dc] in foll 3ch sp, 8ch, 1sc in next 3ch sp, rep from * 3 more times omitting last sc, ss in first sc.

10th round Ss in first 3ch sp, 1ch, 1sc in same sp, * 3ch, 1sc in next 3ch sp, 10ch, [2dc, 3ch, 2dc] in foll 3ch sp, 10ch, 1sc in next 3ch sp, rep from * 3 more times omitting last sc, ss in first sc.

11th round Ss in first 3ch sp, 1ch, 1sc in same sp, 3ch, * [1dc in next 10ch sp, 1ch] 5 times, miss 1dc, 1dc in next dc, 1ch, [1dc, 3ch, 1dc] in 3ch sp, 1ch, 1dc in next dc, 1ch, miss 1dc, [1dc in next 10ch sp, 1ch] 5 times, 1dc in next 3ch sp, 1ch, rep from * 3 more times omitting last dc and ch, ss in 2nd ch. Fasten off.

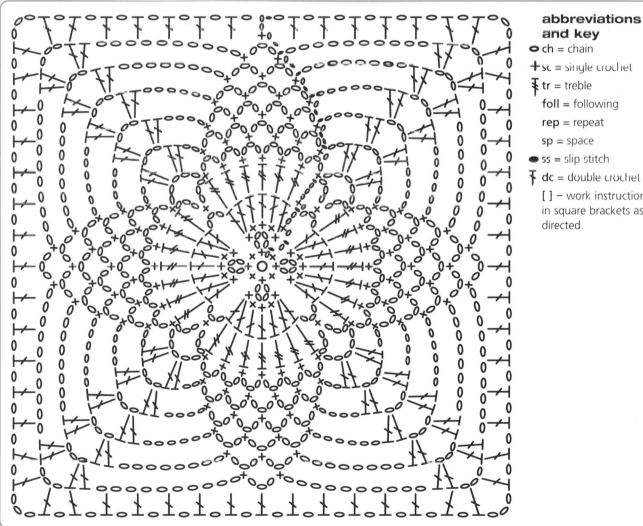

abbreviations and key

○ ch = chain
+ sc = single crochet
⊤ tr = treble
foll = following
rep = repeat
sp = space
● ss = slip stitch
⊤ dc = double crochet
[ ] – work instructions in square brackets as directed.

little shell circle

This motif uses half double crochet instead of the more familiar double crochet to give a delicate openwork effect. A chain, a single crochet stitch, and another chain stand in place of the first half double crochet. The first chain is made to reach the height of the single crochet, so always join at the end of the round into the chain after the single crochet.

instructions

Wind yarn around finger to form a ring.

1st round 1ch, 1sc in ring, 1ch, 11hdc in ring, ss in ch before first hdc.

2nd round 1ch, 1sc in same place as ss, 2ch, [1hdc in next hdc, 1ch] 11 times, ss in first of 2ch.

3rd round Ss in first 1ch sp, 1ch, 1sc in same 1ch sp, 3ch, 1hdc in same 1ch sp, [1hdc, 2ch, 1hdc] in each of next 11 sps, ss in first of 3ch.

4th round Ss in first 2ch sp, 1ch, 1sc in same 1ch sp, 3ch, 1hdc in same 1ch sp, 1ch, * [1hdc, 2ch, 1hdc] in next 2ch sp, 1ch, rep from * 10 more times, ss in first of 3ch.

5th round Ss in first 2ch sp, 1ch, 1sc in same 2ch sp, 3ch, 2hdc in same 2ch sp, ss in next 1ch sp, * [2hdc, 2ch, 2hdc] in next 2ch sp, ss in foll 1ch sp, rep from * 10 more times, 1hdc in first 2ch sp, ss in first of 3ch.

Fasten off.

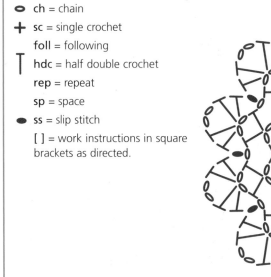

rosette hexagon

This quick-to-work little motif has just three rounds: a little flower in the center made from treble clusters linked with chain, the second round is just double crochet groups as simple as a granny square, and a final round of chain loops making it easy to join the motifs together to work a throw or a garment.

instructions

Wind yarn around finger to form a ring.

1st round 1ch, 1sc in ring, 3ch, 1tr in ring, 3ch, [2trtog in ring, 3ch] 5 times, ss in first tr.

2nd round Ss in first 3ch sp, 1ch, 1sc in same sp, 4ch, 2dc in same sp, 2ch, *[2dc, 2ch] twice in next sp, rep from * 4 more times, 1dc in first 3ch sp, ss in 2nd ch.

3rd round Ss in first 2ch sp, 1ch, 1sc in same sp, 4ch, [1sc in next sp, 4ch] 11 times, ss in first sc.

Fasten off.

abbreviations and key

- **ch** = chain
- **sc** = single crochet
- **foll** = following
- **hdc** = half double crochet
- **rep** = repeat
- **sp** = space
- **ss** = slip stitch
- [ ] = work instructions in square brackets as directed.

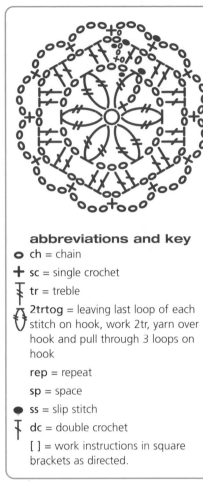

abbreviations and key

o ch = chain

+ sc = single crochet

T tr = treble

2trtog = leaving last loop of each stitch on hook, work 2tr, yarn over hook and pull through 3 loops on hook

rep = repeat

sp = space

● **ss** = slip stitch

T dc = double crochet

[ ] = work instructions in square brackets as directed.

shamrock octagon

The design elements of trefoil loops and airy, open spaces of this motif are made almost entirely in quick-to-work chain stitch linked by single crochet, double crochet, and trebles.

instructions

Make 4ch, ss in first ch to form a ring.

1st round 1ch, 8sc in ring, ss in first sc.

2nd round 1ch, 2sc in same place as ss, 2sc in each sc, ss in first sc. 16 sts.

3rd round 1ch, 1sc in same place as ss, 7ch, [miss 1sc, 1dc in next sc, 5ch] 7 times, miss 1sc, ss in 2nd ch.

4th round 1ch, 1sc in same place as ss, * 3ch, 1dc in sp, [5ch, ss in top of dc] 3 times, 3ch, 1sc in next dc, rep from * 7 more times omitting last sc, ss in first sc.

5th round 1ch, 1sc in same place as ss, 8ch, [1sc in next center 5ch loop, 5ch, 1tr in next sc, 5ch] 7 times, 1sc in last center 5ch loop, 5ch, ss in 3rd ch.

Fasten off.

abbreviations and key

o ch = chain

+ sc = single crochet

T tr = treble

rep = repeat

sp = space

● **ss** = slip stitch

sts = stitches

T dc = double crochet

[ ] = work instructions in square brackets as directed.

chain mesh square

This easy-to-work motif uses just chain and single crochet to create an Irish crochet-style square. After working one motif as given in the sample, you'll see how easy it would be to make a larger or smaller square.

instructions

Make 5ch, ss in first ch to form a ring.

1st round 1ch, 1sc in ring, [5ch, 1sc in ring] 3 times, 5ch, ss in first sc.

2nd round Ss in first sp, 1ch, 1sc in first sp, * [5ch, 1sc in same sp] twice, 2ch, 1sc in next sp, rep from * 3 more times omitting last sc, ss in first sc.

3rd round Ss in first sp, 1ch, 1sc in first sp, * 5ch, 1sc in same sp, 5ch, 1sc in next 5ch, sp, 5ch, 1sc in same sp, 3ch, 1sc in next 5ch sp, rep from * 3 more times omitting last sc, ss in first sc.

4th round Ss in first sp, 1ch, 1sc in first sp, * 5ch, 1sc in same sp, [5ch, 1sc in next 5ch sp] twice, 5ch, 1sc in same sp, 4ch, 1sc in next 5ch sp, rep from * 3 more times omitting last sc, ss in first sc.

5th round Ss in first sp, 1ch, 1sc in first sp, * 5ch, 1sc

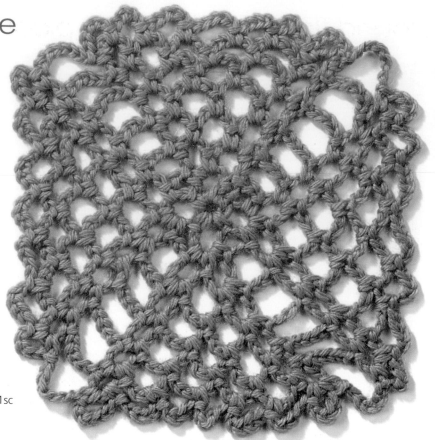

in same sp, [5ch, 1sc in next 5ch sp] 3 times, 5ch, 1sc in same sp, 5ch, 1sc in next 5ch sp, rep from * 3 more times omitting last sc, ss in first sc.

6th round Ss in first sp, 1ch, 1sc in first sp, * 5ch, 1sc in same sp, [5ch, 1sc in next 5ch sp] 4 times, 5ch, 1sc in same sp, 6ch, miss next 5ch sp, 1sc in next 5ch sp, rep from * 3 more times omitting last sc, ss in first sc.

7th round Ss in first sp, 1ch, 1sc in first sp, * 5ch, 1sc in same sp, [5ch, 1sc in next 5ch sp] 5 times, 5ch, 1sc in same sp, 7ch, 1sc in next 5ch sp, rep from * 3 more times omitting last sc, ss in first sc.

Fasten off.

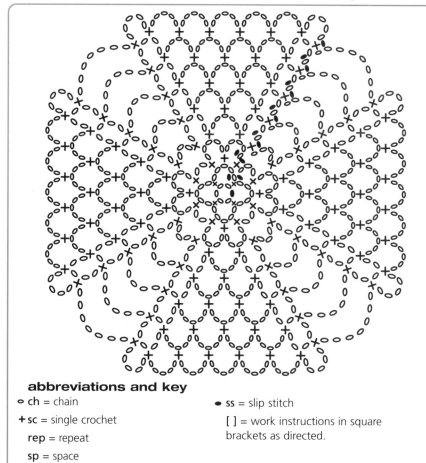

abbreviations and key

∘ ch = chain

+ sc = single crochet

   rep = repeat

   sp = space

● ss = slip stitch

[ ] = work instructions in square brackets as directed.

round flower

Treble groups and treble clusters make the center of this octagonal motif work up very quickly. On the second round, pull the first chain stitch after each cluster as tightly as you can for a really neat finish.

instructions

Wind yarn around finger to form a ring.

1st round 1ch, 1sc in ring, 3ch, 4tr in ring, 5ch, [5tr in ring, 5ch] 3 times, ss in 3rd ch.

2nd round 1ch, 1sc in same place as ss, 2ch, 4trtog, 8ch, 1sc in next 5ch sp, 8ch, [5trtog, 8ch, 1sc in next 5ch sp, 8ch] 3 times, ss in 4trtog.

3rd round Ss in first 8ch sp, 1sc, 2ch, 8dc in same 8ch sp, 2ch, [9dc in next 8ch sp, 2ch] 7 times, ss in 2nd ch.

Fasten off.

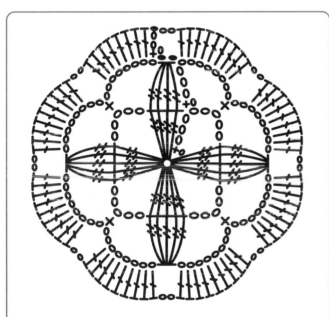

abbreviations and key

o ch = chain

+ sc = single crochet

Ŧ tr = treble

4trtog = leaving last loop of each stitch on hook, work 4tr, yo and pull through 5 loops on hook

5trtog = leaving last loop of each stitch on hook, work 5tr, yo and pull through 6 loops on hook

● ss = slip stitch

Ŧ dc = treble

yo = yarn over

[ ] = work instructions in square brackets as directed.

picot mesh square

This motif is based on the kind of picot mesh often worked in rows as a background in Irish crochet. Working separate squares makes it easy to carry your crochet around and easy to link the squares on the last round with a single crochet stitch between picots. Combine this motif with raised flowers for a patchwork Irish crochet afghan.

instructions

Wind yarn around finger to form a ring.

To work ss in first sp neatly, remove hook, insert from back in first sp, and catch loop.

1st round 1ch, [1sc in ring, 5ch, ss in 3rd ch from hook, 6ch, ss in 3rd ch from hook, 2ch] 4 times, ss in first sc.

2nd round Ss in first sp, 1ch, [1sc before first picot, * 5ch, ss in 3rd ch from hook, 6ch, ss in 3rd ch from hook, 2ch *, 1sc between picots, rep from * to *, 1sc after 2nd picot, 2ch] in each of 4 sps, ss in first sc.

3rd round Ss in first sp, 1ch, [1sc before first picot of first sp, rep from * to * of 2nd round, 1sc between picots of same sp, rep from * to * of 2nd round, 1sc between picots of next sp, rep from * to * of 2nd round, 1sc after 2nd picot of same sp, 2ch] 4 times, ss in first sc.

4th round Ss in first sp, 1ch, [1sc before first picot of first sp, rep from * to * of 2nd round, 1sc between picots of first sp, rep from * to * of 2nd round, 1sc between picots of 2nd sp, rep from * to * of 2nd round, 1sc between picots of 3rd sp, rep from * to * of 2nd round, 1sc after 2nd picot of 3rd sp, 2ch] 4 times, ss in first sc.

Fasten off.

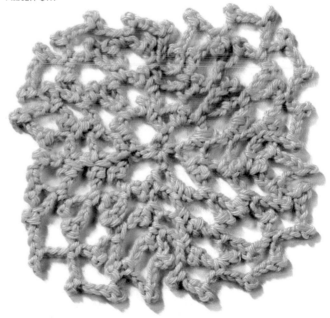

abbreviations

ch = chain	ss – slip stitch
sc = single crochet	[ ] = work instructions in
rep = repeat	square brackets as directed.
sp = space	

fan border medallion

All the stitches for this motif are very simple, but the result looks intricate because the number of repeats moves from twenty-four to twelve, then to sixteen, eight, and finally to forty-eight.

instructions

Make 8ch, ss in first ch to form a ring.

1st round 1ch, 24sc in ring, ss in first sc.

2nd round 1ch, 1sc in same place as ss, 5ch, [miss 1sc, 1dc in next sc, 3ch] 11 times, ss in 2nd ch.

3rd round Ss in each of next 2ch, 1ch, 1sc in same 5ch sp as ss, 3ch, [1sc in next 3ch sp, 3ch] 11 times, ss in first sc.

4th round 1ch, 1sc in same place as ss, 2ch, [3dc in next 3ch sp, 1dc in next sc] 11 times, 3dc in last 3ch sp, ss in 2nd ch.

5th round 1ch, 1sc in same place as ss, 1ch, 2dctog, 7ch, [3dctog, 7ch] 15 times, ss in 2dctog.

6th round Ss in first 7ch sp, 1ch, 1sc in same 7ch sp, 4ch, [1dc, 2ch] 4 times in same 7ch sp, * 1sc in next 7ch sp, 2ch, 1dc in next 7ch sp, [2ch, 1dc in same 2ch sp] 4 times, 2ch, rep from * 6 more times, 1sc in last 7ch sp, 2ch, ss in 2nd ch.

7th round Ss in first 2ch sp, 1ch, 1sc in same 2ch sp, [4ch, 1sc in next 2ch sp] 47 times, 4ch, ss in first sc.

Fasten off.

abbreviations and key

- **ch** = chain
- **sc** = single crochet
- **ss** = slip stitch
- **dc** = double crochet
- **2dctog** = leaving last loop of each stitch on hook, work 2dc, yo and pull through 3 loops on hook
- **3dctog** = leaving last loop of each stitch on hook, work 3dc, yo and pull through 4 loops on hook
- **yo** = yarn over hook
- **[ ]** = work instructions in square brackets as directed.

cobweb

This motif is very flexible; left to itself it's a circle, but joined with a space at each corner and three spaces along each side it'll pull into a square. When you've completed the five rounds given here, you'll see how the motif could easily be extended.

instructions

Wind yarn around finger to form a ring.

1st round 1ch, 1sc in ring, 2ch, 15dc in ring, ss in 2nd ch.

2nd round 1ch, 1sc in same place as ss, 3ch, [1dc in next dc, 1ch] 15 times, ss in 2nd ch.

3rd round 1ch, 1sc in same place as ss, 4ch, [1dc in next dc, 2ch] 15 times, ss in 2nd ch.

4th round 1ch, 1sc in same place as ss, 5ch, [1dc in next dc, 3ch] 15 times, ss in 2nd ch.

5th round 1ch, 1sc in same place as ss, 6ch, [1dc in next dc, 4ch] 15 times, ss in 2nd ch.

Fasten off.

shell-edged filet square

A simple square of filet mesh is made in rows first, then finished with a shell edging that has convenient chain spaces for joining it to other squares. Note that the filet mesh begins with a single crochet and two chain to stand for the first treble; this gives a neater edge.

instructions

Center Make 16 ch.

1st row (RS) 1dc in 6th ch from hook, [1ch, miss 1ch, 1dc in next ch] 5 times.

2nd row 1sc in first dc, 3ch, [1dc in next dc, 1ch] 5 times, miss 1ch, 1dc in next ch.

2nd row forms filet pattern. Work 4 more rows.

Border. 1st round (RS) 1ch, 2sc in first corner sp, * 2sc in each of next 4 sps along top edge, [2sc, 2ch, 2sc] in corner sp, 2sc in each of 4 sps along left side *, [2sc, 2ch, 2sc] in corner sp, rep from * to * along lower edge and right side, 2sc in first corner sp, 2ch, ss in first sc.

2nd round * Miss 1sc, [2dc, 2ch, 2dc] in next sc, miss 1sc, ss in next sc, rep from * two more times, placing last ss in corner 2ch sp, 1sc in corner sp, 6ch, ss in side of sc, ss in next sc, rep from * 3 more times omitting last ss.

Fasten off, joining end in last ss of 1st round when darning in ends.

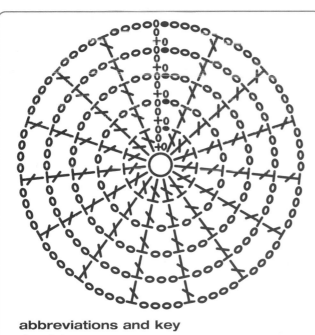

abbreviations and key

● ch = chain

✚ sc = single crochet

● ss = slip stitch

T dc = double crochet

[ ] = work instructions in square brackets as directed.

abbreviations

ch = chain

sc = single crochet

rep = repeat

RS = right side

ss = slip stitch

dc = double crochet

[ ] = work instructions in square brackets as directed.

pointed arches octagon

The only stitches you need to know to work this delicate motif are chain, single crochet, and treble, with slip stitches to join the rounds. Because it's so open, the motif is quick to work but looks very impressive.

instructions

Wind yarn around finger to form a ring.

1st round 1ch, 8sc in ring, ss in first ch.

2nd round 1ch, [1sc, 4ch, 1tr] in same place as ss, * 10ch, miss next sc, [1tr, 1ch, 1tr] in foll sc, rep from * two more times, 10ch, ss in 3rd ch.

3rd round Ss in first 1ch sp, 1ch, [1sc, 3ch, 1sc] in same 1ch sp, * [6sc, 3ch, 6sc] in next 10ch sp, [1sc, 3ch, 1sc] in foll 1ch sp, rep from * two more times, [6sc, 3ch, 6sc] in last 10ch sp, ss in first sc.

4th round Ss in first 3ch sp, 1ch, [1sc, 2ch, 4dctog] in same 3ch sp, [10ch, 1sc in next 3ch sp, 10ch, 5dctog in foll 3ch sp] 3 times, 10ch, 1sc in last 3ch sp, 10ch, ss in 4dctog.

5th round Ss in first 10ch sp, 1ch, [6sc, 3ch] twice in each 10ch sp, ss in first sc.

6th round Ss in last 3ch sp of 5th round, 1ch, 1sc in same 3ch sp, [7ch, 1sc in next 3ch sp] 15 times, 7ch, ss in first sc. Fasten off.

abbreviations and key

● **ch** = chain

✛ **sc** = single crochet

‡ **tr** = treble

foll = following

rep = repeat

sp = space

● **ss** = slip stitch

🖐 **4dctog** = leaving last loop of each stitch on the hook work 4dc, yarn over hook and pull through 5 loops on hook

🖐 **5dctog** = leaving last loop of each stitch on the hook work 5dc, yarn over hook and pull through 6 loops on hook

[ ] = work instructions in square brackets as directed.

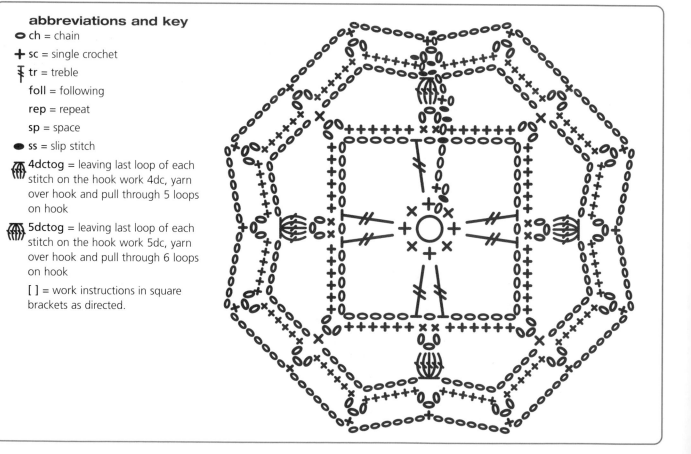

shell-edged flower medallion

This quick-to-work motif has a six-petal flower in the center that develops into a final round of twelve pointed shells. You could use just the one-round flower as a trim or as part of a corsage; in which case, work the last petal in the same way as the others, joining in first sc before fastening off.

instructions

4ch, ss in first ch to form a ring.

1st round 1ch, 1sc in ring, [5ch, 1dtr in ring, 5ch, 1sc in ring] 5 times, 5ch, placing first part st in ring and 2nd part st in first sc, work 2dtrtog.

2nd round 1ch, 1sc in 2dtrtog, [6ch, 1sc in next dtr] 5 times, 6ch, ss in first sc.

3rd round 1ch, 1sc in same place as ss, 5ch, 2dc in same place as ss, * [1sc, 6ch, 1sc] in next 6ch sp, [2dc, 3ch, 2dc] in next sc, rep from * 4 more times, [1sc, 6ch, 1sc] in last 6ch sp, 1dc in same place as first sc, ss in 2nd ch.

4th round Ss in first 3ch sp, 1ch, 1sc in same 3ch sp, [6ch, 1sc in next sp] 11 times, 3ch, 1dc in first sc.

5th round 1ch, 1sc in dc sp, 5ch, 3dc in dc sp, ss in next sc, * [3dc, 3ch, 3dc] in next 6ch sp, ss in next sc, rep from * 10 more times, 2dc in first sp, ss in 2nd ch.

Fasten off.

abbreviations and key

◦ **ch** = chain

✛ **sc** = single crochet

 rep = repeat

 sp = space

● **ss** = slip stitch

 st(s) = stitch(es)

⊤ **dc** = double crochet

 dtr = double treble

 2dtrtog = placing part sts as directed and leaving last loop of each st on the hook, work 2dtr, yarn over hook and pull through 3 loops on hook

 [ ] = work instructions in square brackets as directed.

simple lace block

This block uses panels of double crochet outlined with chain spaces to make an openwork square that is very quick to do. This small square is easily expanded to make the pink lace cushion in the projects section (see page 117).

instructions

Make 6ch, ss in first ch to form a ring.

1st round 3ch, 2dctog in ring, [3ch, 3dctog in ring, 2ch, 3dctog in ring] 3 times, 3ch, 3dctog in ring, 2ch, ss in 3rd ch.

2nd round, Ss in 3ch sp, 3ch, 2dctog in 3ch sp, [3ch, 3dctog in same sp, 1ch, 3dc in 2ch sp, 1ch, 3dctog in next 3ch sp] 3 times, 3ch, 3dctog in same sp, 1ch, 3dc in 2ch sp, 1ch, ss in 3rd ch.

3rd round Ss in 3ch sp, 3ch, 2dctog in 3ch sp, [3ch, 3dctog in same sp, 2ch, 1dc in 1ch sp, 1dc in each of next 3dc, 1dc in 1ch sp, 2ch, 3dctog in next 3ch sp] 3 times, 3ch, 3dctog in same sp, 2ch, 1dc in 1ch sp, 1dc in each of next 3dc, 1dc in 1ch sp, 2ch, ss in 3rd ch.

4th round Ss in 3ch sp, 3ch, 2dctog in 3ch sp, [3ch, 3dctog in same sp, 2ch, 1dc in 2ch sp, 1dc in each of next 5dc, 1dc in 2ch sp, 2ch, 3dctog in next 3ch sp] 3 times, 3ch, 3dctog in same sp, 2ch, 1dc in 2ch sp, 1dc in each of next 5dc, 1dc in 2ch sp, 2ch, ss in 3rd ch.

Edging. 1st round Ss in 3ch sp, 3ch, 2dctog in 3ch sp, * 3ch, 3dctog in same sp, 2ch, 1dc in 2ch sp, 1ch, 1dc in next dc, 1ch, [miss 1dc, 1dc in next dc, 1ch] 3 times, 1dc in 2ch sp, 2ch, 3dctog in next 3ch sp, rep from * two more times, 3ch, 3dctog in same

sp, 2ch, 1dc in 2ch sp, 1ch, 1dc in next dc, 1ch, [miss 1dc, 1dc in next dc, 1ch] 3 times, 1dc in 2ch sp, 2ch, ss in 3rd ch.

2nd round Ss in 3ch sp, 3ch, 2dctog in 3ch sp, * 3ch, 3dctog in same sp, [2ch, 3dctog in next sp] 8 times, rep from * two more times, 3ch, 3dctog in same sp, [2ch, 3dctog in next sp] 7 times, 2ch, ss in 3rd ch. Fasten off.

abbreviations and key

- **ch** = chain
- **rep** = repeat
- **sp** = space
- **ss** = slip stitch
- **dc** = double crochet
- **2dctog** = leaving last loop of each st on hook work 2dc, yo and pull through 3 loops on hook
- **3dctog** = leaving last loop of each st on hook, work 3dc, yo and pull through 4 loops on hook
- **yo** = yarn over hook
- **[ ]** = work instructions in square brackets as directed.

trefoil square

Ridged single crochet makes a firm center, then chain loops and picots speed up the work. A single crochet and picot edging finishes the motif neatly and gives convenient places for joining motifs.

instructions

Make 8ch, ss in first ch to form a ring.

1st round 1ch, 16sc in ring, remove hook, insert hook in back of first sc, catch loop and pull through. 16 sts.

2nd round 1ch, taking hook behind work 1sc around the stem of each sc, ss in first sc.

3rd round 1ch, 2sc in each sc, ss in first sc. 32 sts.

4th round 1ch, 1sc in same place as ss, [9ch, ss in 9th ch from hook, 10ch, ss in same ch as previous ss, 8ch, ss in same ch as previous ss *, 1sc in same sc as last sc, 1sc in each of next 4sc, 4ch, 1sc in same sc as last sc, 1sc in each of next 4sc] 4 times omitting last sc, ss in first sc.

Fasten off. Join yarn in a 4ch sp.

5th round 1ch, 1sc in same 4ch sp as join, [3ch, 1sc in next 8ch sp, 5ch, 1sc in foll 10ch sp, 5ch, 1sc in next 8ch sp, 3ch, 1sc in next 4ch sp] 4 times omitting last sc, ss in first sc.

6th round Ss in first 3ch sp, 1ch, 3sc in same 3ch sp, [6sc in each of next two 5ch sps, 3sc in each of foll two 3ch sps] 4 times omitting last 3sc, ss in first sc.

7th round 1ch, 1sc in same sc as ss, 1sc in each of foll 3sc, * [1sc

in next sc, 4ch, 1sc in same sc, 1sc in each of foll 2sc] 3 times, 1sc in next sc, 4ch, 1sc in same sc **, 1sc in each of next 8sc, rep from * two more times, then rep from * to **, 1sc in each of next 4sc, ss in first sc. Fasten off.

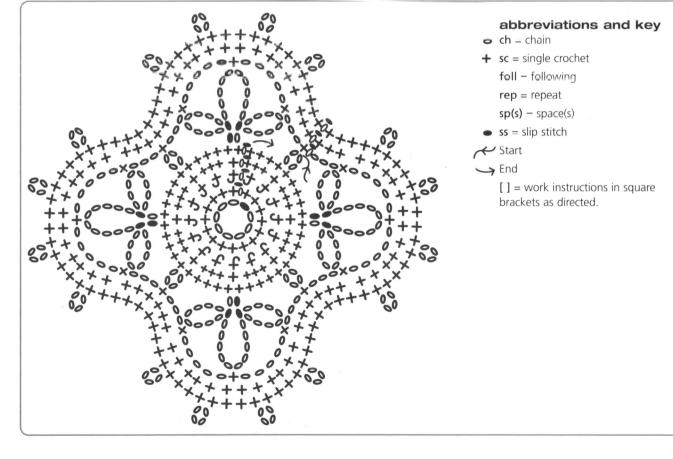

abbreviations and key

◦ **ch** – chain

✛ **sc** = single crochet

foll – following

rep = repeat

sp(s) – space(s)

● **ss** = slip stitch

↰ Start

↳ End

[ ] = work instructions in square brackets as directed.

alphabet

You can create the entire alphabet with combinations of simple crochet stitches —perfect to appliqué on a nursery throw.

A

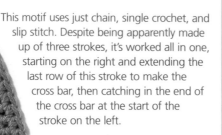

This motif uses just chain, single crochet, and slip stitch. Despite being apparently made up of three strokes, it's worked all in one, starting on the right and extending the last row of this stroke to make the cross bar, then catching in the end of the cross bar at the start of the stroke on the left.

instructions

Make 16ch.

Right stroke. 1st row (WS) 1sc in 2nd ch from hook, [1sc in each ch] to end. 15 sts.

2nd row 1ch, [1sc in each sc] to end.

Cross bar. 3rd row 1ch, 1sc in each of next 8sc, 6ch, 1sc in 2nd ch from hook, 1sc in each of next 4ch, 1sc in each of next 6sc of 2nd row, ss in last sc.

Left stroke.1st row Make 6ch, ss in end ch of cross bar, ss in base of next ch, make 8ch.

2nd row 1sc in 2nd ch from hook, 1sc in each of next 6ch, 1sc in each of next 2ss, 1sc in each of next 6ch, 1sc in each of next 3 row-ends. 18 sts.

3rd and 4th rows 1ch, [1sc in each sc] to end. Fasten off.

Edging With RS facing, join yarn in first sc of 1st row of right stroke, 1ch, 2sc in same place as join, 16sc up outer edge of right stroke, 3sc in corner sc, 16sc down outer edge of left stroke, 3sc in corner sc, 1sc in row-end, 3sc in corner sc, 7sc up inner edge of left stroke, 5sc along lower edge of cross bar, 7sc down inner edge of right stroke, 3sc in corner sc, 1sc in row-end, 1sc in same place as first 2sc, ss in first sc. Fasten off.

B

The vertical stroke is worked first using just chain and single crochet. The curves use single crochet with double crochet stitches to fill out the shape; they're worked over a chain extending from the last row of the vertical and joined with double crochet at the center of the stroke.

instructions

Make 19ch.

Vertical stroke. 1st row (WS) 1sc in 2nd ch from hook, [1sc in each ch] to end. 18 sts.

2nd and 3rd rows 1ch, [1sc in each sc] to end.

Curves. 1st row Ss in each of first 3sc, 10ch, miss next 5sc, 1dc in each of next 2sc, miss next 5sc, 10ch, ss in each of next 2sc, turn.

2nd row [5sc, 5hdc, 3sc] in upper 10ch sp, ss between next 2dc, [3sc, 5hdc, 5sc] in lower 10ch sp, ss in each of next 2ss, turn.

3rd row 1sc in each of first 5sc, 2hdc in each of next 5hdc, 1sc in next sc, ss in foll sc, miss 1sc, ss and 1sc, ss in next sc, 1sc in foll sc, 2hdc in each of next 5hdc, 1sc in each of last 5sc, ss in last sc of 3rd row of vertical stroke. Fasten off.

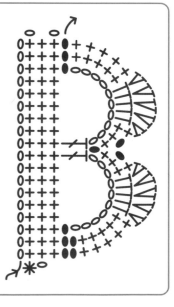

Edging With RS facing, join yarn in first sc at lower edge of 1st row of vertical stroke. 1ch, 2sc in same place as join, 2sc in row-ends along lower edge of vertical stroke, 1sc in each of next 15 sts around lower curve, miss next sc, ss between ss, miss foll sc, 1sc in each of next 15 sts, 2sc in row-ends along upper edge of vertical stroke, 3sc in corner sc, 16sc down outer edge of vertical stroke, 1sc in same place as first 2sc, ss in first sc. Fasten off.

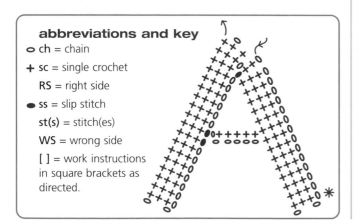

abbreviations and key

○ ch = chain

+ sc = single crochet

 RS = right side

● ss = slip stitch

 st(s) = stitch(es)

 WS = wrong side

 [ ] = work instructions in square brackets as directed.

abbreviations and key

○ ch = chain

+ sc = single crochet

 foll = following

T hdc = half double crochet

 RS = right side

 sp = space

● ss = slip stitch

 st(s) = stitch(es)

T dc = double crochet

 WS = wrong side

 [ ] = work instructions in square brackets as directed.

C

Single crochet is worked into a chain base with a few increases to establish the shape. More increases and half double crochet stitches fill out the curve of the letter on the following rows.

instructions

Make 23ch.

1st row (WS) 2sc in 2nd ch from hook, 2sc in next ch, 1sc in each of foll 2ch, 2sc in each of next 2ch, 1sc in each of foll 10ch, 2sc in each of next 2ch, 1sc in each of foll 2ch, 2sc in each of last 2ch. 30 sts.

2nd row 2ch, 1hdc in each of first 2sc, 2hdc in next sc, 1hdc in foll sc, 1sc in each of next 2sc, 1hdc in foll sc, 2hdc in next sc, 1hdc in each of foll 4sc, 2hdc in each of next 2sc, 1hdc in each of foll 2sc, 2hdc in each of next 2sc, 1hdc in each of foll 4sc, 2hdc in next sc, 1hdc in foll sc, 1sc in each of next 2sc, 1hdc in foll sc, 2hdc in next sc, 1hdc in each of last 2sc. 38 sts.

3rd row 2ch, 2hdc in first hdc, 1hdc in each of next 4hdc, 2hdc in each of next 2sc, 1hdc in each of next 4hdc, [2hdc in next hdc, 1hdc in foll hdc] 3 times, 1hdc in each of next 5hdc, [2hdc in next hdc, 1hdc in foll hdc] 3 times, 1hdc in each of next 3hdc, 2hdc in each of next 2sc, 1hdc in each of next 4 hdc, 2hdc in last hdc. 50 sts. Fasten off.

Edging With RS facing, join yarn in first sc at inner top edge of 1st row, 1ch, 1sc in same place as join, 3sc in row-ends along top edge, 3sc in first hdc, 1sc in each of next 48hdc around curve, 3sc in corner hdc, 4sc in row-ends across lower edge. Fasten off.

D

The construction for the D is similar to the letter B. The vertical stroke is worked first using chain and single crochet, then a large curve is made from a length of chain covered with single crochet and half double crochet to fill out the shape.

instructions

Make 19ch.

Vertical stroke. 1st row (WS) 1sc in 2nd ch from hook, [1sc in each ch] to end. 18 sts.

2nd and 3rd rows 1ch, [1sc in each sc] to end.

Curve. 1st row Turn and ss in each of first 3sc, make 20ch, miss 12sc, ss in each of next 2sc, turn.

2nd row [5sc, 14hdc, 5sc] in 20ch sp, miss first ss of vertical stroke, ss in each of last 2ss. 24 sts.

3rd row 1sc in each of first 5sc, 1hdc in each of next 4hdc, 2hdc in each of foll 6hdc, 1hdc in each of next 4hdc, 1sc in each of last 5sc, ss in last sc of vertical stroke. 30 sts.

Fasten off.

Edging With RS facing, join yarn in first sc at outer lower edge of vertical stroke, 1ch, 2sc in same place as join, 2sc in row-ends along lower edge, 1sc in each of next 30 sts around curve, 2sc in row-ends along top edge of vertical stroke, 3sc in corner sc, 16sc down outer edge of vertical, 1sc in same place as first 2sc, ss in first sc. Fasten off.

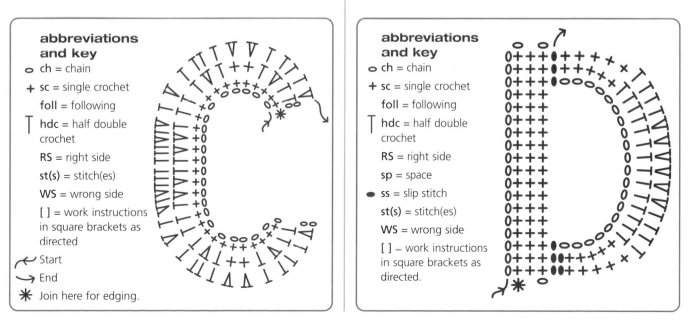

E

Two rows of the vertical stroke are worked first using just chain and single crochet, then the three horizontal strokes are added as extensions to the third row.

instructions
Make 19ch.

Vertical stroke. 1st row (WS) 1sc in 2nd ch from hook, [1sc in each ch] to end. 18 sts.

2nd row 1ch, [1sc in each sc] to end.

3rd row Make 9ch for top horizontal stroke, 1sc in 2nd ch from hook, 1sc in each of next 7ch, ss in first and 2nd sc of 2nd row, turn, 1sc in each of 8sc of horizontal, turn, 1ch, 1sc in each of 8sc of horizontal, ss in next sc of 2nd row, 1sc in each of foll 5sc of 2nd row, make 6ch for center horizontal stroke, 1sc in 2nd ch from hook, 1sc in each of next 4ch, ss in next sc of 2nd row, 1sc in each of foll 6sc of 2nd row, make 9ch for lower horizontal stroke and complete lower horizontal stroke in same way as top horizontal stroke, joining into last 3sc of 2nd row. Fasten off.

Edging With RS facing, join yarn in first sc at outer lower edge of vertical stroke, 1ch, 2sc in same place as join, 8sc along lower edge of horizontal, 3sc in corner sc, 1sc in row-end, 3sc in corner sc, 6sc along upper edge of lower stroke, 6sc up inner edge of vertical, 4sc along lower edge of center stroke, 3sc in sc at end, 4sc along upper edge of center stroke, 4sc up inner edge of vertical, 6sc along lower edge of top stroke, 3sc in corner sc, 1sc in row-end, 3sc in corner sc, 8sc along upper edge of top stroke, 3sc in corner sc, 16sc down outer edge of vertical, 1sc in same place as 2sc, ss in first sc. Fasten off.

abbreviations and key
- **o** ch = chain
- **+** sc = single crochet
- foll = following
- RS = right side
- **●** ss = slip stitch
- st(s) = stitch(es)
- WS = wrong side
- [ ] = work instructions in square brackets as directed
- ↵ Start
- ↳ End
- ✳ Join here for edging.

F

The letter F is constructed in the same way as the E, but without the lower stroke.

instructions
Make 19ch.

Vertical stroke. 1st row (WS) 1sc in 2nd ch from hook, [1sc in each ch] to end. 18 sts.

2nd row 1ch, [1sc in each sc] to end.

3rd row Make 9ch for top horizontal stroke, 1sc in 2nd ch from hook, 1sc in each of next 7ch, ss in first and 2nd sc of 2nd row, turn, 1sc in each of 8sc of horizontal, turn, 1ch, 1sc in each of 8sc of horizontal, ss in next sc of 2nd row, 1sc in each of foll 5sc of 2nd row, make 6ch for center horizontal stroke, 1sc in 2nd ch from hook, 1sc in each of next 4ch, ss in next sc of 2nd row, 1sc in each of last 9sc of 2nd row. Fasten off.

Edging With RS facing, join yarn in first sc at outer lower edge of vertical stroke, 1ch, 2sc in same place as join, 1sc in row-end, 3sc in corner sc, 8sc up inner edge of vertical, 4sc along lower edge of center stroke, 3sc in sc at end, 4sc along upper edge of center stroke, 4sc up inner edge of vertical, 6sc along lower edge of top stroke, 3sc in corner sc, 1sc in row-end, 3sc in corner sc, 8sc along upper edge of top stroke, 3sc in corner sc, 16sc down outer edge of vertical, 1sc in same place as 2sc, ss in first sc. Fasten off.

abbreviations and key
- **o** ch = chain
- **+** sc = single crochet
- foll = following
- RS = right side
- **●** ss = slip stitch
- st(s) = stitch(es)
- WS = wrong side
- [ ] = work instructions in square brackets as directed
- ↵ Start
- ↳ End
- ✳ Join here for edging

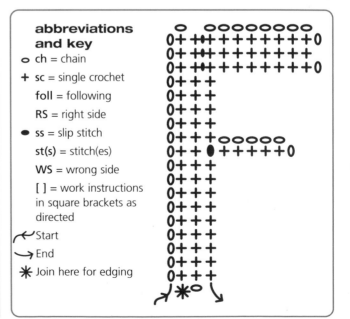

G

The letter G is based on the C; the cross bar is added when working the edging.

instructions

Make 23ch.

1st row (WS) 2sc in 2nd ch from hook, 2sc in next ch, 1sc in each of foll 2ch, 2sc in each of next 2ch, 1sc in each of foll 10ch, 2sc in each of next 2ch, 1sc in each of foll 2ch, 2sc in each of last 2ch. 30 sts.

2nd row 2ch, 1hdc in each of first 2sc, 2hdc in next sc, 1hdc in foll sc, 1sc in each of next 2sc, 1hdc in foll sc, 2hdc in next sc, 1hdc in each of foll 4sc, 2hdc in each of next 2sc, 1hdc in each of foll 2sc, 2hdc in each of next 2sc, 1hdc in each of foll 4sc, 2hdc in next sc, 1hdc in foll sc, 1sc in each of next 2sc, 1hdc in foll sc, 2hdc in next sc, 1hdc in each of last 2sc. 38 sts.

3rd row 2ch, 2hdc in first hdc, 1hdc in each of next 4hdc, 2hdc in each of next 2sc, 1hdc in each of next 4hdc, [2hdc in next hdc, 1hdc in foll hdc] 3 times, 1hdc in each of next 5hdc, [2hdc in next hdc, 1hdc in foll hdc] 3 times, 1hdc in each of next 3hdc, 2hdc in each of next 2sc, 1hdc in each of next 4 hdc, 2hdc in last hdc. 50 sts. Fasten off.

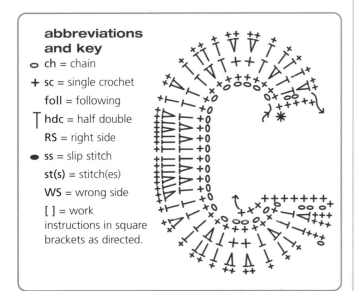

Edging and cross bar With RS facing, join yarn in first sc at inner top edge of 1st row, 1ch, 1sc in same place as join, 3sc in row-ends along top edge, 3sc in first hdc, 1sc in each of next 49hdc around curve, turn, 1ch, 1sc in each of first 3sc, turn, 1ch, 1sc in each of first 2sc, 3sc in corner sc, 4sc in row-ends across lower edge, 3sc in corner sc, [1sc between next 2sc along inner edge] twice. Fasten off

H

This letter is constructed from two pieces: the left vertical stroke has an extension in the third row for the center stroke, then the end of the bar is joined when working the base chain for the right vertical stroke.

instructions

Make 19ch.

Left vertical and center stroke.
1st row (WS) 1sc in 2nd ch from hook, [1sc in each ch] to end. 18 sts.

2nd row 1ch, [1sc in each sc] to end.

3rd row 1ch, 1sc in each of first 8sc, make 6ch for center horizontal stroke, 1sc in 2nd ch from hook, 1sc in each of next 4ch, 1sc in next sc of 2nd row, 1sc in each of foll 9sc of 2nd row. Fasten off.

Right vertical stroke Make 9ch, ss in end ch and in next ch of center stroke, make 8ch.

1st row (WS) 1sc in 2nd ch from hook, 1sc in each of next 6ch, 1sc in each of next 2ss, 1sc in each of last 9ch. 18 sts.

2nd and 3rd rows 1ch, [1sc in each sc] to end. Fasten off.

Edging With RS facing, join yarn in first sc at outer lower edge of left vertical stroke, 1ch, 2sc in same place as join, 1sc in row-end, 3sc in corner sc, 8sc up inner edge of left vertical, 4sc along lower edge of center stroke, 8sc down inner edge of right vertical, 3sc in corner sc, 1sc in row-end, 3sc in corner sc, 16sc up outer edge of right vertical, 3sc in corner sc, 1sc in row-end, 3sc in corner sc, 6sc down inner edge of right vertical stroke, 4sc along upper edge of center stroke, 6sc up inner edge of left vertical, 3sc in corner sc, 1sc in row-end, 3sc in corner sc, 16sc down outer edge of left vertical, 1sc in same place as 2sc, ss in first sc. Fasten off.

---

abbreviations and key

o   ch = chain

\+   sc = single crochet

   foll = following

T   hdc = half double

   RS = right side

●   ss = slip stitch

   st(s) = stitch(es)

   WS = wrong side

   [ ] = work instructions in square brackets as directed.

abbreviations and key

o   ch = chain

\+   sc = single crochet

   foll = following

   RS = right side

●   ss = slip stitch

   st(s) = stitch(es)

   WS = wrong side

   [ ] = work instructions in square brackets as directed.

I

This letter is the basic vertical stroke made using just chain and single crochet.

instructions
Make 19ch.

Vertical stroke. 1st row (WS) 1sc in 2nd ch from hook, [1sc in each ch] to end. 18 sts.

2nd and 3rd rows 1ch, [1sc in each sc] to end. Fasten off.

Edging With RS facing, join yarn in first sc at outer lower edge of vertical. 1ch, 2sc in same place as join, 1sc in row-end, 3sc in corner sc, 16sc up edge of vertical, 3sc in corner sc, 1sc in row-end, 3sc in corner sc, 16sc down edge of vertical, 1sc in same place as 2sc, ss in first sc. Fasten off.

abbreviations and key
o ch = chain
+ sc = single crochet
RS = right side
ss = slip stitch
st(s) = stitch(es)
WS = wrong side
[ ] = work instructions in square brackets as directed.

abbreviations and key
o ch = chain
+ sc = single crochet
foll = following
RS = right side
ss = slip stitch
st(s) = stitch(es)
WS = wrong side
[ ] = work instructions in square brackets as directed.

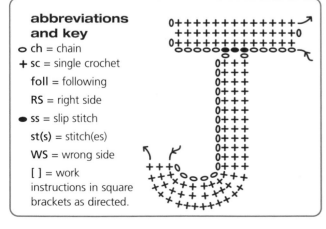

J

This letter is based on the vertical stroke made using just chain and single crochet and the lower curve of the letter U. The top horizontal stroke is the same as the letter T.

instructions
Make 18ch.

Lower curve and vertical stroke. 1st row (WS) 1sc in 2nd ch from hook, 1sc in each of next 10ch, 2sc in each of next 2ch, 1sc in each of foll 2ch, 2sc in each of next 2ch. 21 sts.

2nd row 1ch, 1sc in each of first 2sc, 2sc in foll sc, 1sc in each of next 4sc, 2sc in foll sc, 1sc in each of last 13sc. 23 sts.

3rd row 1ch, 1sc in each of first 13sc, [2sc in next sc, 1sc in each of foll 2sc, 2sc in next sc] twice, 1sc in each of last 2sc. 27 sts. Fasten off.

Top horizontal stroke
Make 5ch, with RS facing, ss in each row-end across top edge of vertical, make 6ch.

1st row (WS) 1sc in 2nd ch from hook, 1sc in each of next 4ch, 1sc in each of next 3ss, 1sc in each of last 5ch. 13 sts.

2nd and 3rd rows 1ch, [1sc in each sc] to end.

Do not fasten off if working edging in the same color.

Edging (RS) 1ch, 2sc in corner sc, 11sc along upper edge of top horizontal, 3sc in corner sc, 1sc in row-end, 3sc in corner sc, 4sc along lower edge of top horizontal, 18sc around inner edge of vertical and curve, 3sc in corner sc, 1sc in row-end, 3sc in corner sc, 26sc around outer edge of curve and vertical, 4sc along lower edge of top horizontal, 3sc in corner sc, 1sc in row-end, 1sc in same place as 2sc, ss in first sc. Fasten off.

K

The basic vertical stroke is made using just chain and single crochet, then the upper and lower diagonal strokes are added.

instructions
Make 19ch.

Vertical stroke. 1st row (WS) 1sc in 2nd ch from hook, [1sc in each ch] to end. 18 sts.

2nd and 3rd rows 1ch, [1sc in each sc] to end. Fasten off.

Upper diagonal stroke Make 8ch, with WS facing, ss in 8th sc from top inner edge of vertical, ss in next sc.

1st row 1sc in each of first 7ch, 2sc in last ch. 9 sts.

2nd row 1ch, [1sc in each sc] to end, ss in each of next 2sc of vertical.

3rd row 1sc in each of first 8sc, 2sc in last sc. 10 sts. Fasten off.

Lower diagonal stroke Make 9ch, with RS facing, ss in same place as ss at end of 2nd row of upper stroke, ss in next sc of upper stroke.

1st row 1sc in each of first 8ch, 2sc in last ch. 10 sts.

2nd row 1ch, [1sc in each sc] to end, ss in each of next 2sc of upper stroke.

3rd row 1sc in each of first 9sc, 2sc in last sc. 11 sts. Fasten off.

abbreviations and key
o ch = chain
+ sc = single crochet
RS = right side
ss = slip stitch
st(s) = stitch(es)
WS = wrong side
[ ] = work instructions in square brackets as directed.

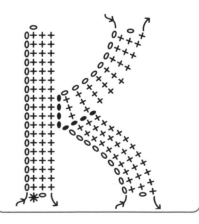

Edging With RS facing, join yarn in first sc at outer lower edge of vertical stroke, 1ch, 2sc in same place as join, 1sc in row-end, 3sc in corner sc, 7sc up inner edge of vertical, 8sc down inner edge of lower diagonal, 3sc in corner sc, 1sc in row-end, 3sc in corner sc, 10sc up outer edge of lower diagonal, 6sc up outer edge of upper diagonal, 3sc in corner, 1sc in row-end, 3sc in corner, 7sc down inner edge of upper diagonal, 6sc up inner edge of vertical, 3sc in corner sc, 1sc in row-end, 3sc in corner sc, 16sc down outer edge of vertical, 1sc in same place as 2sc, ss in first sc. Fasten off.

L

This letter starts with the basic vertical stroke made using just chain and single crochet, then the lower horizontal is added at the end of the third row, in the same way as for the E.

instructions

Make 19ch.

Vertical stroke. 1st row (WS) 1sc in 2nd ch from hook, [1sc in each ch] to end. 18 sts.

2nd row 1ch, [1sc in each sc] to end.

3rd row 1ch, 1sc in each of first 15sc, make 9ch for lower horizontal stroke, 1sc in 2nd ch from hook, 1sc in each of next

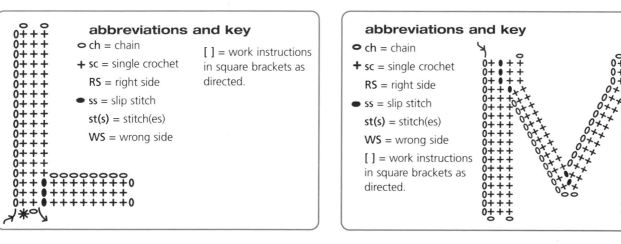

7ch, ss in each of next 2sc of 2nd row, turn, 1sc in each of 8sc of horizontal, turn, 1ch, 1sc in each of 8sc of horizontal, ss in last sc of 2nd row. Fasten off.

Edging With RS facing, join yarn in first sc at outer lower edge of vertical, 1ch, 2sc in same place as join, 8sc along lower edge, 3sc in corner sc, 1sc in row-end, 3sc in corner sc, 6sc along upper edge of horizontal, 14sc up inner edge of vertical, 3sc in corner, 1sc in row-end, 3sc in corner, 16sc down outer edge of vertical, 1sc in same place as 2sc, ss in first sc. Fasten off.

M

The M is made all in one piece. The first vertical is worked in the same way as the other vertical strokes, but with the second and third rows shortened to allow for adding the two-row down stroke. The two-row up stroke extends from the down stroke, then ends with another three-row vertical.

instructions

Make 19ch.

First vertical stroke. 1st row (RS) 1sc in 2nd ch from hook, [1sc in each ch] to end. 18 sts.

2nd row Ss in each of first 3sc, 1sc in each of last 15sc.

3rd row 1ch, 1sc in each of first 14sc, ss in next sc.

Down stroke Make 13ch.

1st row 1sc in 2nd ch from hook, 1sc in each of next 11ch, 1sc in ss at end of 3rd row of vertical, 1sc in each of 3ss at beginning of 2nd row of vertical. 16 sts.

2nd row 1ch, 1sc in each of first 14sc, ss in next sc, leave last sc.

Up stroke Make 14ch.

1st row 1sc in 2nd ch from hook, 1sc in each of next 12ch, 1sc in ss at end of 2nd row of down stroke, ss in first sc of 1st row of down stroke. 14 sts.

2nd row 1ch, 1sc in ss, 1sc in each of next 10sc, ss in next sc.

Last vertical stroke Make 15ch.

1st row 1sc in 2nd ch from hook, 1sc in each of next 13ch, 1sc in ss at end of 2nd row of up stroke, 1sc in each of next 2sc of 1st row of up stroke, ss in last sc.

2nd row 1ch, 1sc in ss, [1sc in each sc] to end. 18 sts.

3rd row 1ch, [1sc in each sc] to end.

Do not fasten off if working edging in the same color.

Edging (RS) 1ch, 2sc in corner sc, 1sc in row-end, 3sc in corner sc, 12sc down outer edge of up stroke, 13sc up outer edge of down stroke, 3sc in corner sc, 1sc in row-end, 3sc in corner sc, 16sc down outer edge of first vertical, 3sc in corner sc, 1sc in row-end, 3sc in corner sc, 13sc up inner edge of first vertical, 11sc down inner edge of down stroke, 2sc in each of next 2 corner sc, 10sc up inner edge of up stroke, 13sc down inner edge of last vertical, 3sc in corner sc, 1sc in row-end, 3sc in corner sc, 16sc up outer edge of last vertical, 1sc in same place as 2sc, ss in first sc. Fasten off.

abbreviations and key

○ **ch** = chain

+ **sc** = single crochet

RS = right side

● **ss** = slip stitch

st(s) = stitch(es)

WS = wrong side

[ ] = work instructions in square brackets as directed.

abbreviations and key

○ **ch** = chain

+ **sc** = single crochet

RS = right side

● **ss** = slip stitch

st(s) = stitch(es)

WS = wrong side

[ ] = work instructions in square brackets as directed.

N

The N is based on the M and is also made all in one piece.

instructions

Make 19ch.

Left vertical stroke. 1st row (RS) 1sc in 2nd ch from hook, [1sc in each ch] to end. 18 sts.

2nd row Ss in each of first 3sc, 1sc in each of last 15sc.

3rd row 1ch, 1sc in each of first 14sc, ss in next sc.

Down stroke Make 14ch.

1st row 1sc in 2nd ch from hook, 1sc in each of next 12ch, 1sc in ss at end of 3rd row of vertical, 1sc in each of 3ss at beginning of 2nd row of vertical. 17 sts.

2nd row 1ch, 1sc in each of first 14sc, ss in next sc, leave last 2sc.

Right vertical stroke Make 15ch.

1st row 1sc in 2nd ch from hook, 1sc in each of next 13ch, 1sc in ss at end of 2nd row of down stroke, 1sc in next sc of 1st row of down stroke, 2sc in last sc.

2nd and 3rd rows 1ch, [1sc in each sc] to end. 18 sts.

Do not fasten off if working edging in the same color.

Edging (RS) 1ch, 2sc in corner sc, 16sc up outer edge of right vertical stroke, 3sc in corner sc, 1sc in row-end, 3sc in corner sc, 12sc down inner edge of right vertical, 13sc up upper edge of down stroke, 3sc in corner sc, 1sc in row-end, 3sc in corner sc, 16sc down outer edge of left vertical, 3sc in corner sc, 1sc in row-end, 3sc in corner sc, 13sc up inner edge of left vertical, 13sc down lower edge of down stroke, 3sc in corner sc, 1sc in row-end, 1sc in same place as 2sc, ss in first sc. Fasten off.

abbreviations and key

- o ch = chain
- + sc = single crochet
  - RS = right side
- • ss = slip stitch
  - st(s) = stitch(es)
  - WS = wrong side
  - [ ] = work instructions in square brackets as directed.

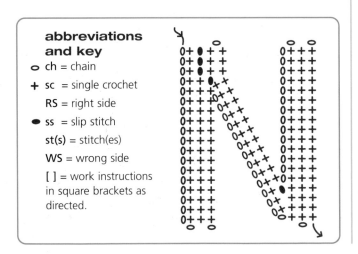

O

The first round of single crochet is worked into a circle of chain to make the basic O shape. Different-height stitches on the next round, and increases on the third round, gently shape the circle into an oval.

instructions

Make 36ch, ss in first ch to form a ring.

1st round (WS) 1ch, 48sc in ring, ss in first sc, turn. 48 sts.

2nd round 1ch, 1sc in each of first 5sc, 1hdc in each of foll 14sc, 1sc in each of next 10sc, 1hdc in each of foll 14sc, 1sc in each of last 5sc, ss in first sc, turn.

3rd round 1ch, 1sc in each of first 5sc, * 1hdc in each of next 4hdc, 2hdc in each of foll 6hdc, 1hdc in each of next 4hdc *, 1sc in each of next 10sc, rep from * to *, 1sc in each of last 5sc, ss in first sc, turn. 60 sts.

Do not fasten off if working edging in same color.

Edging (RS) 1ch, 1sc in each of 60 sts around edge, ss in first sc. Fasten off.

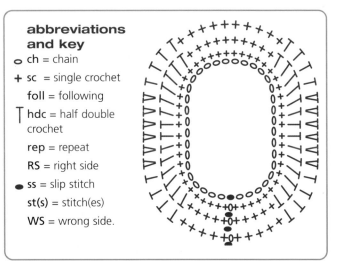

abbreviations and key

- o ch = chain
- + sc = single crochet
  - foll = following
- T hdc = half double crochet
  - rep = repeat
  - RS = right side
- • ss = slip stitch
  - st(s) = stitch(es)
  - WS = wrong side.

P

The upright of this letter P is the basic vertical stroke made using just chain and single crochet. The curve is shared with the letter R.

instructions

Make 19ch.

Vertical stroke. 1st row (WS) 1sc in 2nd ch from hook, [1sc in each ch] to end. 18 sts.

2nd and 3rd rows 1ch, [1sc in each sc] to end. Fasten off.

Curve With RS facing, join yarn in 10th sc from end of 3rd row of vertical, make 12ch, miss next 5sc of 3rd row of vertical, ss in each of next 2sc, turn.

1st row (WS) [5sc, 5hdc, 5sc] in 12ch sp, ss in each of next 2sc of 3rd row of vertical.

2nd row 1sc in each of first 5sc, 2hdc in each of foll 5hdc, 1sc in each of last 5sc, ss in last sc of 3rd row. Fasten off.

Edging With RS facing, join yarn in first sc at outer lower edge of vertical, 1ch, 2sc in same place as join, 1sc in row-end, 3sc in corner sc, 7sc up edge of vertical, 20sc around curve, 2sc in row-ends at top edge of vertical, 3sc in corner sc, 16sc down edge of vertical, 1sc in same place as 2sc, ss in first sc. Fasten off.

Q

The O is used as the basis for the Q, with extensions to form the tail.

instructions
Make 36ch, ss in first ch to form a ring.

1st round (WS) 1ch, 48sc in ring, ss in first sc, turn. 48 sts.

2nd round 1ch, 1sc in each of first 5sc, 1hdc in each of foll 14sc, 1sc in each of next 10sc, 1hdc in each of foll 14sc, 1sc in each of last 5sc, ss in first sc, turn.

3rd round 1ch, 1sc in each of first 5sc, * 1hdc in each of next 4hdc, 2hdc in each of foll 6hdc, 1hdc in each of next 4hdc *, 1sc in each of next 10sc, rep from * to *, 1sc in each of last 5sc, ss in first sc. 60 sts. Fasten off.

Outer tail With RS facing, join yarn in 6th st from join in 3rd round.

1st row 1ch, 1sc in same place as join, 1sc in each of next 2hdc, turn. 3 sts.

2nd row 1ch, 2sctog, 2sc in last sc.

3rd row 1ch, 2sc in first sc, 2sctog.

4th row 1ch, 2sctog, 1sc in last sc. 2 sts.

5th row 1ch, 2sctog. Fasten off.

Inner tail With RS facing, join yarn between 7th and 8th sc to the right of join in 1st round.

1st row 1ch, 1sc in same place as join, [1sc between next 2sc] twice. 3 sts.

2nd and 3rd rows As 4th and 5th rows of outer tail.

Do not fasten off if working edging in same color.

Inner edging (RS) 1ch, 1sc in each of next 3 row-ends of inner tail, [miss space between next 2sc, 1sc between foll 2sc of first round] 5 times, 1sc between each of next 12sc, [miss space between next 2sc, 1sc between foll 2sc] 6 times, 1sc between each of next 10sc, 1sc in each of next 3 row-ends of inner tail, ss in first sc. Fasten off.

Outer edging With RS facing, join yarn in 2sctog of 5th row of outer tail, 1ch, 3sc in same place as join, 1sc in each of next 4 row-ends of outer tail, 57sc around outer edge, 1sc in each of next 4 row-ends of outer tail, ss in first sc. Fasten off.

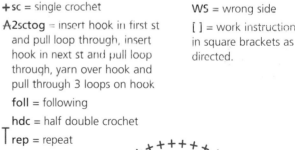

abbreviations and key
o ch = chain

+ sc = single crochet

A 2sctog = insert hook in first st and pull loop through, insert hook in next st and pull loop through, yarn over hook and pull through 3 loops on hook

foll = following

hdc = half double crochet

T rep = repeat

RS = right side

● ss = slip stitch

st(s) = stitch(es)

WS = wrong side

[ ] = work instructions in square brackets as directed.

abbreviations and key
o ch = chain

+ sc = single crochet

foll = following

T hdc = half double crochet

RS = right side

sp = space

● ss = slip stitch

st(s) = stitch(es)

WS = wrong side

[ ] = work instructions in square brackets as directed.

R

The R combines the letter P with the lower diagonal stroke of the letter K.

instructions

Make 19ch.

Vertical stroke. 1st row (WS) 1sc in 2nd ch from hook, [1sc in each ch] to end. 18 sts.

2nd and 3rd rows 1ch, [1sc in each sc] to end. Fasten off.

Curve With RS facing, join yarn in 10th sc from end of 3rd row of vertical, make 12ch, miss next 5sc of 3rd row of vertical, ss in each of next 2sc, turn.

1st row (WS) [5sc, 5hdc, 5sc] in 12ch sp, ss in each of next 2sc of 3rd row of vertical.

2nd row 1sc in each of first 5sc, 2hdc in each of foll 5hdc, 1sc in each of last 5sc, ss in last sc of 3rd row. Fasten off.

Lower diagonal stroke Make 9ch, ss in same place as 2nd ss at end of 1st row of curve, ss in next sc of curve.

1st row 1sc in each of first 8ch, 2sc in last ch. 10 sts.

2nd row 1ch, [1sc in each sc] to end, ss in each of next 2sc of curve.

3rd row 1sc in each of first 9sc, 2sc in last sc. 11 sts. Fasten off.

Edging With RS facing, join yarn in first sc at outer lower edge of vertical, 1ch, 2sc in same place as join, 1sc in row-end, 3sc in corner sc, 7sc up inner edge of vertical, 8sc down inner edge of lower diagonal, 3sc in corner sc, 1sc in row-end, 3sc in corner sc, 10sc up outer edge of diagonal, 16sc around curve, 2sc in row-ends at top of vertical, 3sc in corner sc, 16sc down outer edge of vertical, 1sc in same place as 2sc, ss in first sc. Fasten off.

abbreviations and key

o **ch** = chain

+ **sc** = single crochet

foll = following

T **hdc** = half double crochet

RS = right side

sp = space

● **ss** = slip stitch

st(s) = stitch(es)

WS = wrong side

[ ] = work instructions in square brackets as directed.

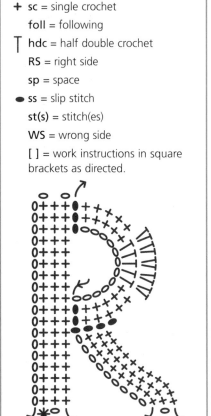

S

The base chain forms the inner edge of the lower curve and the outer edge of the upper curve. Carefully spaced increases and decreases on the following rows coax the chain into the curvy S shape.

instructions

Make 35ch.

1st row (WS) 1sc in 2nd ch from hook, 1sc in next ch, [2sctog] twice over next 4ch, 1sc in each of foll 4ch, [2sctog] twice over next 4ch, 1sc in each of foll 4ch, 2sctog over next 2ch, 1sc in each of next 5ch, 2sc in foll ch, [1sc in each of next 2ch, 2sc in each of foll 2ch] twice. 34 sts.

2nd row 1ch, 1sc in each of first 2sc, 2sc in foll sc, 1sc in each of next 4sc, 2sc in foll sc, [1sc in each of next 2sc, 2sc in foll sc] twice, 1sc in each of next 4sc, [2sctog] twice, 1sc in next sc, [2sctog] twice, 1sc in each of next 2sc, [2sctog] twice, 1sc in last

sc. 32 sts.

3rd row 1ch, 1sc in each of first 22 sts, [2sc in next sc, 1sc in each of foll 2sc, 2sc in next sc] twice, 1sc in each of last 2sc. 36 sts.

Do not fasten off if working edging in same color.

Edging (RS) 1ch, 2sc in corner sc, 34sc around outer lower and inner upper curves, 3sc in corner sc, 1sc in row-end, 3sc in corner sc, 34sc around outer upper and inner lower curves, 3sc in corner sc, 1sc in row-end, 1sc in same place as 2sc, ss in first sc. Fasten off.

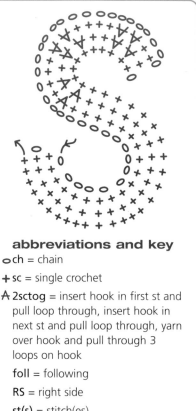

abbreviations and key

o **ch** = chain

+ **sc** = single crochet

A **2sctog** = insert hook in first st and pull loop through, insert hook in next st and pull loop through, yarn over hook and pull through 3 loops on hook

foll = following

RS = right side

st(s) = stitch(es)

ss = slip stitch

WS = wrong side

[ ] = work instructions in square brackets as directed.

T

This letter is made from a shorter vertical stroke and a top horizontal stroke that's the same as for the letter J.

instructions

Make 16ch.

Vertical stroke. **1st row** (WS) 1sc in 2nd ch from hook, 1sc in each of next 14ch. 15 sts.

2nd and 3rd rows 1ch, [1sc in each sc] to end.

Fasten off.

Top horizontal stroke Make 5ch, with RS facing, ss in each row-end across top edge of vertical, make 6ch.

1st row (WS) 1sc in 2nd ch from hook,

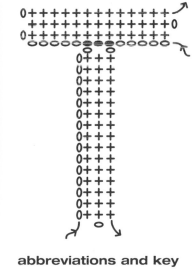

1sc in each of next 4ch, 1sc in each of next 3ss, 1sc in each of last 5ch. 13 sts.

2nd and 3rd rows 1ch, [1sc in each sc] to end.

Do not fasten off if working edging in the same color.

Edging (RS) 1ch, 2sc in corner sc, 11sc along upper edge of top horizontal, 3sc in corner sc, 1sc in row-end, 3sc in corner sc, 4sc along lower edge of top horizontal, 13sc down edge of vertical, 3sc in corner sc, 1sc in row-end, 3sc in corner sc, 13sc up edge of vertical, 4sc along lower edge of horizontal, 3sc in corner sc, 1sc in row-end, 1sc in same place as 2sc, ss in first sc. Fasten off.

U

The base chain forms the inner edge—so the down vertical, the curve, and the up vertical for the letter U are worked all in one piece. The curve is made in a similar way to the curve on the letter J.

instructions

Make 35ch.

1st row (WS) 1sc in 2nd ch from hook, 1sc in each of next 13ch, 2sc in each of foll 2ch, 1sc in each of next 2ch, 2sc in each of foll 2ch, 1sc in each of last 14ch. 38 sts.

2nd row 1ch, 1sc in each of first 15sc, 2sc in each of foll 2sc, 1sc in each of next 4sc, 2sc in each of foll 2sc, 1sc in each of last 15sc. 42 sts.

3rd row 1ch, 1sc in each of first 16sc, [2sc in each of next 2sc, 1sc in each of foll

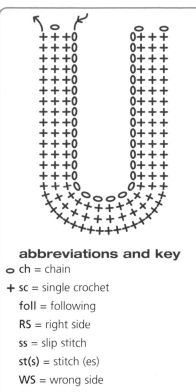

abbreviations and key

o **ch** = chain

+ **sc** = single crochet

foll = following

RS = right side

ss = slip stitch

st(s) = stitch (es)

WS = wrong side

[ ] = work instructions in square brackets as directed.

2sc] twice, 2sc in each of next 2sc, 1sc in each of foll 16sc, turn. 48 sts.

Do not fasten off if working edging in same color.

Edging (RS) 1ch, 2sc in corner sc, 46sc around outer edge, 3sc in corner sc, 1sc in row-end, 3sc in corner sc, 36sc around inner edge, 3sc in corner, 1sc in row-end, 1sc in same place as 2sc, ss in first sc. Fasten off.

V

This letter V is constructed with a shorter left diagonal worked first, then extended into the longer right diagonal.

instructions

Left diagonal Make 16ch.

1st row (WS) 1sc in 2nd ch from hook, [1sc in each ch] to end. 15 sts.

2nd row 1ch, [1sc in each sc] to end.

3rd row 1ch, 1sc in each of first 14sc, ss in last sc.

Right diagonal Make 15ch.

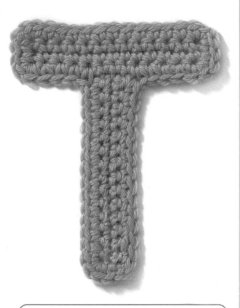

abbreviations and key

o **ch** = chain

+ **sc** = single crochet

RS = right side

ss = slip stitch

st(s) = stitch (es)

WS = wrong side

[ ] = work instructions in square brackets as directed.

1st row 1sc in 2nd ch from hook, 1sc in each of next 13ch, 1sc in each of next 3 row-ends. 17 sts.

2nd and 3rd rows 1ch, [1sc in each sc] to end.

Do not fasten off if working edging in same color.

Edging (RS) 1ch, 2sc in corner sc, 14sc up outer edge of right diagonal, 3sc in corner sc, 1sc in row-end, 3sc in corner sc, 12sc down inner edge of right diagonal, 12sc up inner edge of left diagonal, 3sc in corner sc, 1sc in row-end, 3sc in corner sc, 16sc down outer edge of left diagonal, 1sc in same place as 2sc, ss in first sc. Fasten off.

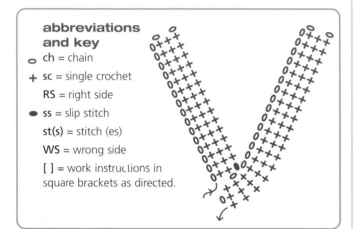

abbreviations and key

- ○ ch = chain
- ＋ sc = single crochet
- RS = right side
- ● ss = slip stitch
- st(s) = stitch (es)
- WS = wrong side
- [ ] = work instructions in square brackets as directed.

W

The W is simply the M used the other way up.

X

The top-left-to-bottom-right diagonal is worked first, then the upper right and lower left diagonals are added to complete the X.

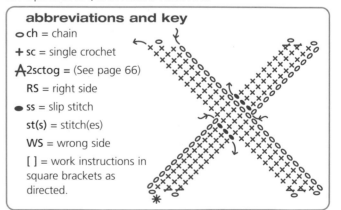

instructions

First diagonal stroke Make 25ch.

1st row (WS) 1sc in 2nd ch from hook, [1sc in each ch] to end. 24 sts.

2nd row 1ch, 2sc in first sc, 1sc in each of next 21sc, 2sctog.

3rd row 1ch, 2sctog, 1sc in each of next 21sc, 2sc in last sc. Fasten off.

Upper right diagonal With RS facing, join yarn between 12th and 13th sc from lower right of first diagonal. Make 12ch.

1st row 1sc in 2nd ch from hook, 1sc in each of next 10ch, ss in same place as join, ss between next 2 sts of first diagonal, turn. 11 sts.

2nd row 1sc in each of first 9sc, 2sctog.

3rd row 1ch, 2sctog, 1sc in each of next 8sc, ss between next 2 sts of first diagonal. Fasten off.

Lower left diagonal With RS facing, join yarn in 13th sc from top left of first diagonal. Make 13ch.

1st row 1sc in 2nd ch from hook, 1sc in each of next 11ch, ss in same place as join, ss in next sc of first diagonal, turn. 12 sts.

2nd row 1sc in each of next 10sc, 2sctog.

3rd row 1ch, 2sctog, 1sc in each of next 9sc, ss in next sc of first diagonal. Fasten off.

Edging With RS facing, join yarn in first sc at outer edge of lower left diagonal, 1ch, 2sc in same place as join, 1sc in row-end, 3sc in corner sc, 9sc up inner edge of lower left diagonal, 9sc down inner edge of lower right diagonal, 3sc in corner sc, 1sc in row-end, 3sc in corner sc, 10sc up outer edge of lower right diagonal, 10sc up outer edge of upper right diagonal, 3sc in corner sc, 1sc in row-end, 3sc in corner sc, 9sc down inner edge of upper right diagonal, 9sc up inner edge of upper left diagonal, 3sc in corner sc, 1sc in row-end, 3sc in corner sc, 10sc down outer edge of upper left diagonal, 10sc down outer edge of lower left diagonal, 1sc in same place as 2sc, ss in first sc. Fasten off.

abbreviations and key

- ○ ch = chain
- ＋ sc = single crochet
- ⋀ 2sctog = (See page 66)
- RS = right side
- ● ss = slip stitch
- st(s) = stitch(es)
- WS = wrong side
- [ ] = work instructions in square brackets as directed.

Y

This letter is worked all in one piece. It starts with a stroke that forms the short straight vertical and the diagonal to the left, then the diagonal to the right is extended from the third row of the first stroke.

instructions

Vertical and left diagonal Make 22ch.

1st row (WS) 1sc in 2nd ch from hook, 1sc in each of next 10ch, 2sc in next ch, 1sc in each of last 9ch. 22 sts.

2nd row 1ch, 1sc in each of first 9sc, 2sc in each of foll 2sc, 1sc in each of next 9sc, 2sctog. 23 sts.

3rd row 1ch, 2sctog, 1sc in each of next 9sc.

Right diagonal Make 11ch.

1st row 1sc in 2nd ch from hook, 1sc in each of next 9ch, ss in each of next 2sc of 2nd row of vertical and left diagonal, turn. 10 sts.

2nd row 1sc in each of next 9sc, 2sc in last sc.

3rd row 1ch, 2sc in first sc, 1sc in each of next 10sc of right diagonal, 1sc in each of last 10sc of 2nd row of vertical.

Do not fasten off if working edging in same color.

Edging (RS) 1ch, 2sc in corner sc, 20sc up outer edge of vertical and right diagonal, 3sc in corner sc, 1sc in row-end, 3sc in corner sc, 8sc down inner edge of right diagonal, 8sc up edge inner edge of left diagonal, 3sc in corner sc, 1sc in row end, 3sc in corner sc, 20sc down outer edge of left diagonal and vertical, 3sc in corner sc, 1sc in row-end, 1sc in same place as 2sc, ss in first sc.

Fasten off.

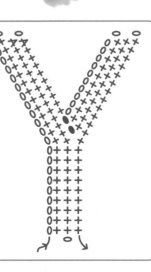

abbreviations and key

o **ch** = chain

+ **sc** = single crochet

A **2sctog** = (See page 66)

RS = right side

● **ss** = slip stitch

st(s) = stitch(es)

WS = wrong side

[ ] = work instructions in square brackets as directed.

Z

The top-right-to-bottom-left diagonal is worked first, with the lower horizontal stroke extended from the last stitch of the third row of the diagonal. Then the upper horizontal stroke is added to complete the Z.

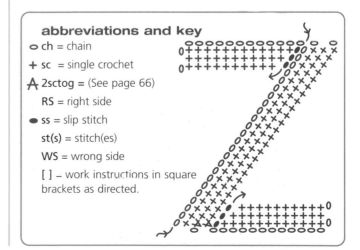

instructions

Diagonal stroke Make 25ch.

1st row (WS) 1sc in 2nd ch from hook, [1sc in each ch] to end. 24 sts.

2nd row 1ch, 2sctog, 1sc in each of next 21sc, 2sc in last sc.

3rd row 1ch, 2sc in first sc, 1sc in each of next 21sc, 2sctog.

Lower horizontal Make 13ch.

1st row 1sc in 2nd ch from hook, 1sc in each of next 11ch, ss in first and 2nd sts of diagonal, turn. 12 sts.

2nd row Miss first sc of lower horizontal, 1sc in each of next 11sc.

3rd row 1ch, 1sc in each of next 10sc, miss last sc, ss in next sc of diagonal. Fasten off.

Upper horizontal With RS facing, join yarn in first sc at top left of diagonal. Make 13ch.

Work as lower horizontal joining between sts of first row of first diagonal. Fasten off.

Edging With RS facing, join yarn in first sc at lower left outer edge of diagonal, 1ch, 2sc in same place as join, 13sc along lower edge, 3sc in corner sc, 1sc in row-end, 3sc in corner sc, 9sc along upper edge of lower horizontal, 20sc up edge of diagonal, 3sc in corner sc, 13sc along upper edge, 3sc in corner sc, 1sc in row-end, 3sc in corner sc, 9sc along lower edge of upper left horizontal, 20sc down edge of diagonal, 1sc in same place as 2sc, ss in first sc. Fasten off.

abbreviations and key

o **ch** = chain

+ **sc** = single crochet

A **2sctog** = (See page 66)

RS = right side

● **ss** = slip stitch

st(s) = stitch(es)

WS = wrong side

[ ] = work instructions in square brackets as directed.

shapes

Each shape stands alone or can be combined with other motifs to create larger blocks or a repeat fabric. Try spirals linked together in Celtic designs; shells and scallops joined to make a border or insertion.

simple paisley block

Here the characteristic paisley shape is reduced to the simplest curl and outlined to make an oblong block, so it's easy to keep your place and easy to join the motifs. The sample shown here is worked in just three colors, but you could use a different color for each round if you want a jazzier effect.

instructions

Colors: Two shades of purple (A) and cream (B).

Motif Using A, make 9ch, ss in 5th ch from hook, turn.

1st round 8sc in ring, 1sc in each of next 3ch, ss in last ch, turn.

2nd round (RS) 1ch, 1sc in ss, [1ch, 1dc in next sc] 11 times, 1ch, ss in first ch of 1st round. Fasten off.

With RS facing join B in same ch as ss at end of 1st round.

3rd round 3ch, 2dc in same place as join, [1ch, 2dc in next 1ch sp] 11 times, 1ch, ss in next sp, ss in base of each of next 3 starting ch. Fasten off.

With RS facing, join A in 3ch sp at beg of 3rd round.

4th round [3ch, 3dc] in same sp as join, [1ch, 3dc in next 1ch sp] 12 times, ss in same ch as ss at end of first round, 3ch, ss in first ch of this round. Fasten off.

With RS facing, join B in 3ch sp at end of 4th round.

5th round 1ch, 1sc in same sp as join, 3ch, 1sc in 3ch sp at beg of 4th round, [4ch, 1sc in next 1ch sp] 12 times, 3ch, 1sc in ss, 3ch, ss in first sc.

6th round Ss in first 3ch sp, 1ch, [1sc, 1dc, 2ch, 1dc, 1sc] in first 3ch sp, [1sc, 1dc, 2ch, 1dc, 1sc] in each of foll twelve 4ch sps, 1sc, 1dc in next 3ch sp, 2ch, 1dc, 1sc in last 3ch sp, ss in first sc. Fasten off.

With RS facing, join A in first 2ch sp of 6th round.

7th round 1ch, 1sc in same 2ch sp, 9ch, [1sc in next 2ch sp, 4ch] twice, 1sc in foll 2ch sp, 9ch, [1sc in next 2ch sp, 4ch] 3 times, 1sc in foll 2ch sp, 9ch, [1sc in next 2ch sp, 4ch] twice, 1sc in foll 2ch sp, 9ch, [1sc in next 2ch sp, 4ch] 3 times, ss in first sc.

8th round Ss in first 9ch sp, 1ch, 1sc in same sp, 3ch, 1dc in same sp, 1ch, 1dc in same sp, 3ch, [1dc in same sp, 1ch] 3 times, [1dc in next sp, 1ch, 1dc in same sp, 1ch] twice, * 1dc in next 9ch sp, [1ch, 1dc in same 9ch sp] twice, 3ch, [1dc in same 9ch sp, 1ch] 3 times *, [1dc in next 4ch sp, 1ch, 1dc in same 4ch sp, 1ch] 3 times, rep from * to *, work instructions in last square brackets twice, rep from * to *, work instructions in last square brackets 3 times, ss in 2nd ch. Fasten off.

abbreviations

beg = beginning

ch = chain

dc = double crochet

foll = following

rep = repeat

sp(s) = space(s)

sc = single crochet

ss = slip stitch

[ ] = work instructions in square brackets as directed.

swirling heart

Two spirals are extended, joined, filled in, and edged to make this pretty heart. If you made this motif in green and turned it the other way up, it would also make a good leaf.

instructions

First spiral Wind yarn around finger to form a ring.

1st round 1ch, [2sc, 2hdc, 6dc] in ring. 10 sts.

2nd round 2dc in each st. 20 sts.

Fasten off.

Second spiral Work as given for first spiral but do not fasten off.

With WS of first spiral facing, join spare yarn in same dc as the last dc of 2nd round was worked, make 15ch, with RS facing of 2nd spiral facing, join yarn with ss in same dc as the last dc of 2nd round was worked.

Joining row Continue with yarn from 2nd spiral and inserting hook in top loop of chain only, work 1dc in each of first 7ch, [2dc, 2ch, 2dc] in next ch, 1dc in each of last 7ch, ss in last dc of first spiral. Fasten off.

Center With RS facing, join yarn in top loop of 2nd ch along from first spiral, 1ch, 1sc in same ch as join, 3ch, leaving last loop of each st on hook and working into top loop of chain only, miss 1ch, 1tr in next ch, miss 1ch, 1dtr in next ch, miss 1ch, 1trtr in next ch, miss 1ch, 1dtr in next ch, [miss 1ch, 1tr in next ch] twice, yo and pull through 7 loops on hook, 1ch.

Pull ch tight and leaving a long end, fasten off. Thread a blunt-pointed needle with yarn end, stitch around the stem of 2nd dc of first spiral and through top of cluster, around stem of 2nd dc of 2nd spiral and through cluster, then with 2nd spiral on top, stitch through each of next 2dc of each spiral. Fasten off.

Border Join yarn in 2ch sp at lower point.

1st round 1ch, 1sc in 2ch sp, 4ch, 1dc in 2ch sp, [1ch, miss 1dc, 1dc in next dc] 8 times, [1ch, 1dc in next dc] 3 times, 1ch, miss 1dc, 1dc in next dc, 1ch, miss 1dc, placing first st in next dc of first spiral and 2nd st in corresponding dc of 2nd spiral work 2dctog, [1ch, miss 1dc, 1dc in next dc] twice, [1ch, 1dc in next dc] 3 times, [1ch, miss 1dc, 1dc in next dc] 7 times, 1ch, ss in 2nd ch. Fasten off.

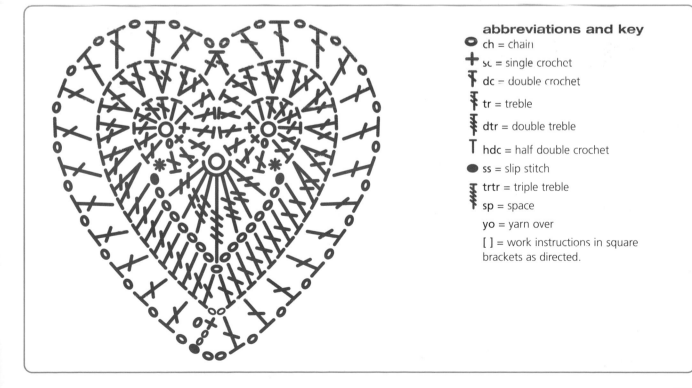

abbreviations and key

O ch = chain

+ sc = single crochet

Ŧ dc = double crochet

Ŧ tr = treble

Ŧ dtr = double treble

T hdc = half double crochet

● ss = slip stitch

Ŧ trtr = triple treble

Ŧ sp = space

yo = yarn over

[ ] = work instructions in square brackets as directed.

two-color spiral

Have you ever made the mistake of carrying on working instead of joining a round? This interesting motif exploits that mistake to show the curved, shell-like shape that's formed when you work in a spiral. Using two colors helps you to see exactly where to work and how many stitches to make for this small motif. If you want to make a bigger spiral and you continue increasing in every stitch, you'll make a cupped or domed shape, so you'll need to space the increases one stitch farther apart on each extra round to make sure that it lies flat.

instructions

Colors: Cream (A) and green (B).

Using A, wrap yarn around finger to make a ring.

1st round (RS) Cont in A, work 1ch, 1sc, 1hdc, 2dc in ring, remove hook, join B in ring, work 1ch, 1sc, 1hdc, 2dc in ring.

2nd round Cont in B, work 2dc in sc in A, 2dc in hdc in A and 2dc in each of 2dc in A, remove hook and return to last st in A, cont in A, work 2dc in sc in B, 2dc in hdc in B and 2dc in each of 2dc in B.

3rd round Cont in A, work 2dc in each of next 8dc in B, remove hook, return to last st in B, work 2dc in each of next 8dc in A.

4th round Cont in B, work 2dc in each of next 3dc in A, fasten off, return to last st in A, cont in A, work 2dc in each of next 3dc in B.

Fasten off.

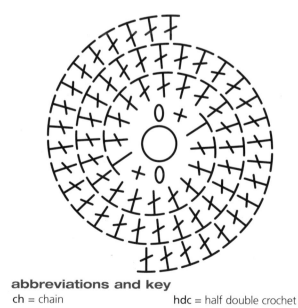

abbreviations and key

ch = chain

cont = continue

sc = single crochet

hdc = half double crochet

dc = double crochet

three-color spiral

Working out from the center in a spiral with three starting points makes a swirling, three-armed motif that can be joined to make a variety of Celtic-style designs. When planning a design, remember that changing the order the colors are worked in will link the motifs together differently.

instructions

Colors: Cream (A), light blue (B), and dark blue (C).

Using A, wind yarn around finger to form a ring.

1st round Using A, * [1ch, 1sc, 1hdc, 2dc] in ring, remove hook*, join B in ring and rep from * to *, join C in ring and rep from * to *.

2nd round Return hook to loop in A, * 2dc in each of next 4 sts, remove hook *, return hook to loop in B, rep from * to *, return hook to loop in C, rep from * to *.

3rd round Return hook to loop in A, * 2dc in each of next 8dc *, return hook to loop in B, rep from * to *, return hook to loop in C, rep from * to *.

Fasten off all colors.

abbreviations

ch = chain

dc = double crochet

hdc = half double crochet

rep = repeat

sc = single crochet

[ ] = work instructions in square brackets as directed.

four-color spiral

The four-armed spiral is a favorite Celtic motif. The motifs can be joined to make a fabric—giving "S" spirals in each color—or you could continue working outward to make a larger motif, spacing the increases one double crochet stitch farther apart on following rounds to keep the work flat.

instructions

Colors: Cream (A), pale duck egg (B), dark duck egg (C), and teal (D). When removing hook to work in following color, pull loop up so stitches do not unravel. Pull end to close loop on hook on following rounds.

Using A, wind yarn around finger to form a ring.

1st round *[1ch, 1sc, 1hdc, 2dc] in ring, remove hook, joining B, C, and D in ring in turn, rep from *.

2nd round Cont in A, * 2dc in next sc, 1dc in next hdc, 2dc in next dc, 1dc in foll dc, using B, C, and D in turn, rep from *.

3rd round Cont in A, * [2dc in next dc, 1dc in foll dc] 3 times, using B, C, and D in turn, rep from *.

4th round Cont in A, * [2dc in next dc, 1dc in foll dc] 4 times, 2dc in next dc, using B, C, and D in turn, rep from *.

Fasten off all colors.

oak leaf

Working fans at each side of a central chain stem makes a curvy, scalloped oak leaf shape.

instructions

Make 15ch.

1st round Working into back loop of chain only, [2dc, 1hdc] in 4th ch from hook. * 1sc in next ch, ss in foll ch, 1sc in next ch, [1hdc, 1dc, 1hdc] in foll ch, rep from * once, 1sc in next ch, ss in each of last 2ch, 1sc in same ch as last ss, working into top loop of chain only, ss in same ch as sc, ** ss in next ch, 1sc in foll ch, [1hdc, 1dc, 1hdc] in next ch, 1sc in foll ch, rep from ** once, ss in next ch, 1sc in next ch, [1hdc, 2dc] in foll ch, ss in last ch.

2nd round 1ch, 1sc in same place as ss, 2ch, 2dc in each of next 2dc, 1dc in hdc, * 3sctog, 1dc in next hdc, 3dc in dc, 1dc in hdc, rep from * once, 1hdc in sc, 1sc in ss, ss in next ss, [ss, 2ch, ss] in sc, ss in next ss, 1sc in foll ss, 1hdc in sc, ** 1dc in hdc, 3dc in dc, 1dc in hdc, 3sctog, rep from ** once, 1dc in hdc, 2dc in each of next 2dc, 2dc in same place as sc at beg, ss in 2nd ch.

Fasten off.

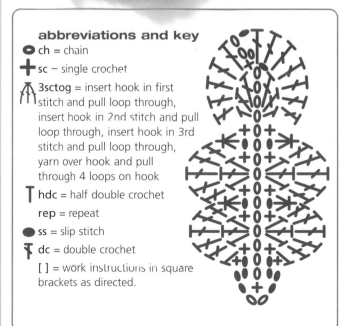

abbreviations

ch = chain

sc = single crochet

foll = following

hdc = half double crochet

rep = repeat

dc = double crochet

[ ] work instructions in square brackets as directed.

abbreviations and key

● **ch** = chain

✚ **sc** – single crochet

⋀ **3sctog** = insert hook in first stitch and pull loop through, insert hook in 2nd stitch and pull loop through, insert hook in 3rd stitch and pull loop through, yarn over hook and pull through 4 loops on hook

⊤ **hdc** = half double crochet

rep = repeat

● **ss** = slip stitch

↑ **dc** = double crochet

[ ] = work instructions in square brackets as directed.

single crochet heart

This neat motif grows out from three center starting points, shaped to make the classic rounded and pointed heart shape.

instructions

Make 4ch, ss in first ch, [3ch, ss in same ch as first ss] twice.

1st round Ss in first 3ch sp, 1ch, 5sc in each 3ch sp, ss in first sc. 15 sc.

2nd round 1ch, 1sc in same place as ss, 1sc in next sc, 2sc in each of foll 2sc, ss between next 2sc, 2sc in each of foll 2sc, 1sc in each of next 4sc, 3sc in foll sc, 1sc in each of last 2sc, ss in first sc. 19 sc.

3rd round 1ch, 1sc in same place as ss, 1sc in next sc, 2sc in each of foll 3sc, miss next sc, ss in same place as ss, miss next sc, 2sc in each of foll 3sc, 1sc in each of next 5sc, 3sc in foll sc, 1sc in each of last 3sc, ss in first sc. 25 sc.

4th round 1ch, 1sc in same place as ss, 1sc in each of next 2sc, 2sc in each of foll 3sc, 1sc in next sc, ss in foll sc, ss in same place as ss, ss in next sc, 1sc in foll sc, 2sc in each of next 3sc, 1sc in each of next 7sc, 3sc in foll sc, 1sc in each of last 4sc, ss in first sc. 31 sc.

5th round 1ch, 1sc in same place as ss, 1sc in each of next 4sc, 2sc in each of foll 3sc, 1sc in each of next 2sc, ss in same place as each of next 3ss, 1sc in each of next 2sc, 2sc in each of foll 3sc, 1sc in each of next 10sc, 3sc in foll sc, 1sc in each of last 5sc, ss in first sc. 39 sc.

Fasten off.

star

This star is worked in half double crochet; it has a pentagon at the center with each of the five points worked separately. Used alone, it makes a decorative motif, but you'll need to add diamonds and hexagons to join the stars for an afghan.

instructions

Make the 4-round half double crochet pentagon as given in the geometric motifs section (page 104), do not fasten off at the end of the last round.

First point On 3rd, 5th, 7th, and 9th rows, work into the strand as well as the front loop of each half double crochet.

1st row (RS) 1ch, 1sc in same place as ss at end of 4th round of pentagon, 1ch, 1hdc in each of next 8 hdc, turn. 9 sts.

2nd row 1sc in first hdc, 1ch, 1hdc in each of next 7hdc, 1hdc in top ch.

3rd row 1sc in first hdc, 1hdc in each of next 6hdc, 2hdctog. 7 sts.

4th row 1sc in first st, 1ch, 1hdc in each of next 6hdc.

5th row 1sc in first hdc, 1hdc in each of next 4hdc, 2hdctog. 5 sts.

6th row 1sc in first st, 1ch, 1hdc in each of next 4hdc.

7th row 1sc in first hdc, 1hdc in each of next 2hdc, 2hdctog. 3 sts.

8th row 1sc in first st, 1ch, 1hdc in each of next 2hdc.

9th row 1sc in first hdc, 2hdctog.

10th row 1sc in 2hdctog, 1ch. Fasten off.

2nd, 3rd, 4th, and 5th points Joining yarn in same place as last hdc of first row of previous point each time, work 4 more points in the same way.

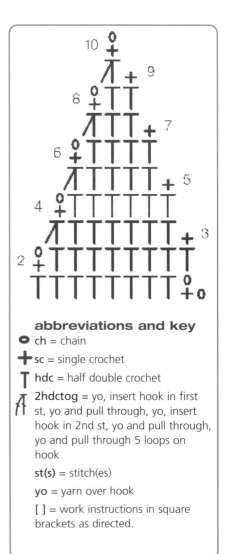

abbreviations and key

- **○ ch** = chain
- **+ sc** = single crochet
- **T hdc** = half double crochet
- **⋀ 2hdctog** = yo, insert hook in first st, yo and pull through, yo, insert hook in 2nd st, yo and pull through, yo and pull through 5 loops on hook
- **st(s)** = stitch(es)
- **yo** = yarn over hook
- **[ ]** = work instructions in square brackets as directed.

abbreviations

ch = chain

foll = following

sc = single crochet

sp = space

ss = slip stitch

[ ] = work instructions in square brackets as directed.

paisley

The characteristic curled paisley shape translates beautifully into crochet. The center is made up of leaf shapes branching out from a stem and the border has a curled tail that's joined to the edging in the last round. To make a three-color motif, work the center in the first color, the 1st, 2nd, 4th, and 5th rows of the border in the second color, and the 3rd row in the third color, or work it in one shade of fine yarn to emphasize the delicate lacy tracery.

instructions

Colors: Pink (A), black (B), and purple (C).

Center Using A, make 8ch, 1sc in 5th ch from hook, * 10ch, ** 1sc in 3rd ch from hook, 1dc in 4th ch, 1tr in 5th ch, 1dc in 6th ch, 1sc in 7th ch ***, [11ch, **** 1sc in 3rd ch, 1dc in 4th ch, 1tr in each of 5th and 6th ch, 1dc in 7th ch, 1sc in 8th ch *****] twice, rep from * to ***, [7ch, rep from ** to ***] twice, [1sc in each of next 3ch, 8ch, rep from **** to *****] twice, 1sc in each of next 3ch, 7ch, rep from ** to ***, 1sc in each of next 3ch, 5ch, 1sc in end ch, 1sc in each of last 3ch, turn.

Fasten off.

Border Join B in last sc at end of stalk.

1st row (WS) 3ch, 1sc in tip of 1st leaf, [3ch, 1sc in next leaf tip] twice, 4ch, 1sc in 4th leaf tip, 4ch, 1sc in 5th leaf tip, 8ch, 1sc in 6th leaf tip, 10ch, 1sc in 7th leaf tip, 6ch, 1sc in 8th leaf tip, 5ch, 1sc in 9th leaf tip, [4ch, 1sc in next leaf tip] twice, 6ch, ss in end of stalk, make 25ch, turn.

2nd row 2sc in 2nd ch from hook, [1sc in next ch, 2sc in foll ch] 11 times, 1sc in last ch, 7sc in 6ch sp, 6sc in first 4ch sp, 5sc in next 4ch sp, 6sc in 5ch sp, 6sc in 6ch sp, 11sc in 10ch sp, 9sc in 8ch sp, 5sc in 4ch sp, 4sc in 4ch sp, 4sc in next 3ch sp, 3sc in each of foll two 3ch sps, ss in first ch of tail, turn.

Fasten off. Join C in same place as ss

3rd row [7ch, miss 2sc, 1sc in next sc, turn, 4sc in 7ch sp, turn] 34 times, 7ch, miss 2sc, 1sc in last sc, turn.

Fasten off. Join B in last sc.

4th row 4sc in first 7ch sp, 3ch, 4sc in same 7ch sp, [4sc in each 7ch sp] to end, ss in 5th ch of tail, turn.

5th row 1sc in each of first 2sc, 4ch, 1sc in each of next 4sc, 1ch, 1sc in 25th ch of tail, 1ch, 1sc in each of next 4sc, 1ch, 1sc in 3ch sp of tail; [1sc in each of next 4sc, 4ch] to last 2sc, 1sc in each of last 2sc, ss in 3ch sp.

Fasten off.

abbreviations and key

- ● ch = chain
- ✛ sc = single crochet
- ⌡ tr = treble crochet
- ● ss = slip stitch;
- ⊤ dc = double crochet
- rep = repeat
- [ ] = work instructions in square brackets as directed.

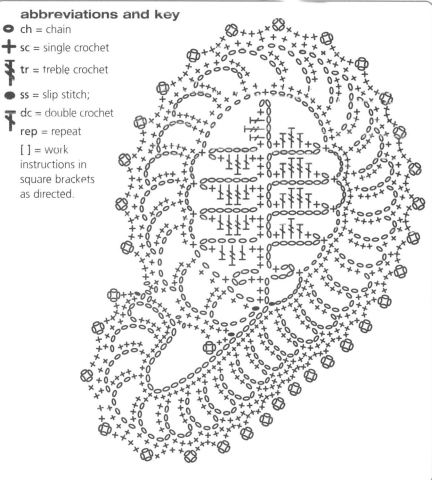

windmill

Each sail is a block of four rows of doubles linked together around a central circle to make a whirling, four-armed windmill.

instructions

Make 4ch, ss in first ch to form a ring.

1st round 1ch, 8sc in ring, ss in first sc.

2nd round 1ch, 2sc in same place a ss, [2sc in each sc] to end, ss in first sc.

3rd round 13ch, miss next sc, 1sc in foll sc, turn, [** 1sc in sc, 2ch, 1dc in each of next 7ch, * turn, 1sc in first dc, 2ch, 1dc in each of next 6dc, 1dc in 2nd ch *, rep from * to * twice **, miss 1sc of 2nd round, 1dtr in next sc, 8ch, miss 1sc, 1sc in next sc, turn] 3 times, rep from ** to **, sc in 5th ch.

4th round 1ch, 1sc in first sc, [12ch, 1sc in 2nd ch at top of block, 12ch, 1sc in dtr] 3 times, 12ch, 1sc in 2nd ch at top of last block, 12ch, ss in first sc.

5th round Ss in first 12ch sp, 1ch, 1sc in 12ch sp, 3ch, * [1dc in 12ch sp, 1ch] 5 times, [1dc, 3ch, 1dc] in corner sc, [1ch, 1dc in 12ch sp] 5 times, 1ch, placing first dc in same 12ch sp and 2nd dc in next 12ch sp, work 2dctog, 1ch, rep from * 3 more times omitting last 2dctog, 1dc in last 12ch sp, ss in 2nd ch. Fasten off.

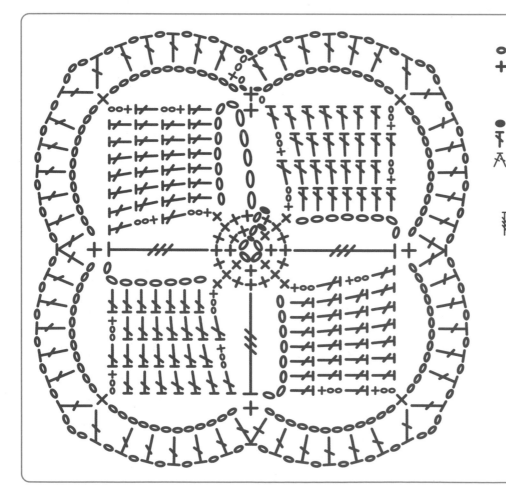

abbreviations and key

- **ch** = chain
- **sc** = single crochet
- **rep** = repeat
- **sp** = space
- **ss** = slip stitch
- **dc** = double crochet
- **2dctog** = leaving last loop of each stitch on hook, work 2dc, yarn over hook and pull through 3 loops on hook
- **dtr** = double treble

[ ] = work instructions in square brackets as directed.

interlocked four-rings square

Linked rings of single crochet form the center of this motif. An edging of single crochet finished with doubles and spaces turns the circles into a square. When working the first round of the edging, arrange the rings so the joins are hidden behind the overlaps in the center.

instructions

Colors: Green (A), blue (B), yellow (C), red (D), and navy (E).

Center. 1st ring
Using A, make 15ch, ss in first ch to form a ring.

1st round 1ch, 24sc in ring, ss in first sc.

2nd round 1ch, [1sc in each sc] to end, ss in first sc. Fasten off.

2nd ring Using B, make 15 ch, thread end of chain length from back to front through 1st ring and complete as 1st ring.

3rd ring Using C, make 15ch, thread end of chain length from back to front through 2nd ring and complete as 1st ring.

4th ring Using D, make 15ch, thread end of chain length from back to front, through 3rd ring and through 1st ring, complete as 1st ring.

Edging Join E in a sc of 4th ring.

1st round 1ch, 1sc in same place as join, 3ch, miss next sc, 1sc in each of foll 4sc, 3ch, 1sc in a sc of 1st ring, * 1sc in each of next 3sc, 3ch, miss 1sc, 1sc in each of foll 4sc, 3ch *, 1sc in a sc of 2nd ring, rep from * to *, 1sc in a sc of 3rd ring, rep from * to *, count back 3sc from first sc in 4th ring, 1sc in 3rd sc, 1sc in each of next 2sc, ss in first sc.

2nd round Ss in first 3ch sp, 1ch, [1sc, 3ch, 1sc] in same 3ch sp, * 1sc in each of next 4sc, 3sc in next 3ch sp, 1sc in each of foll 4sc, [1sc, 3ch, 1sc] in corner 3ch sp, rep from * two more times, 1sc in each of next 4sc, 3sc in next 3ch sp, 1sc in each of foll 4sc, change to B, ss in first sc.

Continue in B.

3rd round Ss in first 3ch sp, 1ch, * [1sc, 3ch, 1sc] in corner 3ch sp, * 1sc in each of next 13sc, rep from * 3 more times, change to E, ss in first sc. Fasten off B.

4th round Ss in first 3ch sp, 1ch, * [1sc, 3ch, 1sc] in corner 3ch sp, * 1sc in each of next 15sc, rep from * 3 more times, ss in first sc.

5th round Ss in first 3ch sp, 1ch, [1sc, 5ch, 1dc] in same 3ch sp, * [1ch, miss next sc, 1dc in foll sc] 8 times, 1ch, miss 1sc, [1dc, 3ch, 1dc] in corner 3ch sp, rep from * two more times, [1ch, miss next sc, 1dc in foll sc] 8 times, 1ch, miss next sc, ss in 2nd ch.

Fasten off.

abbreviations

ch = chain

dc = double crochet

foll = following

rep = repeat

sc = single crochet

sp = space

ss = slip stitch

[ ] = work instructions in square brackets as directed.

spiral shell

For this motif the stitches get progressively taller and each round continues working into the stitches of the previous round without a join, to make a smooth, continuous spiral. Appliqué this motif on a plain background or join motifs to make a shell fabric.

instructions

Wind yarn around finger to form a ring.

1st round 1ch, 2sc, 2hdc, 8dc in ring.

2nd round 2dc in each of next 2sc and 2hdc, 2tr in each of foll 6dc, 2dtr in each of next 2dc.

3rd round 2dtr in each of next 8dc.

Fasten off.

abbreviations and key

○ ch = chain

● sc = single crochet

↑ tr = treble

foll = following

↑ hdc = half double crochet

↑ dc = double crochet

↑ dtr = double treble.

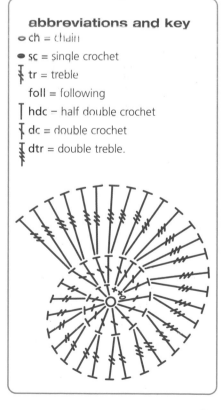

trefoil leaf

Each chain loop has stitches with spaces between worked into it to create a rounded leaf shape. If you want to make a lucky four-leaf clover, simply make one more chain loop on the first round and repeat the instructions one more time on the following rounds before making the stem.

instructions

Wind yarn around finger to form a ring.

1st round 1ch, [1sc in ring, 6ch, 1sc in ring] 3 times, turn.

2nd round (RS) Ss in first 6ch sp, 1ch, * 1sc, [1ch, 1dc] 5 times, 1ch, 1sc, all in first 6ch sp *, 1sc in ring, rep from * to * in next 6ch sp, 1sc in ring, rep from * to * in foll 6ch sp, 1ch, ss in first sc.

3rd round * 1sc in first 1ch sp of next leaf, [1ch, 1dc in next 1ch sp, 1ch, 1dc in same 1ch sp] 4 times, 1ch, 1sc in last 1ch sp, rep from * two more times, ss in last 1ch sp, make 10ch, 1sc in 2nd ch from hook, 1sc in each of next 8ch, ss in same 1ch sp. Fasten off.

long hexagon carpet motif

This motif was inspired by an Anatolian carpet design. Three little blocks are joined to make a central strip and are surrounded with different-height stitches on the first edging round to make a long hexagonal shape. The striped round is just double crochet in alternating colors—remember to pull through the last loop of each stitch with the next color for a neat finish—and the last round has little loops to make it easy to join motifs.

instructions

Colors: Dark red (A), natural (B), black (C), and yellow ocher (D).

Center Using A, wind yarn around finger to form a ring.

1st motif (RS) 1ch, [2sc in ring, 3ch] 4 times, ss in first sc. Fasten off.

2nd motif Work as first motif joining into a 3ch sp of first motif by working 1ch, 1sc in sp, 1ch, ss in first sc instead of last 3ch.

3rd motif Work as 2nd motif joining into 2nd motif sp opposite first join.

Edging With RS facing, join B in 3ch sp at top of first motif opposite first join.

1st round 1ch, [1sc, 3ch, 1sc] in same sp as join, 2ch, [1sc, 3ch, 1sc] in next 3ch sp, 2ch, * placing first part st in joined 3ch sp of same motif and 2nd part st in joined sp of next motif work 2dctog *, 2ch, [1sc, 3ch, 1sc] in next 3ch sp, 2ch, rep from * to *, 2ch, [1sc, 3ch, 1sc, 2ch] in each of next three 3ch sps, rep from *

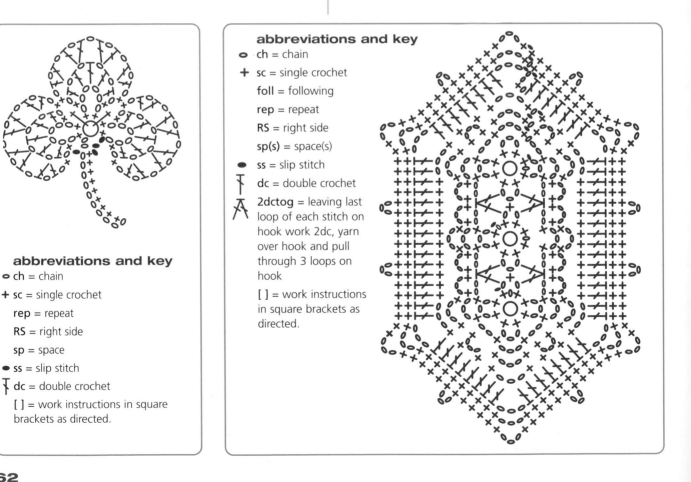

abbreviations and key
o ch = chain
+ sc = single crochet
rep = repeat
RS = right side
sp = space
• ss = slip stitch
┬ dc = double crochet
[ ] = work instructions in square brackets as directed.

abbreviations and key
o ch = chain
+ sc = single crochet
foll = following
rep = repeat
RS = right side
sp(s) = space(s)
• ss = slip stitch
┬ dc = double crochet
⋀ 2dctog = leaving last loop of each stitch on hook work 2dc, yarn over hook and pull through 3 loops on hook
[ ] = work instructions in square brackets as directed.

to *, 2ch, [1sc, 3ch, 1sc] in next 3ch sp, 2ch, rep from * to *, 2ch, [1sc, 3ch, 1sc] in last 3ch sp, 2ch, ss in first sc.

2nd round Ss in first 3ch sp, 1ch, [1sc, 3ch, 1sc] in same 3ch sp, [1sc, 3ch, 1sc] in each of next 19 sps, ss in first sc. Fasten off.

With RS facing, join C in first 3ch sp of 2nd round.

3rd round 1ch, [1sc, 3ch, 1sc] in same 3ch sp, 2sc in next 3ch sp, [1sc, 3ch, 1sc] in foll 3ch sp, 2sc in each of next 5 sps, * [1sc, 3ch, 1sc] in next sp, 2sc in foll sp, rep from * once more, [1sc, 3ch, 1sc] in next sp, 2sc in each of next 5 sps, [1sc, 3ch, 1sc] in foll sp, 2sc in last sp, ss in first sc.

4th round Ss in first 3ch sp, 1ch, [1sc, 4ch, change to D, 1ch, 1dc, change to C, 1dc] all in same 3ch sp, alternating D and C, work 1dc in each of next 4sc, [2dc, 3ch, 2dc] in next 3ch sp, 1dc in each of next 12sc, * [2dc, 3ch, 2dc] in foll 3ch sp, 1dc in each of next 4dc, rep from * once more, [2dc, 3ch, 2dc] in next 3ch sp, 1dc in each of next 12sc, [2dc, 3ch, 2dc] in last 3ch sp, 1dc in each of last 4sc, 1dc in first 3ch sp, ss in 2nd ch.

5th round Using D, ss in first 3ch sp, 1ch, [1sc, 3ch, 1sc] in same 3ch sp, 1sc in each of next 8dc, [1sc, 3ch, 1sc] in foll 3ch sp, 1sc in each of next 16dc, * [1sc, 3ch, 1sc] in foll 3ch sp, 1sc in each of next 8dc, rep from * once more, [1sc, 3ch, 1sc] in foll 3ch sp, 1sc in each of next 16dc, [1sc, 3ch, 1sc] in last 3ch sp, 1sc in each of next 8 sts, ss in first sc. Fasten off D.

6th round Using C, ss in first 3ch sp, 1ch, * [1sc, 3ch, 1sc] in 3ch sp, 1sc in each of next 5sc, 3ch, 1sc in each of foll 5sc, [1sc, 3ch, 1sc] in next 3ch sp, [1sc in each of next 6sc, 3ch] twice, 1sc in each of foll 6sc, [1sc, 3ch, 1sc] in next 3ch sp, 1sc in each of next 5sc, 3ch, 1sc in each of foll 5sc, rep from * once more, ss in first sc. Fasten off.

celtic knot

This intertwined knot design looks complex, but all you have to do is tie knots in the foundation chain before joining it in a ring, then pass the ball of yarn through the knots as the following rows are worked. The center and the border are worked afterward to hold the knots in place.

instructions

Knots Make 200ch, tie four overhand knots loosely in the chain, checking that the chain is not twisted, ss in strand behind first ch to form a ring.

1st round 1ch, 1sc in same place as ss, opening up knots to pass the ball of yarn through when necessary, work [1sc in strand behind each ch] to end, check that this row is not twisted, ss in first sc, turn.

2nd round (RS) 1ch, 1sc in same place as ss, [1sc in each sc] to end, ss in first sc, do not turn.

3rd round 1ch, 1sc in same place as ss, 3ch, [1dc in next sc, 1ch] to end, ss in 2nd ch. Fasten off.

Lay ring of knots flat and arrange knots as equal in size as possible, hiding the join in the ring behind an overlap. Using lengths of contrast yarn, mark a space between dc in the center of the top edge between two knots, then count along and mark every 25th space. If necessary, adjust knots so that four of the markers fall between knots around the outer edge and four are in the center at the base of each knot.

Center With RS facing, join yarn in a marked sp at center of a knot.

1st round 1ch, 1sc in same sp as join, [1ch, 2sc in marked sp at center of next knot] 3 times, 1ch, 1sc in first sp, ss in first sc.

2nd round Ss in next 1ch sp, 1ch, work 2sc in each 1ch sp, ss in first sc. Fasten off.

Edging Count and mark 13th sp at each side of each center joined sp. There will be two markers at the top curves of each knot. With RS facing, join yarn in sp before first marker at top right knot.

1st round 1ch, 1sc in same sp as join, * 7ch, 1sc in sp after 2nd marker of same knot, 1ch, [1sc in next sp, 1ch] 4 times, 1sc in 2nd sp before marker between knots, 1ch, [1sc in next sp, 1ch] 4 times, [1sc, 1ch] in each of 5 sps before 1st

abbreviations

ch = chain

dc = double crochet

foll = following

rep = repeat

RS = right side

sc = single crochet

ss = slip stitch

sp(s) = space(s)

[ ] = work instructions in square brackets as directed.

marker of next knot, rep from * 3 more times, ending last rep [1sc, 1ch] in each of 4 sps before first sc, ss in first sc.

2nd round Ss in 7th sp, 1ch, * [4sc, 3ch, 4sc] in corner 7ch sp, [2sc in each of next four 1ch sps, miss next 1ch sp] twice, 2sc in each of next four 1ch sps, rep from * 3 more times, ss in first sc, turn.

3rd round 1ch, 1sc in same place as ss, 1sc in each of next 28sc, * [1sc, 3ch, 1sc] in next 3ch sp, 1sc in each of next 32sc, rep from * two more times, [1sc, 3ch, 1sc] in last 3ch sp, 1sc in each of next 3sc, ss in first sc, turn.

4th round 4ch, miss first sc, 1dc in next sc, 1ch, miss next sc, 1dc in foll sc, 1ch, * [1dc, 3ch, 1dc] in next 3ch sp, [1ch, miss next sc, 1dc in foll sc] 17 times, 1ch, rep from * two more times, [1dc, 3ch, 1dc] in last 3ch sp, [1ch, miss next sc, 1dc in foll sc] 14 times, 1ch, ss in 3rd ch. Fasten off.

popcorn paisley

Two flower shapes joined and surrounded by popcorns form the center teardrop shape, as shown on the chart. Follow the written instructions for the single crochet edging with the characteristic curved tail.

instructions

Colors: Blue (A) and cream (B).

Center. Large flower Using A, make 6ch, ss in first ch to form a ring.

1st round (RS) 1ch, [1sc in ring, 3ch, 1tr in ring, 3ch] 7 times, ss in first sc. Fasten off.

Small flower Using A, wind yarn around finger to form a ring.

1st round (RS) 1ch, [1sc in ring, 3ch] 3 times, 1sc in ring, 1ch, remove hook, insert in back of a tr of large flower, catch loop and pull through, 1ch, ss in first sc. Fasten off.

Inner edging With RS facing, join B in 2nd 3ch sp of small flower.

1st round 1ch, 1sc in same 3ch sp as join, 2ch, 1sc in next 3ch sp of small flower, [4ch, 1sc in next tr of large flower] 6 times, 4ch, 1sc in last 3ch sp of small flower, 2ch, 1sc in same 3ch sp as first sc in small flower, 4ch, ss in first sc, turn.

2nd round Ss in first 4ch sp, 1ch, [3sc, 6ch, ss in 6th ch from hook, 3sc] in first 4ch sp, 3sc in next 2ch sp, 6sc in each of foll seven 4ch sps, 3sc in last 2ch sp, ss in first sc. Fasten off.

With RS facing, join A in the 6ch sp.

3rd round 1ch, [1sc, 2ch, 4dc] in 6ch sp, remove hook, insert in 2nd ch, catch loop and pull through to close first popcorn, 3ch, 5dcpc in same 6ch sp, miss next 4sc, [3ch, 5dcpc in foll sc, miss next 2sc] 16 times, 3ch, 5dcpc in foll sc, 3ch, 5dcpc in first 6ch sp, 5ch, ss in first popcorn. Fasten off.

Outer edging and tail With RS facing, join B in the 5ch sp.

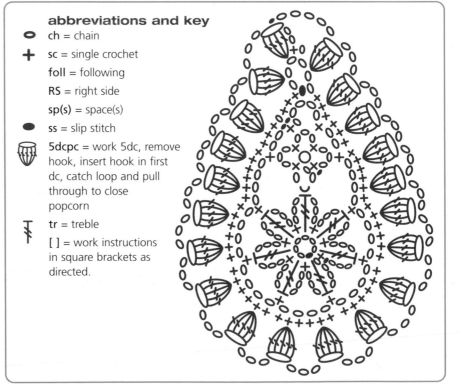

abbreviations and key

○ **ch** = chain

✛ **sc** = single crochet

foll = following

RS = right side

sp(s) = space(s)

● **ss** = slip stitch

5dcpc = work 5dc, remove hook, insert hook in first dc, catch loop and pull through to close popcorn

tr = treble

[ ] = work instructions in square brackets as directed.

1st round 1ch, 1sc in 5ch sp, 3sc in each of next four 3ch sps, 4sc in each of foll fifteen 3ch sps, 5sc in first 5ch sp, ss in first sc, turn. 78 sts.

2nd round 1ch, 1sc in each of 78sc, make 9ch, 5sc in 2nd ch from hook, 1sc in each of next 7ch, ss in first sc, turn. Fasten off.

With RS facing, join A in first sc at left after tail.

3rd round 1ch, 1sc in each of next 78sc, 1sc in each of foll 12sc around outer edge of tail, ss in 7th sc from start of round, 1sc in base of each of next 7ch, ss in first sc. Fasten off.

holly leaf

A center chain is the stem of this leaf. Stitches of different heights are worked around the chain and finished with little picots to give a pointed holly-leaf shape.

instructions

Make 17ch.

1st round Ss in 2nd ch from hook, ss in each of next 3ch, [1hdc in next ch, 1dc in foll ch, 1tr in next ch, 1dc in foll ch, 1hdc in next ch, 1sc in foll ch] twice, 3ch, now work in base of ch, [1sc in next ch, 1hdc in foll ch, 1dc in next ch, 1tr in foll ch, 1dc in next ch, 1hdc in foll ch] twice, ss in next ch, turn.

2nd round (RS) 1sc in next hdc, 1sc in foll dc, * [1sc, 3ch, ss in 3rd ch from hook, 1sc] * in next tr, 1sc in each of foll 5 sts, rep from * to * in next tr, 1sc in each of foll 3 sts, rep from * to * in 3ch sp, 1sc in each of next 3 sts, rep from * to * in foll tr, 1sc in each of next 5 sts, rep from * to * in foll tr, 1sc in each of next 2 sts, ss in next ss. Fasten off.

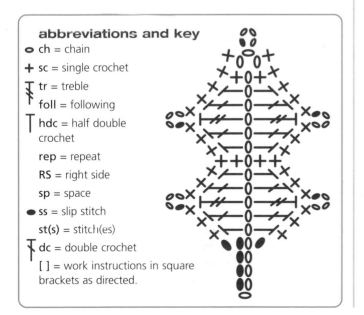

abbreviations and key

- **o** ch = chain
- **+** sc = single crochet
- **T** tr = treble
- **↑** foll = following
- **T** hdc = half double crochet
- **rep** = repeat
- **RS** = right side
- **sp** = space
- **●** ss = slip stitch
- **st(s)** = stitch(es)
- **↑** dc = double crochet
- **[ ]** = work instructions in square brackets as directed.

woven ribbon block

This is a lovely carry-about crochet motif. Just make little single and double crochet strips for the ribbons whenever you have a moment, then at home, weave them under and over and add an edging to make a cozy, padded block.

instructions

Colors: Pink (A), blue (B), and cream (C).

1st ribbon Using A, make 21ch loosely.

1st row (RS) Work into strand behind ch, 1sc in 2nd ch from hook, 1sc in each of next 19ch. 20 sts.

2nd row 1sc in first sc, 2ch, 1dc in each sc.

3rd row 1ch, 1sc in each dc, 1sc in 2nd ch. Fasten off.

Make 3 more ribbons in A and 4 ribbons in B.

With RS facing, placing A ribbons vertically and B ribbons horizontally, weave ribbons over and under to make a square. Baste to hold ribbons in place.

Edging With RS facing, join C in first row-end in A at top right corner.

1st round 1ch, [4sc in row-ends of each of next 4 ribbons in A, 2ch, 4sc in each of next 4 ribbons in B, 2ch] twice, remove hook, insert from back in first sc, catch loop and pull through.

2nd round 1ch, taking hook behind, [1sc around the stem of each of next 16sc, 2ch] 4 times, ss in first sc, turn.

3rd round Ss in first 2ch sp, 1ch, * [1sc, 2ch, 1sc] in 2ch sp, 1sc in each of next 16sc, rep from * 3 more times, ss in first sc.

Fasten off. Remove basting threads.

abbreviations

ch = chain	st(s) = stitch(es)
sc = single crochet	dc = double crochet
rep = repeat	[ ] = work instructions in square brackets as directed.
RS = right side	
ss = slip stitch	

eight-ring circle

Eight interlocked rings of chain and single crochet are worked first. Two practical and pretty edging rounds hold the rings in place, then the center is filled with a simple chain motif.

instructions

1st ring Make 15ch, ss in first ch to form a ring.

1st round 1ch, 24sc in ring, ss in first sc.

2nd round 1ch, 1sc in same place as ss, 1sc in each of next 23sc, ss in first sc. Fasten off.

2nd ring Make 15ch, thread end of chain length from front to back through first ring, ss in first ch to form a ring. Complete as given for first ring.

3rd, 4th, 5th, 6th, and 7th rings As 2nd ring, joining each ring to the previous ring.

8th ring Make 15ch, check that RS is facing on all rings, thread end of chain length from front to back through 7th and 1st rings, ss in first ch to form a ring. Complete as given for first ring.

Edging Join yarn in a sc of one ring.

1st round 1ch, 1sc in same place as join, 3ch, miss 2sc, 1sc in next sc of same ring, * 3ch, 1sc in a sc of next ring, [3ch, miss 2sc, 1sc in next sc of same ring] twice, rep from * 6 more times, 3ch, 1sc in 3rd sc from join in first ring, 3ch, ss in first sc.

2nd round Ss in first 3ch sp, 1ch, [2sc, 3ch, 2sc] in each 3ch sp, ss in first sc. Fasten off.

Center With RS facing, count on 9sc from a 1st edging round sc in each ring and mark this sc. Make 4ch, ss in first ch to form a ring.

1st round 1ch, 1sc in 4ch ring, 2ch, 1sc in marked sc of an interlocked ring, [2ch, 1sc in 4ch ring, 2ch, 1sc in marked sc of next interlocked ring] 7 times, 2ch, ss in first sc. Fasten off.

abbreviations

ch = chain	**ss** = slip stitch
rep = repeat	**sp** = space
RS = right side	**[ ]** = work instructions in square brackets as directed.
sc = single crochet	

baby's blocks diamond

Usually it's really annoying when a crochet fabric slips into a bias, but this motif exploits that tendency to turn a square worked from point to point in single crochet into a diamond. See the projects section for how to assemble the diamonds to create the traditional optical-effect baby's blocks pattern (page 134) or a blazing star (page 135).

instructions

Make 2ch.

1st row (RS) 1sc in 2nd ch from hook.

2nd row 1ch, 2sc in sc. 2 sts.

3rd row 1ch, 1sc in first sc, 2sc in last sc. 3 sts.

4th row 1ch, 1sc in each of first 2sc, 2sc in last sc. 4 sts.

5th row 1ch, 1sc in each of first 3sc, 2sc in last sc. 5 sts.

6th row 1ch, 1sc in each of first 4sc, 2sc in last sc. 6 sts.

7th row 1ch, 1sc in each of first 5sc, 2sc in last sc. 7 sts.

8th row 1ch, 1sc in each of first 6sc, 2sc in last sc. 8 sts.

9th row 1ch, 1sc in each of first 7sc, 2sc in last sc. 9 sts.

10th row 1ch, 1sc in each of first 8sc, 2sc in last sc. 10 sts.

11th row 1ch, 1sc in each of first 8sc, 2sctog. 9 sts.

12th row 1ch, 1sc in each of first 7sc, 2sctog. 8 sts.

13th row 1ch, 1sc in each of first 6sc, 2sctog. 7 sts.

14th row 1sc in each of first 5sc, 2sctog. 6 sts.

15th row 1sc in each of first 4sc, 2sctog. 5 sts.

16th row 1sc in each of first 3sc, 2sctog. 4 sts.

17th row 1sc in each of first 2sc, 2sctog. 3 sts.

18th row 1sc in first sc, 2sctog. 2 sts.

19th row 2sctog, do not fasten off.

Edging (RS) 2sc in 2sctog, * 1sc in each of next 8 row-ends, 3sc in next row-end, 1sc in each of next 8 row-ends *, 3sc in base of ch, rep from * to *, 1sc in 2sctog, ss in first sc. Fasten off.

abbreviations

ch = chain	hook and pull through 3 loops on hook
sc = single crochet	**rep** = repeat
2sctog = insert hook in first st and pull loop through, insert hook in 2nd st and pull loop through, yarn over	**RS** = right side
	st(s) = stitch(es).

four feathers

Each curled feather is made by working rows of gradated-height and spaced stitches along one edge of a base chain. The feathers are joined in the center, then the edging is worked to hold the feathers in place.

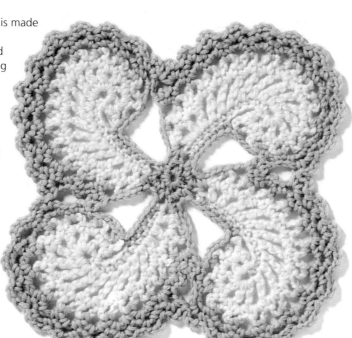

fan

This is the ultimate in little carry-about crochet motifs, just make sure that you leave ends long enough to sew the fans together to make a fabric. The motif given here is a three-quarters-open fan; if you want a half circle to decorate a straight edge, work twelve spokes and eleven scallops.

instructions

Wind yarn around finger to form a ring.

1st row (RS) 1ch, 1sc in ring, 3ch, 8tr in ring, turn.

2nd row 1sc in first tr, 4ch, [1tr in next tr, 1ch] 7 times omitting last ch.

3rd row 1sc in first tr, [3ch, 1sc in next tr] 6 times, 3ch, 1sc in 3rd ch. Fasten off.

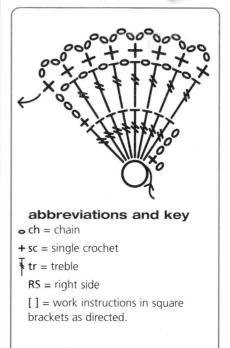

instructions

Colors: Cream (A) and turquoise (B).

1st feather Using A, make 15ch loosely.

1st row Work into strand behind ch, 1sc in 5th ch from hook, 1sc in each of next 9ch, ss in last ch.

2nd row 1ch, miss ss, [1dc in next sc, 1ch] 3 times, [1tr in next sc, 1ch] 7 times, [1tr, 1ch] twice in 4ch sp, [1dc, 1ch] 3 times in same 4ch sp, ss in base of first foundation ch, turn.

3rd row (RS) Ss in first 1ch sp, 1ch, [1sc, 4ch, 1sc] in each of 15 sps, ss in last 1ch sp. Fasten off.

Make 3 more feathers.

Center Using B, wind yarn around finger to form a ring. Arrange feathers with RS facing.

Joining round (RS) [1ch, 1sc in ring, 1ch, 1sc in same sp as ss at end of 3rd row of a feather, 1ch, 1sc in ring] 4 times, ss in first sc. Fasten off.

Edging With RS facing, join B in first 4ch sp at top of a feather.

1st round 1ch, 1sc in first 4ch sp, * [3ch, 1sc in next 4ch sp] 14 times, 3ch, 1sc in same sp as center sc, 1sc in each of next 2sc of center, 1sc in base of each of foll 6ch and first 4ch sp of next feather, rep from * 3 more times omitting last sc, ss in first sc.

Fasten off. With RS facing, join B in 4th 3ch sp of 1st edging round.

2nd round 1ch, 1sc in same sp as join, [1sc, 3ch, 1sc] in each of next ten 3ch sps, * 1ch, miss first 3ch sp of next feather, 1sc in next 3ch sp, 1ch, 1sc in last 3ch sp of previous feather, 1ch, 1sc in same 3ch sp as first sc of next feather **, [1sc, 3ch, 1sc] in each of next twelve 3ch sps, rep from * 3 more times, then rep from * to **, [1sc, 3ch, 1sc] in next 3ch sp, 1sc in first 3ch sp, 3ch, ss in first sc.

3rd round Ss in first 3ch sp, 1ch, missing last 3ch sp of each feather, work [1sc, 3ch, 1sc] in all other 3ch sps, ss in first sc. Fasten off.

abbreviations and key

o ch = chain

+ sc = single crochet

⸓ tr = treble

RS = right side

[ ] = work instructions in square brackets as directed.

abbreviations

ch = chain

dc = double crochet

foll = following

rep = repeat

RS = right side

sc = single crochet

sp(s) = space(es)

ss = slip stitch

tr = treble

[ ] = work instructions in square brackets as directed.

pictures

These motifs range from cute animals and insects to seaside themes and seasonal images. Worked as blocks, they would combine well for a themed throw.

butterfly

The body and wings that make the butterfly itself are worked first, then the background is added to turn the shape into a block. The first round of the background has stitches of varying heights and the second round has decreases at each side and at the tail to even out the shape. The background then settles into a simple repeat, so you could easily work more rounds if you want to add a contrast border. To make an appliqué butterfly motif, finish after working the wing edgings.

instructions

Colors: Black (A), blue (B), cream (C), and green (D).

Body Using A, make 13ch.

1st row (RS) Starting at tail, work 1sc in 2nd ch from hook, 1hdc in next ch, [1ch,

miss 1ch, 1dc in next ch] 3 times, 1ch, miss 1ch, 1hdc in next ch, 1ch, miss 1ch, ss in last ch, do not turn.

1st round 2ch, 1dc in first sp, 2sc in same sp, [2ch, 2sc in next sp] 4 times, 2ch, 1sc in same ch as hdc, 1sc in same ch as sc, 3sc in next ch, 1sc in next sc, 1sc in next hdc, [2ch, 2sc in next sp] 5 times, ss in dc. Fasten off.

Wing spots (Make 2) Using A, make 6ch, ss in first ch to form a ring.

1st round (RS) 1ch, [1sc in ring, 3ch] 6 times, ss in first sc. Fasten off.

Upper left wing. With RS facing, join B in first 2ch sp down from head on left side of body.

1st row 1ch, [1sc, 2ch, 1sc] in same sp as join and in each of next 2 sps, turn.

2nd row 2ch, [1sc, 2ch, 1sc] in first 2ch sp, [1ch, 1sc, 2ch, 1sc in a 3ch sp of spot, 1ch, 1sc in next 2ch sp of wing] twice, 2ch,

1sc in same 2ch sp as previous sc, turn.

3rd row 2ch, [1sc, 2ch, 1sc] in first 2ch sp of wing, [1sc, 2ch, 1sc] in each of next four 3ch sps of spot, [1sc, 2ch, 1sc] in last 2ch sp of wing, turn.

4th row 2ch, [1sc, 2ch, 1sc] in each of next six 2ch sps, turn.

5th row 2ch, [1sc, 3ch, 1sc] in each of next six 2ch sps. Fasten off.

Upper right wing With RS facing, join B in 3rd 2ch sp down from head on right side of body. Work as given for left upper wing.

Right lower wing With RS facing, join B in first 2ch sp at lower right of body.

1st row 1ch, 1sc in same sp as join, 3ch, 1sc in next 2ch sp, turn.

2nd row 1sc in first sc, 3ch, [1dc, 1ch, 1tr, 1ch, 1tr, 1ch, 1dc, 1ch] in 3ch sp, 1dc in last sc, turn.

3rd row Ss in first 1ch sp, [1sc, 3ch, 1sc] in each 1ch sp., ss in 2nd ch. Fasten off.

Left lower wing With RS facing, join B in 2nd 2ch sp at lower left of body. Work as given for right lower wing.

Right wing edging With RS facing, join C in first 3ch sp of lower wing, 1ch, [1sc, 3ch, 1sc] in each of five 3ch sps of lower wing, miss first two 2ch sps of upper wing, [1sc, 3ch, 1sc] in each of next six 3ch sps and in foll two 2ch sps, ss in sp at end of first row of upper wing. Fasten off.

Left wing edging With RS facing, join C in sp at beginning of first row of upper wing, 1ch, [1sc, 3ch, 1sc] in each of next two 2ch sps and in foll six 3ch sps, miss last two 2ch sps of upper wing, [1sc, 3ch, 1sc] in each of five 3ch sps of lower wing. Fasten off.

Background square With RS facing, join D in same dc as ss at tail end.

1st round 1ch, 1sc in same place as join, 3ch, 2dc in first sc in B of lower right wing, 1ch, 2sc in next 3ch sp, 1ch, 2dc in foll 3ch sp, 1ch, [2tr, 3ch, 2tr] in next 3ch sp, 1ch, [2tr in next 3ch sp, 1ch] twice, [2sc in next 3ch sp, 1ch] 4 times, [2dc, 3ch, 2dc] in foll 3ch sp, 1ch, [2sc in next sp, 1ch] twice, 2dc in last 3ch sp of right wing, 1ch, 2dc in center sc of head, 1ch, 2dc in first 3ch sp of left wing, 1ch, [2sc in next 3ch sp, 1ch] twice, [2dc, 3ch, 2dc] in foll 3ch sp, 1ch, [2sc in next 3ch sp, 1ch] 4 times, [2tr in next 3ch sp, 1ch] twice, [2tr, 3ch, 2tr] in foll 3ch sp, 1ch, 2dc in next

3ch sp, 1ch, 2sc in last 3ch sp of left wing, 1ch, 2dc in next sc in B, 1ch, 1dc in same place as join in tail, ss in 2nd ch.

2nd round Ss in first 1ch sp, 1ch, [1sc, 1ch, 1dc] in same sp as join, [1ch, 2dc in next 1ch sp] 3 times, 1ch, [2dc, 3ch, 2dc] in corner 3ch sp, [1ch, 2dc in next 1ch sp] twice, 1ch, 2dctog in each of 2 foll 1ch sps, [1ch, 2dc in next 1ch sp] 3 times, 1ch, [2dc, 3ch, 2dc] in corner 3ch sp, [1ch, 2dc in next 1ch sp] 3 times, 1ch, 2dctog in each of 2 foll 1ch sps, [1ch, 2dc in next 1ch sp] 3 times, 1ch, [2dc, 3ch, 2dc] in corner 3ch sp, [1ch, 2dc in next 1ch sp] 3 times, 1ch, 2dctog in each of 2 foll 1ch sps, [1ch, 2dc in next 1ch sp] twice, 1ch, [2dc, 3ch, 2dc] in corner 3ch sp, [1ch, 2dc in next 1ch sp] 3 times, 1ch, 2dctog in next 1ch sp, ss in first dc.

3rd round Ss in first 1ch sp, 1ch, 1sc in same sp as ss, 3ch, [2dc in next sp, 1ch] 3 times, *[2dc, 3ch, 2dc] in corner 3ch sp, 1ch, [2dc in next 1ch sp, 1ch] to corner, rep from * two more times, [2dc, 3ch, 2dc] in corner 3ch sp, 1ch, [2dc in next 1ch sp, 1ch] 4 times, 1dc in first 1ch sp, ss in 2nd ch.

4th round Ss in first 1ch sp, 1ch, 1sc in same sp as ss, 3ch, [2dc in next sp, 1ch] 3 times, *[2dc, 3ch, 2dc] in corner 3ch sp, 1ch, [2dc in next 1ch sp, 1ch] to corner, rep from * two more times, [2dc, 3ch, 2dc] in corner 3ch sp, 1ch, [2dc in next 1ch sp, 1ch] 5 times, 1dc in first 1ch sp, ss in 2nd ch. Fasten off.

Using A, embroider antennae in chain stitch. Catch gaps together at tail and between wings when darning in ends.

abbreviations

ch = chain

sc = single crochet

dc = double crochet

tr = treble

foll = following

hdc = half double crochet

rep = repeat

RS = right side

ss = slip stitch

sp(s) = space(s)

2dctog = leaving last loop of each stitch on hook work 2dc, yarn over hook and pull through 3 loops on hook

[ ] = work instructions in square brackets as directed.

flower basket

This simple square of single crochet is worked in areas of different colors with rings of surface crochet for the sweet-pea-like flowers. A plait for the basket handle is added afterward.

instructions

Colors: Duck egg (A), camel (B), pale blue (C), green (D) and 5 shades of lilac and pink (E). Each square of the chart represents one sc. Use separate balls of yarn for each color area, pulling through the last loop of the last stitch of each color area with the next color and twisting yarns on the back of the work to link the colors.

Using A, make 26ch.

1st row 1sc in 2nd ch from hook, [1sc in each ch] to end. 25 sts.

2nd row (RS) 1ch, [1sc in each sc] to end.

2nd row forms sc and corresponds to 2nd row of chart.

Cont in sc changing colors as indicated on chart for 27 more rows.

Fasten off.

Handle Cut 6 x 12in strands of B, tie them together with an overhand knot 1¼in from one end, then taking two strands together each time, make a three-strand plait, finishing with another

overhand knot when plait fits around area in green. Trim tassels and sew handle on basket.

Varying the shades of pink and lilac, work flower rings scattered as wished on the green area to fill the basket.

For each flower Join yarn to the stem of an sc in D. Work 6sc up the stem of same sc as join, turn and work 6sc down the stem of next sc in D, ss in first sc of flower. Fasten off.

abbreviations

ch – chain

sc = single crochet

sts = stitches

[ ] work instructions in square brackets as directed.

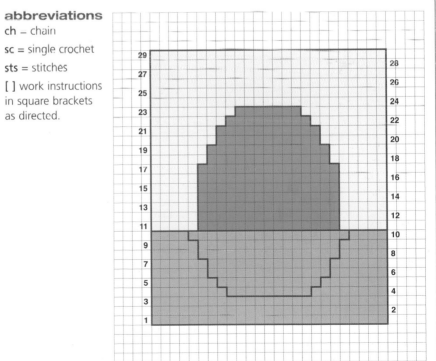

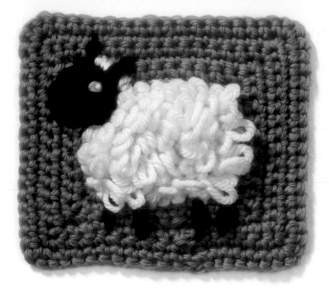

sheep

This sweet sheep is very easy to do. The body of the sheep is a little oval in loop stitch and the green field background is worked in turning rounds of single crochet around the loop stitch body to give a ridged texture. The head is worked separately and sewn on then the details are embroidered.

instructions

Colors: Cream (A), green (B), black (C), and a tiny scrap of yellow.

Body Using A, make 6ch.

Preparation row (RS) 1sc in 2nd ch from hook, [1sc in each ch] to end, turn. 5 sts.

1st round 1ch, 1Lpst in each of 5sc, 1Lpst in side of end sc, 1Lpst in base of each of 5ch, 1Lpst in side of last sc, ss in first st, turn. 12 sts.

2nd round 1ch, 3sc in same place as ss, *1sc in next st, 3sc in foll st, 1sc in each of next 3 sts *, 3sc in foll st, rep from * to *, ss in first sc, turn. 20 sts.

3rd round 1ch, [1Lpst in each sc] to end, ss in first st, turn.

4th round 1ch, 1sc in first st, * 3sc in next st, 1sc in each of foll 3 sts, 3sc in next st *, 1sc in each of foll 5 sts, rep from * to *, 1sc in each of last 4 sts, ss in first st, turn. 28 sts.

5th round 1ch, [1Lpst in each sc] to end, ss in first st. Fasten off.

Field With RS facing, join B in same place as ss in last round in A.

1st round 1ch, 1sc in each of next 2 sts, * 3sc in foll st, 1sc in each of next 5 sts *, 3sc in foll st, 1sc in each of next 7 sts, rep from * to * twice, ss in first sc, turn.

2nd round 1ch, 1sc in each of next 6sc, * 3sc in foll sc, 1sc in each of next 7sc, 3sc in foll sc *, 1sc in each of next 9sc, rep from * to *, 1sc in each of next 3sc, ss in first sc, turn.

3rd round 1ch, 1sc in each of next 4sc, * 3sc in foll sc, 1sc in each of next 9sc, 3sc in foll sc *, 1sc in each of next 11sc, rep from * to *, 1sc in each of next 7sc, ss in first sc, turn.

4th round 1ch, 1sc in each of next 8sc, * 3sc in foll sc, 1sc in each of next 11sc, 3sc in foll sc*, 1sc in each of next 13sc, rep from * to *, 1sc in each of next 5sc, ss in first sc, turn.

5th round 1ch, 1sc in each of next 6sc, * 3sc in foll sc, 1sc in each of next 13sc, 3sc in foll sc *, 1sc in each of next 15sc, rep

from * to *, 1sc in each of next 9sc, ss in first sc, turn.

6th round 1ch, 1sc in each of next 10sc, * 3sc in foll sc, 1sc in each of next 15sc, 3sc in foll sc *, 1sc in each of next 17sc, rep from * to *, 1sc in each of next 7sc, ss in first sc. Fasten off.

Head Using C, wind yarn around finger to form a ring.

1st round 1ch, 6sc in ring, ss in first sc.

2nd round 1ch, 3sc in same place as ss, [1sc in next sc, 3sc in foll sc] twice, 1sc in last sc, ss in first sc. Fasten off.

To complete Sew head on at top left corner of body. Using B, work a long chain stitch for each ear and embroider legs in straight stitch. Using yellow, work a short straight stitch for the eye. Using A, work three short straight stitches between ears and add tiny stab stitch on the right of the yellow stitch to highlight the eye.

abbreviations

ch = chain

sc = single crochet

Lpst = loop stitch, insert hook in sc of previous row, extend left middle finger and catch the strand behind the finger and the strand in front to make a small loop around finger, pull the 2 strands through, yarn over hook and pull through 3 loops on hook, remove finger from loop

rep = repeat

ss = slip stitch

[ ] = work instructions in square brackets as directed.

tiger

The tiger's body is an oblong of orange and black striped single crochet with rounds of single crochet in lime green worked around the body to make the background block. The head is worked separately and sewn on, then the face, legs, and tail are embroidered with simple straight stitches.

instructions

Colors: Orange (A), black (B), green (C), and a tiny scrap of yellow.

When changing colors for the one-row stripes, pull through the last loop of the last stitch of a row in the new color, then lay the old color along the row and work over it ready to change color for the next row.

Using A, make 9ch.

Body. 1st row (WS) 1sc in 2nd ch from hook, [1sc in each ch] to end. 8 sts.

Change to B and work over A.

2nd row 1ch, [1sc in each sc] to end.

Change to A and work over B.

3rd row As 2nd row.

2nd and 3rd rows form the sc stripe patt. Patt 8 more rows. Fasten off.

Background With RS facing, join C in last sc of last row of body.

1st round 1ch, 2sc in same sc as join, 1sc in each of next 6sc, 3sc in last sc, 1sc in each of next 10 row-ends, 3sc in base of first ch,

1sc in base of each of next 6ch, 3sc in base of last ch, 1sc in each of next 10 row-ends, 1sc in same place as first 2sc, ss in first sc. 44 sts.

2nd round 1ch, 2sc in same place as ss, [1sc in each of next 8sc, 3sc in next sc, 1sc in each of next 12sc, 3sc in foll sc] twice, omitting last 2sc, ss in first sc.

Cont in this way working sc in rounds and increasing by working 3sc in each corner sc to make 8 more sc on each round, work 4 more rounds. 84 sts. Fasten off.

Head Using A, make 2ch.

1st row (WS) 3sc in first ch. 3 sts.

2nd row 1ch, 1sc in first sc, 3sc in next sc, 1sc in last sc. 5 sts.

Change to B and work over A.

3rd row 1ch, 1sc in each sc.

Change to A and work over B.

4th row 1ch, 1sc in first sc, [3sc in next sc, 1sc in foll sc] twice. 9 sts.

Change to B and work over A.

5th row 1ch, 1sc in each sc. Fasten off B.

6th row 1ch, ss in each of first 2sc, * [1sc, 1hdc, 2dc, 1hdc, 1sc] in next sc *, ss in each of next 3sc, rep from * to *, ss in each of last 2sc. Fasten off.

To complete With join in background rounds to top left, slip stitch head in place over the join and at an angle to the body. Using yellow, embroider eyes, then using black, embroider pupils and nose. Using short straight stitches set horizontally to the body and alternating two or three stitches in A and B for stripes, embroider legs and tail.

abbreviations

ch = chain
dc = double crochet
sc = single crochet
foll = following
hdc = half double

rep = repeat
ss = slip stitch
[ ] = work instructions in square brackets as directed.

grapes

The raised bunch of grapes is made with popcorns on a background of rows of double and single crochet. The single crochet edging is worked in the round and the finishing touches are embroidered afterward.

instructions

Colors: Green (A), purple (B), and small amount of brown for embroidery.

Center Using A, make 20ch.

1st row Working into back loop of ch, 1sc in 2nd ch from hook, [1sc in each ch] to end. 19 sts.

2nd row (RS) 1sc in first sc, 2ch, 1dc in each of next 8sc, change to B, 5trpc in next sc, change to A, 1dc in each of next 9sc.

3rd and every WS row 1ch, [1sc in each st] to end.

4th row 1sc in first sc, 2ch, 1dc in each of next 7sc, change to B, 5trpc in next sc, change to A, 1dc in foll sc, change to B, 5trpc in next sc, change to A, 1dc in each of next 8sc.

6th row 1sc in first sc, 2ch, 1dc in each of next 6sc, [change to B, 5trpc in next sc, change to A, 1dc in foll sc] twice, change to B, 5trpc in next sc, change to A, 1dc in each of next 7sc.

8th row 1sc in first sc, 2ch, 1dc in each of next 5sc, [change to B, 5trpc in next sc, change to A, 1dc in foll sc] 3 times, change to B, 5trpc in next sc, change to A, 1dc in each of next 6sc.

10th row 1sc in first sc, 2ch, 1dc in each of next 4sc, [change to B, 5trpc in next sc, change to A, 1dc in foll sc] 4 times, change to B, 5trpc in next sc, change to A, 1dc in each of next 5sc. Fasten off B.

12th row 1sc in first sc, 2ch, [1dc in each sc] to end.

13th row As 3rd row.

Edging. 1st round (RS) Using A, work 19sc along top edge, 2ch, 19sc in row-ends down left edge, 2ch, 19sc in ch along lower edge, 2ch, 19sc in row-ends up right edge, 2ch, ss in first sc, turn.

2nd round Ss in 2ch sp, 1ch, * [1sc, 2ch, 1sc] in 2ch sp, 1sc in each of next 19sc, rep from * 3 more times, ss in first sc. Fasten off.

To complete Using brown work two closely spaced lines of chain stitch for the branch and single lines of chain stitch for the stems of the grapes.

abbreviations

ch = chain
dc = double crochet
sc = single crochet
tr = treble crochet
5trpc = work 5tr, remove hook, insert hook in first tr, catch loop and pull through to close popcorn

foll = following
rep = repeat
RS = right side
sp = space
ss = slip stitch
WS = wrong side
[ ] = work instructions in square brackets as directed.

dresden plate

If you like blue-and-white china you'll love this motif. The center is a simple chain flower in blue surrounded with chain and single crochet chevrons in cream. This is followed by a ring of blue chain flower motifs finished with two rounds of double groups and a round of chain loops in cream. The motif is edged with chain loops in blue.

instructions

Colors: Blue (A) and cream (B).

Center Using A, wind yarn around finger to form a ring.

1st round 1ch, [1sc in ring, 8ch] 8 times, ss in first sc. Fasten off.

Join B in an 8ch sp.

2nd round 1ch, 1sc in same place as join, [4ch, 1sc in next 8ch sp] 7 times, 4ch, ss in first sc.

3rd round Ss in each of first 2ch, 1ch, 1sc in first 4ch sp, 2ch, 2sc in same 4ch sp, [2sc, 2ch, 2sc] in each of next seven 8ch sps, 1sc in first 4ch sp, ss in first sc.

4th round Ss in first 2ch sp, 1ch, [1sc, 2ch, 2sc] in first 2ch sp, * 3ch, [2sc, 2ch, 2sc] in next 2ch sp, rep from * 6 more times, 3ch, 1sc in first 2ch sp, ss in first sc. Fasten off.

5th round. 1st flower Using A, wind yarn around finger to form a ring, 1ch, [1sc in ring, 7ch] 5 times, 1sc in ring, 3ch, 1sc in a 2ch sp between sc groups of 4th round, 3ch, 1sc in ring, 3ch, 1sc in next 3ch sp of 4th round, 3ch, 1sc in ring, 3ch, 1sc in next 2ch sp of 4th round, 3ch, ss in first sc. Fasten off.

2nd flower Work as 1st flower until four 7ch petals have been completed, join 5th petal in adjacent petal of previous flower, 6th petal in same 2ch sp of 4th round as previous flower, 7th petal in next 3ch sp of 4th round, and 8th petal in next 2ch sp of 4th round. Make and join 5 more flowers in same way as 2nd flower.

8th flower Work as 1st flower until 3 petals have been completed, join 4th petal in adjacent petal of 7th flower, 5th petal in same 2ch sp as 7th flower, 6th petal in next 3ch sp, 7th petal in same 2ch sp as first flower, and 8th petal in adjacent petal of first flower.

Join B in a center free petal of a flower.

6th round 1ch, 1sc in same place as join, 4ch, 3dc in next petal of same flower, 2ch, * 1sc over next sc join between flowers, 2ch, [3dc, 2ch] in each of next 3 petals, rep from * 6 more times, 1sc over last sc join between flowers, 2ch, 3dc in next petal, 2ch, 2dc in first petal, ss in 2nd ch.

7th round Ss in each of next 2ch, 1ch, 1sc, 4ch, in same 2ch sp, * placing first part st in next 2ch sp and 2nd part st in foll 2ch sp, work 2dctog, 2ch **, [2dc, 2ch] twice in each of next two 2ch sps, rep from * 6 more times, then work from * to **, [2dc, 2ch] twice in last 2ch sp, 2dc in first sp, 2ch, 1dc in same sp, ss in 2nd ch.

8th round Ss in first 2ch sp, 1ch, 1sc in same 2ch sp, [4ch, 1sc in next 2ch sp] 39 times, 4ch, ss in first sc. Fasten off.

Join A in a 2ch sp.

9th round 1ch, 1sc in same place as join, [4ch, 1sc in next 2ch sp] 39 times, 4ch, ss in first sc. Fasten off.

abbreviations

ch = chain

sc = single crochet

dc = double crochet

foll = following

rep = repeat

sp(s) = space(s)

ss = slip stitch

st(s) = stitch(es)

2dctog = placing sts as described and leaving last loop of each st on the hook, work 2dc, yarn over hook and pull through 3 loops on hook

[ ] = work instructions in square brackets as directed.

lion

The body of the lion is an oblong of single crochet. The background is worked around the body in single crochet with a final round of double crochet and spaces to make it easy to join motifs. The head and mane are worked separately and sewn on, then the details are embroidered. If you want to make a pride of lions, just leave out the mane for the lionesses.

instructions

Colors: Yellow ocher (A), sand (B), and brown (C) with a scrap of orange for embroidery.

Body Using A, make 7ch.

1st row 1sc in 2nd ch from hook, [1sc in each ch] to end. 6 sts.

2nd row (RS) 1ch, [1sc in each sc] to end.

2nd row forms sc. Work 11 more rows sc. Fasten off.

Background With RS facing, join B in 2nd row-end at top left of body.

1st round 1ch, 1sc in same place as join, 2ch, miss last row-end, 1sc in base of each of next 6ch, 2ch, miss first row-end, 1sc in each of 11 row-ends, miss last row-end, 2ch, 1sc in each of next 6sc, 2ch, miss first row-end, 1sc in each of next 10 row-ends, ss in first sc.

2nd round Ss in first 2ch sp, 1ch, * [1sc, 2ch, 1sc] in 2ch sp, 1sc in each of next 6sc, [1sc, 2ch, 1sc] in next 2ch sp, 1sc in each of next 11sc, rep from * once more, ss in first sc.

3rd round Ss in first 2ch sp, 1ch, * [1sc, 2ch, 1sc] in 2ch sp, 1sc in each of next 8sc, [1sc, 2ch, 1sc] in next 2ch sp, 1sc in each of next 13sc, rep from * once more, ss in first sc.

4th round Ss in first 2ch sp, 1ch, * [1sc, 2ch, 1sc] in 2ch sp, 1sc in each of next 10sc, [1sc, 2ch, 1sc] in next 2ch sp, 1sc in each of next 15sc, rep from * once more, ss in first sc.

5th round Ss in first 2ch sp, 1ch, * [1sc, 2ch, 1sc] in 2ch sp, 1sc in each of next 12sc, [1sc, 2ch, 1sc] in next 2ch sp, 1sc in each of next 17sc, rep from * once more, ss in first sc.

6th round Ss in first 2ch sp, 1ch, * [1sc, 2ch, 1sc] in 2ch sp, 1sc in each of next 14sc, [1sc, 2ch, 1sc] in next 2ch sp, 1sc in each of next 19sc, rep from * once more, ss in first sc.

7th round Ss in first 2ch sp, 1ch, * [1sc, 2ch, 1sc] in 2ch sp, 1sc in each of next 16sc, [1sc, 2ch, 1sc] in next 2ch sp, 1sc in each of next 21sc, rep from * once more, ss in first sc.

8th round Ss in first 2ch sp, 1ch, [1sc, 4ch, 1dc] in same 2ch sp, * [1ch, miss next sc, 1dc in foll sc] 9 times, 1ch, [1dc, 2ch, 1dc] in next 2ch sp, [1ch, miss next sc, 1dc in foll sc] 11 times, 1ch, miss 1sc *, [1dc, 2ch, 1dc] in next 2ch sp, rep from * to *, ss in 2nd ch.

Fasten off.

Head Using A, make 3ch.

1st row 1sc in 2nd ch from hook, 1sc in next ch. 2 sts.

2nd row (RS) 1ch, 2sc in each sc. 4 sts.

3rd row 1ch, 1sc in each sc.

4th row 1ch, 2sc in first sc, 1sc in each of next 2sc, 2sc in last sc. 6 sts.

5th row As 3rd row.

Ears. 6th row Ss in each of first 2sc, * 3hdc in same sc as last ss,

ss in same sc *, ss in each of next 3sc, rep from * to *, ss in last sc.

Fasten off.

Mane Using C, [make 8ch, 1sc in 8th ch from hook] 8 times.

Fasten off.

To complete Place head at an angle at top left of body, inserting mane behind top half of head, sew on head and mane. Using orange, embroider two small horizontal straight stitches for eyes. Using C embroider two small vertical straight stitches for pupils and a Y shape of straight stitches for the nose. Using A, and closely packed small horizontal straight stitches, embroider legs. Using A embroider tail in chain stitch, then using C, make three small straight stitches at end of tail.

abbreviations

ch = chain
sc = single crochet
dc = double crochet
foll = following
hdc = half double crochet
rep = repeat
RS = right side
sp = space
ss = slip stitch
[ ] = work instructions in square brackets as directed.

waves

This version of the classic zigzag pattern is worked in rows to make the center of the block, then the edging rounds fill in the dips and neaten the sides to make a square.

instructions

Colors: Denim blue (A), bright blue (B), pale blue (C), cream (D), and navy (E).

Using A, make 23ch.

1st row 1dc in 3rd ch from hook, *1dc in each of next 3ch, 3dctog, 1dc in each of foll 3ch *, 3dc in next ch, rep from * to *, 2dc in last ch. 21 sts.

2nd row (RS) 1sc in first dc, 2ch, 1dc in same dc, * 1dc in each of next 3dc, 3dctog, 1dc in each of foll 3dc *, 3dc in next dc, rep from * to *, 2dc in top ch.

2nd row forms the wavy pattern. Work 2 more rows in each of B, C, and D. Fasten off.

Edging With RS facing, join E in first row-end down left edge.

1st round 1ch, 2sc in same row-end as join, 2sc in each of next 7 row-ends down left edge, ss in base of first ch at lower edge, 3ch, 1dc in same place as ss, 1dc in base of next ch, * 1hdc in base of each of next 2ch, 1sc in base of each of foll 3ch, 1hdc in base of each of next 2ch *, 1dc in base of foll 3ch, rep from * to *, 1dc in

base of each of last 2ch, 3ch, ss in same place as last dc, 2sc in each of next 8 row-ends up right edge, 1sc in top ch at start of upper edge, 1sc in next dc, * 1hdc in each of next 2dc, 1dc in each of next 3 sts, 1hdc in each of foll 2dc *, 1sc in each of next 3dc, rep from * to *, 1sc in each of last 2dc, ss in first sc.

2nd round 1ch, 2sc in first sc, 1sc in each of next 15sc, 1sc in ss, 3sc in 3ch sp, 2sc in top ch, 2sc in next dc, 1sc in each of next 19 sts, 2sc in next dc, 2sc in top ch, 3sc in 3ch sp, 1sc in ss, 1sc in each of next 15sc, 2sc in each of next 2sc, 1sc in each of next 19 sts, 2sc in last sc, ss in first sc. 92 sts. Fasten off.

little piggy

The body is a simple oval in single crochet worked in turned rounds. The head is worked separately and sewn on, then the details are embroidered to give character to the pig.

instructions

Colors: Dark pink (A) and green (B) with tiny scraps of black and white for the embroidery.

Body Using A, make 6ch.

1st round 2sc in 2nd ch from hook, 1sc in each of next 3ch, 3sc in last ch, 1sc in base of each of next 4ch, ss in first sc, turn. 12 sts.

2nd round (RS) 1ch, 2sc in same place as ss, 1sc in each of next 5sc, 3sc in foll sc, 1sc in each of next 5sc, 1sc in same place as 2sc, ss in first sc, turn. 16 sts.

3rd round 1ch, 2sc in same place as ss, 1sc in each of next 7sc, 3sc in foll sc, 1sc in each of next 7sc, 1sc in same place as 2sc, ss in first sc. 20 sts. Fasten off.

Background With RS facing and counting along top edge of body, join B in 16th sc from end of 3rd round.

1st round 1ch, 2sc in same place as ss, * 1sc in each of next 3sc, 3sc in foll sc, 1sc in each of next 5sc *, 3sc in foll sc, rep from * to *, 1sc in same place as 2sc, ss in first sc. 28 sts.

Continue in rounds without turning.

2nd round 1ch, 2sc in same place as ss, * 1sc in each of next 5sc, 3sc in foll sc, 1sc in each of next 7sc *, 3sc in foll sc, rep from * to *, 1sc in same place as 2sc, ss in first sc. 36 sts.

3rd round 1ch, 2sc in same place as ss, * 1sc in each of next 7sc, 3sc in foll sc, 1sc in each of next 9sc *, 3sc in foll sc, rep from * to *, 1sc in same place as 2sc, ss in first sc. 44 sts.

4th round 1ch, 2sc in same place as ss, * 1sc in each of next 9sc, 3sc in foll sc, 1sc in each of next 11sc *, 3sc in foll sc, rep from * to *, 1sc in same place as 2sc, ss in first sc. 52 sts.

5th round 1ch, 2sc in same place as ss, * 1sc in each of next 11sc, 3sc in foll sc, 1sc in each of next 13sc *, 3sc in foll sc, rep from * to *, 1sc in same place as 2sc, ss in first sc. 60 sts.

6th round 1ch, 2sc in same place as ss, * 1sc in each of next 13sc, 3sc in foll sc, 1sc in each of next 15sc *, 3sc in foll sc, rep from * to *, 1sc in same place as 2sc, ss in first sc. 68 sts.

7th round 1ch, [1sc, 5ch, 1dc] in same place as ss, * [1ch, miss next sc, 1dc in foll sc] 7 times, 1ch, miss next sc, [1dc, 3ch, 1dc] in foll sc, [1ch, miss next sc, 1dc in foll sc] 8 times, 1ch, miss next sc *, [1dc, 3ch, 1dc] in foll sc, rep from * to *, ss in 2nd ch. Fasten off.

Head Using A, make 3ch.

abbreviations

ch = chain
sc = single crochet
dc = double crochet
foll = following
hdc = half double crochet
rep = repeat
RS = right side
ss = slip stitch

sp = space
st(s) = stitch(es)
3dctog = leaving last loop of each st on hook, work 3dc, yarn over hook and pull through 4 loops on hook
[ ] = work instructions in square brackets as directed.

abbreviations

ch = chain
sc = single crochet
dc = double crochet
foll = following
rep = repeat

RS = right side
ss = slip stitch
[ ] = work instructions as directed.

1st round (RS) 2sc in 2nd ch from hook, 4sc in end ch, 2sc in base of same ch as 2sc, ss in first sc.

1st row (RS) 1ch, 1sc around the stem of same sc as ss, 1sc around the stem of each of next 3sc, turn. 4 sts.

2nd row 1ch, 2sc in first sc, 1sc in each of next 2sc, 2sc in last sc. 6 sts.

3rd row 1ch, [1sc in each sc] to end.

Ears. 4th row Ss in each of first 2sc, * 1ch, 1sc, 1dc, 2ch, ss in 2nd ch from hook, 2ch, ss in same sc of 3rd row *, ss in each of next 3sc, rep from * to *, ss in last sc. Fasten off.

To complete Sew head at an angle at top left corner of body. Fold ears down and stitch to hold in place. Using black, embroider small straight stitches for the eyes and nostrils. Using white, embroider a tiny stab stitch to highlight each eye. Using A and closely packed horizontal small straight stitches embroider legs, then chain stitch a curly tail.

COW

An oblong of single crochet in rows makes the body. The field is worked in rounds, turning after each round to give a ridged texture. The head, nose, legs, and udder are worked separately.

instructions
Colors: Camel (A), green (B), cream (C), pink (D), and brown (E).
Body Using A, make 9ch.

1st row 1sc in 2nd ch from hook, [1sc in each ch] to end. 8 sts.
2nd row (RS) 1ch, [1sc in each sc] to end.

2nd row forms sc. Work 11 more rows sc. Fasten off.

Field With RS facing, join B in base of first ch.

1st round 1ch, 2sc in same place as join, 1sc in each of next 6ch, 3sc in end ch, 1sc in each of next 12 row-ends, 3sc in corner sc, 1sc in each of next 6sc, 3sc in corner sc, 1sc in each of next 12 row-ends, 1sc in first corner, ss in first sc, turn.

Turning each time and working two more sc along each side on every round, work 5 more rounds sc. Fasten off.

Head Using A, make 5ch. Work 1st row as given for body. 4 sts. Work 5 rows sc. Fasten off.

Nose Using C, make 5ch.

1st row 4sc in 2nd ch from hook, 1sc in next ch, 4sc in foll ch, ss in last ch, placing one st in base of each of center 3ch, work 3sctog. Fasten off and darn end into first ch.

1st and 4th legs Make 6ch. Work as 1st row of body. 5 sts. Fasten off.

2nd and 3rd legs Make 5ch. Work as 1st row of body. 4 sts. Fasten off.

Udder With RS facing and join in rounds to top left, join D to sc at end of 7th row along lower edge of body. Work 6dc in sc at end of 9th row. Leaving a long end, fasten off.

To complete Sew head in place at top left of body. Turning chain edge to RS, sew on nose. Using A, embroider 3 bullion knots for top knot and work a long detached chain stitch at each side of head for ears. Using D, embroider nostrils. Using E, work a bullion knot for each eye. With longer legs at front and rear, sew on legs. Sew udder in place over 3rd leg and embroider teats with D. Using A, embroider tail in chain stitch, ending with 3 short straight stitches over the last chain.

abbreviations

ch = chain
sc = single crochet
dc = double crochet
3sctog = pull a loop through for each of 3 sts, yarn over hook and pull through 4 loops on hook

foll = following
RS = right side
ss = slip stitch
st(s) = stitch(es)
[ ] = work instructions in square brackets as directed.

rising sun

Inspired by the fabric patchwork block, but with an Art Deco feel, this motif starts with a quarter-circle sun. The rays are wedges, each worked separately out from the last row of the sun. The sky fills in the spaces to give a scalloped edge. Join four motifs to make a round sun.

instructions

Colors: Yellow (A) and blue (B).

Sun Using A, make 2ch.

1st row 3sc in 2nd ch from hook. 3 sts.

2nd and every RS row 1ch, [1sc in each sc] to end.

3rd row 1ch, [2sc in each sc] to end. 6 sts.

5th row 1ch, [2sc in next sc, 1sc in foll sc] 3 times. 9 sts.

7th row 1ch, [2sc in next sc, 1sc in each of foll 2sc] 12 sts.

9th row 1ch, [2sc in next sc, 1sc in each of foll 3sc] 15 sts.

11th row 1ch, [2sc in next sc, 1sc in each of foll 4sc] 18 sts.

13th row 1ch, [2sc in next sc, 1sc in each of foll 5sc] 21 sts.

1st ray. 1st row (RS) 1ch, 1sc in each of first 5sc, turn.

2nd row 1ch, miss first sc, 1sc in each of last 4sc.

3rd row 1ch, 1sc in each of 4sc.

4th row 1ch, miss first sc, 1sc in each of last 3sc.

5th row 1ch, 1sc in each of 3sc.

6th row 1ch, miss first sc, 1sc in each of last 2sc.

7th row 1ch, 1sc in each of 2sc.

8th row 1ch, miss first sc, 1sc in last sc.

9th row 1ch, 1sc in sc. Fasten off.

2nd, 3rd, and 4th rays With RS facing, join A in next sc of 13th row. Complete as 1st ray.

Sky With RS facing and arc of sun at lower left, join B in same sc of 13th row as first st of 1st ray.

1st row 1ch, [1sc in each of next 8 row-ends, 3sc in next sc, 1sc in each of foll 8 row-ends] 4 times, ss in last sc of 13th row.

2nd row 2ch, miss ss and next 2sc, [* 1sc in each of next 7sc, 3sc in foll sc, 1sc in each of next 7sc *, miss 4sc] 3 times, rep from * to *, ss in next sc, turn.

3rd row 2ch, miss ss and next 2sc, [* 1sc in each of next 6sc, 3sc in foll sc, 1sc in each of next 6sc *, miss 4sc] 3 times, rep from * to *, ss in next sc, turn.

4th row 2ch, miss ss and next 2sc, [* 1sc in each of next 5sc, 3sc in foll sc, 1sc in each of next 5sc *, miss 4sc] 3 times, rep from * to *, ss in next sc, turn.

5th row 2ch, miss ss and next 2sc, [* 1sc in each of next 4sc, 3sc in foll sc, 1sc in each of next 4sc *, miss 4sc] 3 times, rep from * to *, ss in next sc, turn.

6th row 2ch, miss ss and next 2sc, [* 1sc in each of next 3sc, 3sc in foll sc, 1sc in each of next 3sc *, miss 4sc] 3 times, rep from * to *, ss in next sc. Fasten off

Edging With RS facing, join B at beg of 6th row of sky and work 8sc in row-ends down left edge of sky, change to A, work 13sc in row-ends down left edge of sun, 3sc in base of corner ch, and 13sc in row-ends along lower edge of sun, change to B, work 8sc in row-ends along lower edge of sky, ss in last sc of 6th row of sky.
Fasten off.

abbreviations

ch = chain

sc = single crochet

foll = following

rep = repeat

ss = slip stitch

st(s) = stitch(es)

[ ] = work instructions in square brackets as directed.

siamese cat

The arched body of the cat is just a simple curve in single crochet with different-length stitches on the second round of the background to fill in the shape and make an oblong. The head is worked separately and sewn on, then the face, legs, and tail are embroidered.

instructions

Colors: Cream (A), blue (B), and soft brown (C) with scraps of black, bright blue, and pink for the embroidery.

Body Using A, make 14ch.

1st row 1sc in 2nd ch from hook, [1sc in each ch] to end. 13 sts.

2nd row (RS) 1ch, miss first st, 1sc in each of next 4sc, 2sc in next sc, 1sc in foll sc, 2sc in next sc, 1sc in each of foll 3sc, 2sctog.

3rd row 1ch, [1sc in each st] to end.

4th row As 2nd row.

5th row As 3rd row. Fasten off.

Background With RS facing, join B in top left corner sc.

1st round 1ch, [1sc, 2ch, 1sc] in same place as join, 1sc in each of next 3 row-ends, [1sc, 2ch, 1sc] in corner sc, 1sc between each of next 11sc, [1sc, 2ch, 1sc] in corner sc, 1sc in each of next 3 row-ends, [1sc, 2ch, 1sc] in corner sc, 1sc in each of next 11sc, ss in first sc.

2nd round Ss in first 2ch sp, 1ch, [1sc, 4ch, 1sc] in same 2ch sp, 1sc in each of next 5sc, [1sc, 2ch, 1sc] in next 2ch sp, 1sc in each of next 2sc, 1hdc in each of foll 2sc, 1dc in each of next 5sc, 1hdc in each of foll 2sc, 1sc in each of next 2sc, [1sc, 2ch, 1sc] in next 2ch sp, 1sc in each of next 5sc, [1sc, 2ch, 1dc] in next 2ch sp, 1dc in each of next 2sc, 1hdc in each of foll 3sc, 1sc in each of next 3sc, 1hdc in each of foll 3sc, 1dc in each of last 2sc, ss in 2nd ch.

3rd round Ss in first 2ch sp, 1ch, [1sc, 2ch, 1sc] in same 2ch sp, * 1sc in each of next 7sc, [1sc, 2ch, 1sc] in next 2ch sp, 1sc in each of next 15 sts *, [1sc, 2ch, 1sc] in next 2ch sp, rep from * to *, ss in first sc.

4th round Ss in first 2ch sp, 1ch, * [1sc, 2ch, 1sc] in 2ch sp, 1sc in each of next 9sc, [1sc, 2ch, 1sc] in next 2ch sp, 1sc in each of next 17sc, rep from * once more, ss in first sc.

5th round Ss in first 2ch sp, 1ch, * [1sc, 2ch, 1sc] in 2ch sp, 1sc in each of next

11sc, [1sc, 2ch, 1sc] in next 2ch sp, 1sc in each of next 19sc, rep from * once more, ss in first sc.

6th round Ss in first 2ch sp, 1ch, * [1sc, 2ch, 1sc] in 2ch sp, 1sc in each of next 13sc, [1sc, 2ch, 1sc] in next 2ch sp, 1sc in each of next 21sc, rep from * once more, ss in first sc.

7th round Ss in first 2ch sp, 1ch, * [1sc, 2ch, 1sc] in 2ch sp, 1sc in each of next 15sc, [1sc, 2ch, 1sc] in next 2ch sp, 1sc in each of next 23sc, rep from * once more, ss in first sc.

8th round Ss in first 2ch sp, 1ch, * [1sc, 2ch, 1sc] in 2ch sp, 1sc in each of next 17sc, [1sc, 2ch, 1sc] in next 2ch sp, 1sc in each of next 25sc, rep from * once more, ss in first sc.

9th round Ss in first 2ch sp, 1ch, [1sc, 4ch, 1dc] in same 2ch sp, * [1ch, miss 1sc, 1dc in next sc] 9 times, 1ch, miss 1sc, [1dc, 2ch, 1dc] in next 2ch sp, [1ch, miss 1sc, 1dc in next sc] 13 times, 1ch, miss 1sc *, [1dc, 2ch, 1dc] in next 2ch sp, rep from * to *, ss in 2nd ch. Fasten off.

Head Using C, wind yarn around finger to form a ring.

1st row 1ch, 2sc in ring, turn. 2 sts.

2nd row (RS) 1ch, 1sc in each sc.

3rd row 1ch, 2sc in each sc. 4 sts.

4th row As 2nd row.

5th row 1ch, 2sc in first sc, 2hdc in each of next 2sc, 2sc in last sc. 8 sts.

Change to A.

6th row 1ch, 1sc in first sc, 2hdc in next sc, 1hdc in foll hdc, ss in each of next 2hdc, 1hdc in foll hdc, 2hdc in next sc, 1sc

in last sc. 10 sts.

7th row Ss in first sc, 1ch, 1sc in each of next 8 sts, ss in last sc. Fasten off.

1st ear With RS facing, miss ss and join C in first sc.

1st row 1ch, 1sc in same place as join, 1hdc in next sc, 1dc in foll sc, turn. 3 sts.

2nd row 1sc in first st, 2ch, 2dctog. Fasten off.

2nd ear With RS facing, miss center 2sc and join C in next sc.

1st row 1ch, 1sc in same place as join, 2ch, 1hdc in next sc, 1sc in foll sc, turn. 3 sts.

2nd row As 2nd row of 1st ear. Fasten off.

To complete Sew head on at top left of body. Using C make a long straight stitch to place each leg and backstitch a curve for the tail, then using A and C work short horizontal stitches over the stitches to fill in the legs and tail. Using bright blue and black embroider eyes, using black embroider nose, using pink make a tiny chain stitch for tongue.

abbreviations

ch = chain

sc = single crochet

dc = double crochet

foll = following

hdc = half double crochet

rep = repeat

RS = right side

sp = space

ss = slip stitch

st(s) = stitch(es)

2dctog = leaving last loop of each st on hook, work 2dc, yarn over hook and pull through 3 loops on hook

[ ] = work instructions in square brackets as directed.

scallop shell

This shell motif is inspired by antique crochet lace designs. The openwork center is worked in rows and the border, which is not shown on the chart, is worked in the round.

instructions

Center Make 27ch.

1st row (RS) 1dc in 4th ch from hook, 1dc in next ch, 5ch, miss next 3ch, 1dc in each of next 13ch, 5ch, miss next 3ch, 1dc in each of last 3ch.

2nd row 1ch, 1sc in each of first 3dc, 5sc in next 5ch sp, 5ch, miss 3dc, 1dc in each of next 7dc, 5ch, miss 3dc, 5sc in next 5ch sp, 1sc in each of next 2dc, 1sc in next ch.

3rd row 1ch, 1sc in each of first 7sc, 5ch, miss next 1sc and 2dc, [1dc, 3ch, 1dc] in foll dc, 1ch, miss next dc, [1dc, 3ch, 1dc] in foll dc, 5ch, miss next 2dc and 1sc, 1sc in each of last 7sc.

4th row 1ch, 1sc in each of first 6sc, 5ch, miss 1sc, * [1dc, 3ch, 1dc] in next 3ch sp, 1ch, [1dc, 3ch, 1dc] in 1ch sp, 1ch, [1dc, 3ch, 1dc] in last 3ch sp, 5ch, miss 1sc, 1sc in each of last 6sc.

5th row 1ch, 1sc in each of first 5sc, 5ch, miss 1sc, * [1dc, 3ch, 1dc] in next 3ch sp, 1ch, rep from * once more, [1dc, 3ch, 1dc] in last 3ch sp, 5ch, miss 1sc, 1sc in each of last 5sc.

6th row 1ch, 1sc in each of first 4sc, 5ch, miss 1sc, * [1dc, 3ch, 1dc] in next 3ch sp, 1ch, rep from * once more, [1dc, 3ch, 1dc] in last 3ch sp, 5ch, miss 1sc, 1sc in each of last 4sc.

7th row 1ch, 1sc in each of first 3sc, 4ch, miss 1sc, * [1dc, 3ch, 1dc] in next 3ch sp, 1ch, [1dc, 3ch, 1dc] in foll 1ch sp, 1ch, rep from * once more, [1dc, 3ch, 1dc] in last 3ch sp, 4ch, miss 1sc, 1sc in each of last 3sc.

8th row 1ch, 1sc in each of first 2sc, 3ch, miss 1sc, [1dc, 3ch, 1dc, 1ch] in each of next five 3ch sps, work 2 more ch, miss 1sc, 1sc in each of last 2sc.

9th row 1ch, 1sc in first sc, 3ch, miss 1sc, [3dc, 1ch, 3dc] in each of next five 3ch sps, miss 1sc, 1tr in last sc.

10th row 1ch, 1sc in tr, 3ch, 1dc in first 1ch sp, [6ch, 1dc in next 1ch sp] 4 times, 1tr in 3rd ch.

11th row 1ch, 1sc in tr, 3ch, [1dc, 3ch, 1tr, 3ch, 1tr, 3ch, 1dc] in first 6ch sp, [3ch, 1dc] twice in each of next two 6ch sps, 3ch, [1dc, 3ch, 1tr, 3ch, 1tr, 3ch, 1dc] in last 6ch sp, 3ch, ss in 3rd ch. Fasten off.

Edging With RS facing, join yarn at top right in third 3ch sp of 11th row.

1st round 1ch, [1sc, 3ch, 2sc] in same 3ch sp, 3sc in each of next seven 3ch sps, [2sc, 3ch, 2sc] in next 3ch sp, 3sc in each of next two 3ch sps, 1sc in dc, 3sc in next 3ch sp, 1sc in sc, 3sc in tr sp, 1sc in each of next 7 row-ends, 2sc in last row-end, 3ch, 1sc in base of each of next 3ch, 3sc in next 3ch sp, 1sc in base of each of next 13ch, 3sc in foll 3ch sp, 1sc in base of each of next 3ch, 3ch, 2sc in first row-end, 1sc in each of next 7 row-ends, 3sc in next 3ch sp, 1sc in next dc, 3sc in tr sp, 1sc in next sc, 3sc in each of next two 3ch sps, 1sc in first 3ch sp, ss in first sc.

2nd round Ss in first 3ch sp, turn, 1ch, 1sc in same 3ch sp, * 1sc in each of next 25sc, [1sc, 3ch, 1sc] in next 3ch sp, rep from * 3 more

times omitting last sc, ss in first sc, turn.

3rd round Ss in first 3ch sp, 1ch, [1sc, 5ch, 1dc] in same 3ch sp, * [1ch, miss next sc, 1dc in foll sc] 13 times, 1ch, miss next sc, [1dc, 3ch, 1dc] in next 3ch sp, rep from * two more times, [1ch, miss next sc, 1dc in foll sc] 13 times, 1ch, miss last sc, ss in 2nd ch. Fasten off.

goldfish

The body of the fish is worked first in single crochet and a little shell pattern to look like scales, with two wedge-shaped fan stitches for the tail. The watery background uses different-height stitches to even out the shape before falling into regular neat rounds of single crochet. Work this motif in natural or mixed fiber yarns, as the long stitches are a bit wavy until pressed.

instructions

Colors: Orange (A) and green (B) with scraps of black and white for the embroidery.

Head Using A, make 2ch.

1st row 3sc in 2nd ch from hook, turn. 3 sts.

2nd row (RS) 1ch, [1sc in each sc] to end.

3rd row 1ch, 2sc in each sc. 6 sts.

4th and 5th rows As 2nd row.

6th row 1ch, [1sc in each sc] to last sc, 2sc in last sc. 7 sts.

Body. 1st row 1ch, 1sc in first sc, miss next 2sc, 5dc in foll sc, miss next 2sc, 1sc in last sc.

2nd row [1sc, 2ch, 2dc] in first sc, miss next 2dc, 1sc in foll dc, miss next 2dc, 3dc in last sc.

3rd row 1ch, 1sc in first dc, miss next 2dc, 5dc in next sc, miss next 2dc, 1sc in 2nd ch.

4th and 5th rows As 2nd and 3rd rows.

Tail. 1st row Ss in each of first 4 sts, [4ch, 2tr, 5ch, ss, 5ch, 2tr, 4ch, ss] in same dc as last ss, ss in each of last 3 sts. Fasten off.

Edging With RS facing, join A in base of ch at start of head.

1st round 1ch, 2sc in same place as join, 12sc in row-ends along lower edge of fish to tail row, 1sc in each of next 2ss, miss foll ss, ss in center dc of 5th row of body, 1sc in each of next 3ch, 3sc in last ch, 1sc in each of next 2tr, 3sc in first ch, ss in each of next 4ch, miss center ss, ss in each of foll 4ch, 3sc in last ch, 1sc in each of next 2tr, 3sc in first ch, 1sc in each of foll 3ch, ss in center dc of 5th row of body, miss next ss, 1sc in each of foll 2ss, 12sc in row-ends along upper edge of fish, 1sc in same place as join, ss in first sc. 63 sts. Fasten off.

Water With RS facing, join B in first sc of edging round.

1st round 1ch, 2sc in same place as join,

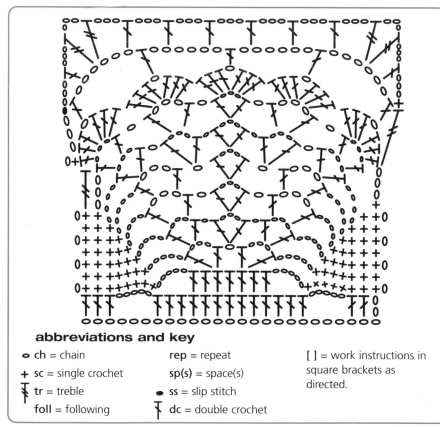

abbreviations and key

o	ch = chain	rep = repeat	[ ] = work instructions in square brackets as directed.
+	sc = single crochet	sp(s) = space(s)	
†	tr = treble	ss = slip stitch	
	foll = following	dc = double crochet	

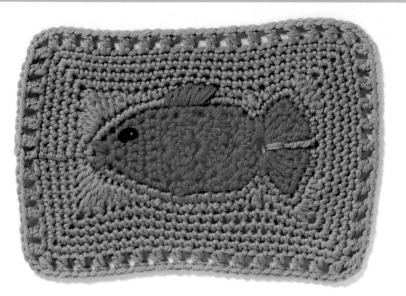

2sc in each of next 13sc, 1sc in each of foll 2sc, miss ss, 1sc in each of next 4sc, 3sc in foll sc, 1sc in each of next 5sc, miss 1sc and next 4ss, 1tr in same dc as tail sts, miss next 4ss and 1sc, 1sc in each of foll 5sc, 3sc in next sc, 1sc in each of foll 4sc, miss ss, 1sc in each of next 2sc, 2sc in each of foll 13sc, 1sc in same place as first 2sc, ss in first sc. 84 sts.

2nd round 1ch, 1sc in same place as ss, 1sc in next sc, 1dc in each of foll 3sc, 3tr in next sc, 1dc in each of foll 3sc, 1sc in each of next 3sc, [miss foll sc, 1sc in next sc] 8 times, miss next sc, 1dc in foll sc, miss next sc, 1sc in next sc, miss foll sc, 1sc in each of next 2sc, [1sc, 2dc] in foll sc, 1dc in each of next 3sc, 1sc in each of foll 7 sts, 1dc in each of next 3sc, [2dc, 1sc] in foll sc, 1sc in each of next 2sc, miss next sc, 1sc in foll sc, miss next sc, 1dc in foll sc, miss next sc, [1sc in foll sc, miss next sc] 8 times, 1sc in each of next 3sc, 1dc in each of foll 3sc, 3tr in next sc, 1dc in each of foll 3sc, 1sc in last sc, 1sc in same place as first sc, ss in first sc. 71 sts.

3rd round 1ch, 1sc in same place as ss, 1sc in each of next 5 sts, 3sc in next tr, 1sc in each of next 21 sts, 3sc in next dc, 1sc in each of next 13 sts, 3sc in next dc, 1sc in each of foll 21 sts, 3sc in next tr, 1sc in each of next 6 sts, 1sc in same place as first sc, ss in first sc. 80 sts.

4th round 1ch, 1sc in same place as ss, 1sc in each of next 6sc, 3sc in foll sc, 1sc in each of next 23sc, 3sc in foll sc, 1sc in each of next 15sc, 3sc in foll sc, 1sc in each of next 23sc, 3sc in foll sc, 1sc in each of next 8sc, ss in first sc.

5th round 1ch, 1sc in same place as ss, 1sc in each of next 7sc, 3sc in foll sc, 1sc in each of next 25sc, 3sc in foll sc, 1sc in each of next 17sc, 3sc in foll sc, 1sc in

each of next 25sc, 3sc in foll sc, 1sc in each of next 9sc, ss in first sc.

6th round 1ch, 1sc in same place as ss, 1sc in each of next 8sc, 3sc in foll sc, 1sc in each of next 27sc, 3sc in foll sc, 1sc in each of next 19sc, 3sc in foll sc, 1sc in each of next 27sc, 3sc in foll sc, 1sc in each of next 10sc, ss in first sc.

7th round 1ch, [miss next sc, 1dc in foll sc, 1ch] 4 times, miss next sc, [1dc, 3ch, 1dc] in foll sc, 1ch, [miss next sc, 1dc in foll sc, 1ch] 14 times, miss next sc, [1dc, 3ch, 1dc] in foll sc, 1ch, [miss next sc, 1dc in foll sc, 1ch] 10 times, miss next sc, [1dc, 3ch, 1dc] in foll sc, 1ch, [miss next sc, 1dc in foll sc, 1ch] 14 times, miss next sc, [1dc, 3ch, 1dc] in foll sc, 1ch, [miss next sc, 1dc in foll sc, 1ch] 5 times, ss in 3rd ch. Fasten off.

To complete Using A, work two chain stitches at the mouth for lips and 5 long chain stitches at center of top edge for fin. Using black make a round chain stitch for the eye and fill eye with two short straight stitches, then using white, embroider a highlight in the eye.

abbreviations
ch = chain

sc = single crochet

dc = double crochet

tr = treble

foll = following

RS = right side

ss = slip stitch

st(s) = stitch(es)

[ ] = work instructions in square brackets as directed.

apple tree

This motif is like a child's drawing of a tree, with a circle of single crochet for the top and a straight strip for the trunk. The sky is worked in rows around three sides of the tree, then the ground is worked in green with longer stitches for the grass. The apples are embroidered afterward.

instructions
Colors: Bright green (A), brown (B), blue (C), lime green (D), warm white (E), and pink for the embroidery.

Top Using A, wind yarn around finger to form a ring.

1st round (RS) 1ch, 6sc in ring, ss in first sc. 6 sts.

2nd round 1ch, 2sc in each sc, ss in first sc. 12 sts.

3rd round 1ch, 1sc in first sc, [2sc in next sc, 1sc in foll sc] 5 times, 2sc in last sc, ss in first sc. 18 sts.

4th round 1ch, 1sc in each of first 2sc, [2sc in next sc, 1sc in each of foll 2sc] 5 times, 2sc in last sc, ss in first sc. 24 sts.

5th round 1ch, 1sc in each of first 3sc, [2sc in next sc, 1sc in each of foll 3sc] 5 times, 2sc in last sc, ss in first sc. 30 sts.

Fasten off.

Tree trunk With RS facing and taking hook behind, join B around the stem of same sc as join in last round of top.

1st row 1ch, 1sc around the stem of same sc as join, 1sc around the stem of each of next 3sc, turn. 4 sts.

2nd row 1ch, [1sc in each sc] to end.

2nd row forms sc. Work 8 more rows sc.

Fasten off.

Sky With RS facing, join C in lower row-end at right of trunk.

1st row 1ch, 1sc in same place as join, 1sc in each of next 9 row-ends, 1sc around the stem of each of next 26sc, 1sc in each of next 10 row-ends, turn. 46 sts.

2nd row 1ch, 1sc in first sc, 2ch, 1dc in each of next 9sc, miss next sc, 1hdc in foll sc, 1sc in each of next 6sc, [1sc, 2ch, 1sc] in foll sc, 1sc in each of next 8sc, [1sc, 2ch, 1sc] in foll sc, 1sc in each of next 6sc, 1hdc in foll sc, miss next sc, 1dc in each of last 10sc.

3rd row 1ch, 1sc in first dc, 2ch, 1dc in each of next 9dc, miss next hdc, 1hdc in foll sc, 1sc in each of next 6sc, [1sc, 2ch, 1sc] in next 2ch sp, 1sc in each of next 10sc, [1sc, 2ch, 1sc] in next 2ch sp, 1sc in each of next 6sc, 1hdc in foll sc, miss next hdc, 1dc in each of next 9dc, 1dc in 2nd ch.

4th row 1ch, 1sc in each of next 18 sts, [1sc, 2ch, 1sc] in first 2ch sp, 1sc in each of next 12sc, [1sc, 2ch, 1sc] in last 2ch sp, 1sc in each of next 18 sts.

5th row 1ch, 1sc in each of next 19sc, [1sc, 2ch, 1sc] in first 2ch sp, 1sc in each of next 14sc, [1sc, 2ch, 1sc] in last 2ch sp, 1sc in each of next 19sc.

6th row 1ch, 1sc in each of next 20sc, [1sc, 2ch, 1sc] in first 2ch sp, 1sc in each of next 16sc, [1sc, 2ch, 1sc] in last 2ch sp, 1sc in each of next 20sc. Fasten off.

Ground With RS facing and tree upside down, join D in first row-end of sky.

1st row 1ch, 1sc in same place as join, work 7sc in row-ends of sky placing hook 2 sts in from edge on alternate sts, 1sc in each sc of trunk, work 7sc in row-ends of sky placing hook 2 sts in from edge on alternate sts. 20 sts.

Work 3 more rows sc. Fasten off.

Edging With RS facing and tree upside down, join E in last sc of ground.

1st round 1ch, [1sc, 2ch, 1sc] in same place as join, 1sc in each of next 18sc, [1sc, 2ch, 1sc] in last sc of lower edge, 1sc in each of next 3 row-ends, 1sc in each of next 21sc, [1sc, 2ch, 1sc] in next 2ch sp, 1sc in each of next 18sc, [1sc, 2ch, 1sc] in next 2ch sp, 1sc in each of next 21sc, 1sc in each of last 3 row-ends, ss in first sc, turn.

2nd round 1ch, * 1sc in each of next 26sc, [1sc, 2ch, 1sc] in next 2ch sp, 1sc in each of next 20sc, [1sc, 2ch, 1sc] in foll 2ch sp, rep from * once more, ss in first sc. Fasten off.

To complete Using pink yarn, embroider scattered detached chain stitches in tree top for apples.

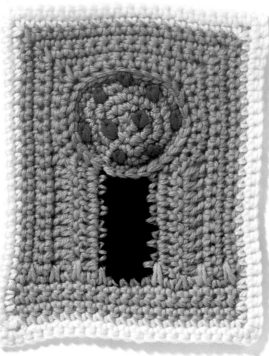

turkish carpet star

This motif is built up in single crochet sections. First, the center square is made then each point is worked separately and outlined to complete the star. Finally, the background triangles and squares are filled in and edged.

instructions

Colors: Red (A), brown (B), natural (C), and pale indigo (D).

Using A, wind yarn around finger to form a ring.

1st round (RS) 1ch, [1sc in ring, 2ch] 4 times, ss in first sc.

2nd round Ss in first 2ch sp, 1ch, * [1sc, 2ch, 1sc] in 2ch sp, 1sc in next sc, rep from * 3 more times, ss in first sc.

3rd round Ss in first 2ch sp, 1ch, * [1sc, 2ch, 1sc] in 2ch sp, 1sc in each of next 3sc, rep from * 3 more times, ss in first sc.

4th round Ss in first 2ch sp, 1ch, * [1sc, 2ch, 1sc] in 2ch sp, 1sc in each of next 5sc, rep from * 3 more times, ss in first sc.

Fasten off. Join B in a 2ch sp.

5th round 1ch, * [1sc, 2ch, 1sc] in 2ch sp, 1sc in each of next 7sc, rep from * 3 more times, ss in first sc. Fasten off.

First point With RS facing, join C in a 2ch sp.

1st row 1ch, 1sc in 2ch sp, 1sc in each of next 4sc, turn. 5 sts.

2nd and every alternate row 1ch, 1sc in each sc.

3rd row 1ch, 1sc in each of next 4sc, turn.

5th row 1ch, 1sc in each of first 3sc, turn.

7th row 1ch, 1sc in each of first 2sc, turn.

9th row 1ch, 1sc in first sc, turn.

10th row 1ch, 1sc in sc. Fasten off.

2nd point With WS facing join C in 2ch sp at other end of same edge as 1st point. Complete as 1st point.

Work 1st and 2nd points along remaining 3 sides.

Outline round With RS facing join B in a sc at tip of a 1st point, 1ch, 2sc in same sc as join, [2sc in each of next 4sc at row-ends down slanted edge of same point, 1sc in next sc of 5th round, 2sc in each of foll 4sc at row-ends up slanted edge of next point, 3sc in sc at tip of point, 9sc in row-ends down straight edge of same point, 1sc in 2ch sp of 5th round, 9sc in row-ends up straight edge of foll point, 3sc in sc at tip of point] 4 times omitting last 2sc, ss in first sc. Fasten off.

Triangle infill With RS facing, join D in center sc of 3sc at tip of a 1st point.

abbreviations

ch = chain	**sp** = space
sc = single crochet	**ss** = slip stitch
foll = following	**st(s)** = stitch(es)
hdc = half double crochet	**dc** = double crochet
rep = repeat	**[ ]** = work instructions in
RS = right side	square brackets as directed.

abbreviations

ch = chain	**RS** = right side
sc = single crochet	**sp** = space
2sctog = pull loops through 1st and 2nd sts, yarn over and pull through 3 loops on hook	**ss** = slip stitch
	st(s) = stitch(es)
foll = following	**WS** = wrong side
rep = repeat	**[ ]** = work instructions in square brackets as directed.

1st row 1ch, 2sctog, 1sc in each of next 7sc, 1ch, miss 3sc, 1sc in each of foll 7sc, 2sctog, turn.

2nd row 1ch, 2sctog, 1sc in each of next 4sc, 1ch, miss next 2sc, 1ch and foll 2sc, 1sc in each of foll 4sc, 2sctog.

3rd row 1ch, 2sctog, 1sc in next sc, 1ch, miss next 2sc, 1ch and foll 2sc, 1sc in foll sc, 2sctog.

4th row 1ch, 1sc in first 2sctog, 1ch, 1sc in last 2sctog. Fasten off.

Work 3 more triangle infills in the same way.

Corner square infill With RS facing, join D in first free sc at tip of a 2nd point.

1st row 1ch, 1sc in each of first 9sc down straight edge of same point, 1ch, miss next 3sc, 1sc in each of foll 9sc up straight edge of foll point.

2nd row 1ch, 1sc in each of first 7sc, 1ch, miss next 2sc, 1ch and foll 2sc, 1sc in each of last 7sc.

3rd row 1ch, 1sc in each first 5sc, 1ch, miss next 2sc, 1ch and foll 2sc, 1sc in each of last 5sc.

4th row 1ch, 1sc in each first 3sc, 1ch, miss next 2sc, 1ch and foll 2sc, 1sc in each of last 3sc.

5th row 1ch, 1sc in first sc, 2ch, 1sc in last sc. Fasten off.

Complete remaining 3 corners in the same way but do not fasten off after last corner.

Edging. 1st round (RS) 1ch, 2sc in 2ch sp of last row of corner infill, * 1sc in each of next 5 row-ends of same corner, 1sc in each of foll 4 row-ends of next triangle, 1sc in 1ch sp, 1sc in each of foll 4 row-ends of same triangle, 1sc in each of next 5 row-ends of next corner, [2sc, 2ch, 2sc] in next 2ch sp, rep from * 3 more times omitting last 2sc, ss in first sc, turn.

2nd round Ss in first 2ch sp, * [1sc, 2ch, 1sc] in 2ch sp, 1sc in each of next 23sc, rep from * 3 more times, ss in first sc. Fasten off.

ladybug on a leaf

The leaf is worked in double crochet with a central ridge of treble worked around the stem. The ladybug is a cluster of raised stitches worked afterward. You could also use this leaf as part of a corsage of flowers.

instructions

Colors: Green (A), red (B), and black (C).

Leaf Using A, make 13ch.

1st row (RS) 1dc in 3rd ch from hook, 1dc in each of next 2ch, 2dctog, 1tr in next ch, 2dctog, 1dc in each of next 2ch, 2dc in last ch.

2nd row 3ch, 1dc in first dc, 1dc in each of next 2dc, 2dctog, taking hook to back 1tr around stem of tr, 2dctog, 1dc in each of next 2dc, 2dc in top ch.

3rd row 3ch, 1dc in first dc, 1dc in each of next 2dc, 2dctog, taking hook to front 1tr around the stem of next tr, 2dctog, 1dc in each of next 2dc, 2dc in top ch.

4th row 3ch, miss first dc, 1dc in each of next 2dc, 2dctog, taking hook to back 1tr around stem of tr, 2dctog, 1dc in each of next 2dc, 1dc in top ch.

5th row 3ch, miss first dc, 1dc in next dc, 2dctog, taking hook to front 1tr around stem of tr, 2dctog, 1dc in next dc, 1dc in top ch.

6th row 3ch, miss first dc, 2dctog, taking hook to back 1tr around stem of tr, 2dctog, 1dc in top ch.

7th row 3ch, miss first 2 sts, taking hook to front 1tr around stem of tr, miss next st, 1dc in top ch.

Edging round (RS) 1ch, 2sc in each of next 7 row-ends, 2sc in base of next ch, 1sc in base of each of foll 4ch, 5ch, ss in 2nd ch from hook, ss in each of next 3ch, 1sc in base of each of next 5ch, 2sc in base of last ch, 2sc in each of next 7 row-ends, ss in first ch. Fasten off.

Ladybug The ladybug can be placed wherever convenient on the leaf. With RS of leaf facing, join B in a st, make 5ch, work 5dtrtog in 5th ch from hook, change to C, yo and pull through 6 loops on hook, 1ch, 1sc in nearest strand of C. Fasten off.

To complete Closing head up to tail to plump up body, catch ladybug down on leaf. Using C, and straight stitches embroider 5 spots.

abbreviations

ch = chain

sc = single crochet

dc = double crochet

tr = treble

foll = following

RS = right side

ss = slip stitch

st(s) = stitch(es)

2dctog = leaving last loop of each stitch on the hook, work 2dc, yo and pull through 3 loops on hook

dtr = double treble

5dtrtog = leaving last loop of each stitch on the hook work 5dtr, yo and pull through 6 loops on hook

yo = yarn over

[ ] = work instructions in square brackets as directed.

purse

The little textured pattern background block echoes the shell pattern used for the purse. The purse is made separately, so you can leave the top of the purse open and pop a decoration into it if you wish.

instructions

Colors: Pink (A) and blue (B).

Purse Using A, make 12ch.

1st row (WS) Miss 3ch, [2dc, 1ch, 3dc] in next ch, * miss 3ch, [3dc, 1ch, 3dc] in next ch, rep from * once more.

2nd row 5ch, [1sc in 1ch sp, 2ch, 1dc in sp below, 2ch] twice, 1sc in 1ch sp, 2ch, 1dc in top ch.

3rd row 3ch, * [3dc, 1ch, 3dc] in next sc, rep from * two more times, 1dc in 3rd ch.

Work 2nd and 3rd rows once more, then work 2nd row again.

7th row * [3dc, 1ch, 3dc] in next sc, rep from * two more times, ss in 3rd ch, do not fasten off.

Edging round (WS) 2sc in each of next 5 sps along side edge, 3sc in corner sp, [1sc in center ch of shell, 3sc in next ch sp] twice, 1sc in center ch of shell, 3sc in corner sp, 2sc in each of next 5 sps along side edge, ss in first dc. Fasten off.

Handle With WS facing, join A in 1ch sp of first shell of 7th row, make 20ch, 1sc in 1ch sp of 3rd shell, turn, work 26sc over ch loop, ss in first 1ch sp. Fasten off.

Background Using B, make 28ch.

1st row (WS) [1dc, 1ch, 1dc] in 5th ch from hook, *miss 2ch, [1dc, 1ch, 1dc] in next ch, rep from * 6 more times, miss 1ch, 1dc in last ch.

2nd row 3ch, [1dc, 1ch, 1dc] in each of next eight 1ch sps, 1dc in top ch.

2nd row forms the pattern. Work 13 more rows, do not fasten off.

Edging round (WS) 1ch, 3sc in corner sp, 2sc in each of next 13 sps down side edge, 5sc in corner sp, 2sc in each of next 7 sps along lower edge, 5sc in corner sp, 2sc in each of next 13 sps up side edge, 5sc in corner sp, 1sc in first sp along top edge, 2sc in each of next 6 sps, 1sc in last sp, 2sc in first corner sp, ss in first sc. Fasten off.

To complete Leaving top edge open, sew purse on background and catch down handle.

sailboat

This motif is all in single crochet; it starts with the boat shape, followed by rows of sky. The motif is turned upside down, a few rows of sea are worked separately at each side, then joined and finished off with rows of yellow sand. The sails are little triangles sewn on afterward with embroidered details.

instructions

Colors: Red (A), blue (B), green (C), yellow (D), cream (E), and a scrap of brown yarn for embroidery.

Boat Using A, make 10ch.

1st row 1sc in 2nd ch from hook, 1sc in each ch. 9 sts.

2nd row (RS) 1ch, 1sc in each of next 8sc, 2sc in last sc. 10 sts.

3rd row 1ch, 2sc in first sc, 1sc in each sc. 11 sts. Fasten off.

Sky Using B, make 7ch for left side of sky, fasten off.

1st row Using B, make 8ch, 1sc in 2nd ch from hook, 1sc in each of next 6ch, with RS of boat facing, 1sc in each of 11sc of boat, 1sc in each of 7ch made for left side of sky. 25 sts.

2nd row 1ch, [1sc in each sc] to end.

2nd row forms sc. Work 12 more rows sc. Fasten off.

Turn work so that sky is at lower edge.

Sea at left (bow) of boat With RS facing, join C in base of first ch in B.

1st row 1ch, 1sc in base of each of next 7ch.

2nd row 1ch, 2sc in first sc, 1sc in each of next 6sc. 8 sts.

3rd row 1ch, 1sc in each of first 7sc, 2sc in last sc. 9 sts. Fasten off.

Sea at right (stern) of boat With RS facing, join C in base of first ch in B.

1st row 1ch, 1sc in base of each of 7ch. 7 sts.

Work 2 more rows sc.

Joining row (WS) 1ch, 1sc in each of next

abbreviations

ch = chain

sc = single crochet

dc = double crochet

rep = repeat

RS = right side

sp(s) = space(s)

ss = slip stitch

[ ] = work instructions in square brackets as directed.

abbreviations

ch = chain

sc = single crochet

foll = following

RS = right side

sp = space

ss = slip stitch

st(s) = stitch(es)

WS = wrong side

[ ] = work instructions in square brackets as directed.

scottie dog

This cute little dog is worked in rows of double crochet with a single crochet edging. To keep the outline neat, don't forget when changing colors to always change on the wrong side and pull through the last part of the last stitch of a color area with the new color. The finishing touch is a plaid ribbon bow.

instructions

Colors: Red (A), black (B), a scrap of lime green yarn, and a short length of plaid ribbon.

Using A, make 25ch.

1st row (RS) 1dc in 4th ch from hook, 1dc in each of next 21ch. 23 sts.

2nd row 1sc in first dc, 2ch, 1dc in each of next 21dc, 1dc in next ch.

2nd row forms dc.

Cont in dc from chart, changing colors as shown, work from 3rd to 10th rows.

Cont in A.

Edging round (RS) 1ch, 1sc in first dc, 1sc in each of next 21dc of top edge, 2sc in top ch, 2sc in each row-end, 2sc in base of first foundation ch, 1sc in base of each of next 21ch, 2sc in last ch, 2sc in each row-end, 1sc in same place as first sc, ss in first sc. Fasten off.

To complete Using B embroider tail and ears with straight stitches and make a French knot for the nose. Using lime yarn, make a small vertical straight stitch for the eye. Tie ribbon in a flat bow and sew on neck.

7sc of sea, 1sc in base of each of next 9ch of boat, 1sc in each of next 9sc of sea. 25 sts.

Work 4 rows sc. Change to D. Work 4 rows sc. Fasten off.

Edging With RS facing, join B in first row-end in B at right edge. When changing colors, pull through last loop of last st in the old color with the new color. On the 1st round, leave the yarns on the WS ready to work the 2nd round.

1st round 1ch, 1sc in each of next 14 row-ends up right edge, 2ch, 1sc in each of next 25 sc along top edge, 2ch, 1sc in each of next 14 row-ends down left edge, change to C, 1sc in each of next 8 row-ends, change to D, 1sc in each of foll 4 row-ends, 2ch, 1sc in each of next 25sc, 2ch, 1sc in each of foll 4 row-ends, change to C, 1sc in each of next 8 row-ends, ss in first sc, turn.

2nd round Using C, 1ch, 1sc in each of next 8sc, change to D, 1sc in each of next 4sc, [1sc, 2ch, 1sc] in next 2ch sp, 1sc in each of next 25sc, [1sc, 2ch, 1sc] in foll 2ch sp, 1sc in each of next 4sc, change to C, 1sc in each of next 8 sc, change to B, 1sc in each of next 14sc, [1sc, 2ch, 1sc] in next 2ch sp, 1sc in each of next 25sc, [1sc, 2ch, 1sc] in foll 2ch sp, 1sc in each of next 14sc, ss in first sc. Fasten off.

Right sail Using F, make 6ch.

1st row (WS) 1sc in 2nd ch from hook, 1sc in each ch. 5 sts.

2nd row 1ch, 1sc in each of 5sc.

3rd row 1ch, 1sc in each of next 4sc, ss in last sc.

4th row 1ch, miss ss, 1sc in each of 4sc. 4 sts.

5th row 1ch, 1sc in each of next 3sc, ss in last sc.

6th row 1ch, miss ss, 1sc in each of 3sc. 3 sts.

7th row 1ch, 1sc in each of next 2sc, ss in last sc.

8th row 1ch, miss ss, 1sc in each of 2sc. 2 sts.

9th row 1ch, 1sc in first sc, ss in last sc.

10th row 1ch, miss ss, 1sc in sc. Fasten off.

Left sail Work as right sail omitting 2nd row so sail is shorter and slants on the left edge

To complete Sew right sail on above boat. Using brown, chain stitch a mast close to and slightly longer than sail. Sew on left sail. Using A, embroider flag.

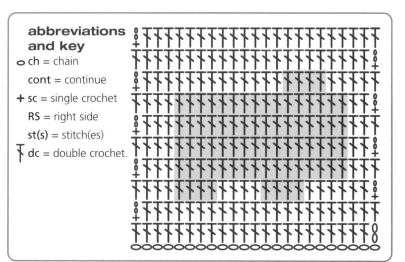

abbreviations and key

o ch = chain

cont = continue

+ sc = single crochet

RS = right side

st(s) = stitch(es)

⊤ dc = double crochet.

bow

Make a crochet ribbon, tie it in a bow, then work around the bow shape to fill in the gaps and create a most unusual motif.

instructions

Colors: Pink (A) and cream (B).

Ribbon Using A, make 81ch.

1st row (RS) 1sc in 2nd ch from hook, [1sc in each ch] to end. 80 sts.

2nd row 1sc in first sc, 2ch, [1dc in each sc] to end.

3rd row 1sc in first tr, 2ch, 1dc in each of next 21dc, 2dc in each of foll 6dc, 1dc in each of next 24dc, 2dc in each of foll 6dc, 1dc in each of last 22dc. 92 sts.

Bow Place markers 9 sts in from each end of ribbon, then after another 7 sts and 21 sts from each end, so leaving 18 sts in the center. For a flat bow, do not tie the bow in the usual way. First tie a loose overhand knot in the center of the ribbon, adjust knot so the markers at each side of the center 18 sts show at each side of knot. The smooth side of the knot should be at the front. With the 3rd row at the outer edge, fold right end, push end of ribbon through back of knot to make first loop on the right, then push the other end through the front of the knot to make the left loop. The ends should twist as they go through the knot so the loops show the RS of the ribbon and the ends the WS still with the 3rd row as the outer edge. Adjust knot so that the markers on the 3rd row for the 21 sts of each loop and the 9 sts of each end show.

Edging With WS of end facing, join B in last st at lower right end.

1st round (RS) 1ch, 1sc in same place as join, 1sc in each of next 8dc up outer edge of right end, starting at next marker of right loop work 1sc in each of next 6dc, 2sc in each of foll 8dc, 1sc in each of next 7dc, 2sc in row-ends of knot, starting at next marker of left loop work 1sc in each of next 7dc, 2sc in each of foll 8dc, 1sc in each of next 6dc, starting at next marker of left end work 1sc in each of next 8dc down outer edge, [1sc, 3ch, 1sc] in corner st, 3sc in row-ends along lower edge, [1sc, 3ch, 1sc] in corner row-end, 9sc between sts up inner edge of left end, 2sc in row-ends of knot, counting back from corner to place first st, work 9sc between sts down inner edge of right end, [1sc, 3ch, 1sc] in corner row-end, 3sc in row-ends across lower edge, 1sc in same place as first sc, 3ch, ss in first sc, turn.

2nd round Ss in first 3ch sp, 1ch, [1sc, 3ch, 1sc] in same 3ch sp, 1sc in each of next 5sc, [1sc, 3ch, 1sc] in foll 3ch sp, 1sc in each of

next 9sc, 4dctog, 1sc in each of next 9sc, [1sc, 3ch, 1sc] in foll 3ch sp, 1sc in each of next 5sc, [1sc, 3ch, 1sc] in foll 3ch sp, 1sc in each of next 7sc, 4dctog, 1sc in each of next 13sc, [1sc, 3ch, 1sc] in foll sc, 1sc in each of next 12sc, 4dctog, 1sc in each of next 12sc, [1sc, 3ch, 1sc] in foll sc, 1sc in each of next 13sc, 4dctog, 1sc in each of next 7sc, ss in first sc, turn.

3rd round 1ch, 1sc in same sc as ss, 3ch, [miss one st, 1dc in next st, 1ch] 11 times, [1dc, 3ch, 1dc] in next 3ch sp, 1ch, 1dc in next st, [1ch, miss one st, 1dc in next st] 13 times, 1ch, [1dc, 3ch, 1dc] in foll 3ch sp, 1ch, 1dc in next st, [1ch, miss one st, 1dc in next st] 11 times, 1ch, [1dc, 3ch, 1dc] in next 3ch sp, 1ch, 1dc in next st, [1ch, miss one st, 1dc in next st] 3 times, 1ch, [1dc, 3ch, 1dc] in next 3ch sp, 1ch, 1dc in next st, [1ch, miss one st, 1dc in next st] 4 times, 1ch, miss 3 sts, 1dc in next st, [1ch, miss one st, 1dc in next st] 4 times, 1ch, [1dc, 3ch, 1dc] in foll 3ch sp, 1ch, 1dc in next st, [1ch, miss one st, 1dc in next st] 3 times, 1ch, [1dc, 3ch, 1dc] in last 3ch sp, 1ch, ss in 2nd ch, do not turn.

4th round Ss in first 1ch sp, 1ch, 2sc in same sp, 2hdc in next sp, 2dc in foll sp, 2tr in each of next 2sps, 2dc in foll sp, 2hdc in next sp, 2sc in each of foll 5 sps, [1sc, 3ch, 1sc] in next 3ch sp, 2sc in each of foll 4 sps, 2hdc in next sp, 2dc in foll sp, 2trtog in next sp, miss foll sp, 2trtog in next sp, 2dc in foll sp, 2hdc in next sp, 2sc in each of foll 4 sps, [1sc, 3ch, 1sc] in next 3ch sp, 2sc in each of foll 5 sps, 2hdc in next sp, 2dc in foll sp, 2tr in each of next 2 sps, 2dc in foll sp, 2hdc in next sp, 2sc in each of foll 2 sps, [1sc, 3ch, 1sc] in next 3ch sp, 2sc in each of foll 5 sps, 2sc in next 3ch sp, * placing first part st in next sp and 2nd part st in foll sp, work 2trtog *, miss next 7 sps, rep from * to *, 2sc in next 3ch sp, 2sc in each of foll 5 sps, [1sc, 3ch, 1sc] in next 3ch sp, 2sc in last sp, ss in first sc, turn.

5th round 1ch, 1sc in same place as ss, 1sc in each of next 3sc, * [1sc, 3ch, 1sc] in next 3ch sp, 1sc in each of next 28 sts, rep from * 3 more times omitting last 4sc, ss in first sc. Fasten off.

abbreviations

ch = chain	**RS** = right side
sc = single crochet	**sp(s)** = space(s)
dc = double crochet	**ss** = slip stitch
tr = treble	**st(s)** = stitch(es)
2trtog = leaving last loop of each st on hook, work 2tr, yarn over hook and pull through 3 loops on hook	**4dctog** = leaving last loop of each st on hook work 4dc, yarn over hook and pull through 5 loops on hook
foll = following	**WS** = wrong side
hdc = half double crochet	**[ ]** = work instructions in square brackets as directed.
rep = repeat	

christmas tree | chick

A little block of red, a simple single crochet green triangle, a white outline—it's a Christmas tree ready to appliqué.

instructions

Colors: Red (A), green (B), and white (C).

Pot Using A, make 6ch.

1st row (WS) 1sc in 2nd ch from hook, 1sc in each of next 4ch. 5 sts.

2nd row 1ch, [1sc in each sc] to end.

2nd row forms sc. Work 2 more rows sc. Fasten off.

Tree Using B, make 5ch.

1st row (WS) 1sc in each of 5sc of pot, make 6ch.

2nd row 1sc in 2nd ch from hook, 1sc in each of next 4ch, 1sc in each of next 5sc, 1sc in each of last 5ch. 15 sts.

3rd row 1ch, 2sctog, [1sc in each sc] to last 2sc, 2sctog. 13 sts.

Cont in sc, dec in same way as 3rd row at each end of next 5 RS rows. 3 sts.

Next row 1ch, 3sctog.

Next row 1ch, 1sc in 3sctog. Fasten off.

With RS facing, join C in last sc at top of tree.

Edging round 1ch, 2sc in same place as join, 14sc in row-ends down left edge of tree, 3sc in base of first ch, 1sc in base of each of next 4ch, 2sc in row-ends down left edge of pot, 3sc in base of first ch, 1sc in base of each of next 3ch, 3sc in base of last ch, 2sc in row-ends up right edge of pot, 4sc in base of each of next 4ch, 3sc in base of last ch, 14sc in row-ends up right edge of tree, 1sc in same place as first 2sc, ss in first sc. Fasten off.

chick

The body of the chick is just a circle of single crochet, then the background is shaped to turn the round into a square. The head, tail, and wing are made separately and sewn on with embroidered details to emphasize the character.

instructions

Colors: Yellow (A), blue (B), deep blue (C), and scraps of rust and brown for the embroidery.

Body Using A, make 4ch, ss in first ch to form a ring.

1st round (RS) 1ch, 8sc in ring, ss in first sc. 8 sts.

2nd round 1ch, 1sc in same sc as ss, [2sc in next sc, 1sc in foll sc] 3 times, 2sc in last sc, ss in first sc. 12 sts.

3rd round 1ch, 1sc in same sc as ss, [2sc in next sc, 1sc in foll sc] 5 times, 2sc in last sc, ss in first sc. 18 sts.

4th round 1ch, 1sc in same sc as ss, [2sc in next sc, 1sc in each of foll 2sc] 5 times, 2sc in next sc, 1sc in last sc, ss in first sc. 24 sts.

Fasten off. With RS facing, join B in same sc as ss.

5th round 1ch, 1sc in same sc as ss, [2sc in next sc, 1sc in each of foll 2sc] 7 times, 2sc in next sc, 1sc in last sc, ss in first sc. 32 sts.

6th round 1ch, 1sc in same sc as ss, [3dc in next sc, 1sc in each of foll 7sc] 3 times, 3dc in next sc, 1sc in each of last 6sc, ss in first sc.

7th round 1ch, 1sc in same sc as ss, 1sc in foll dc, [3sc in next dc, 1sc in each of next 9 sts] 4 times omitting last 2sc, ss in first sc.

8th round 1ch, 1sc in same sc as ss, 1sc in each of next 2sc, [3sc in foll sc, 1sc in each of next 11sc] 4 times omitting last 3sc, ss in first sc.

Fasten off. With RS facing, join C in a corner sc.

9th round 1ch, 2sc in same sc as join, [1sc in each of next 13sc, 3sc in foll sc] 3 times, 1sc in each of next 13sc, 1sc in same sc as first 2sc, ss in first sc. Fasten off.

Head Using A, make 5ch.

1st row 5sc in 3rd ch from hook, ss in last ch.

2nd row 1ch, 1sc in each of next 5sc, 1sc in foll ch. Fasten off.

Wing Using A, make 5ch, ss in 2nd ch from hook, 1sc in foll ch, 1dc in each of last 2ch. Fasten off.

Tail Using A, make 3ch, ss in 2nd ch from hook, 1sc in next ch. Fasten off.

To complete Placing tail at top right over join in 5th round, sew on tail. Gathering straight edge slightly to fit curve, sew head on at top left. Leaving point free, sew on wing. Using rust and straight stitches, embroider legs and beak. Using brown, make a French knot for the eye.

abbreviations

ch = chain

cont = continue

sc = single crochet

2sctog = insert hook in first st and pull loop through, insert hook in next st and pull loop through, yarn over hook and pull through 3 loops on hook

3sctog = insert hook in first st and pull loop through, insert hook in next st and pull loop through, insert hook in foll st and pull loop through, yarn over hook and pull through 4 loops on hook

dec = decrease

RS = right side

ss = slip stitch

st(s) = stitch(es)

WS = wrong side

[ ] = work instructions in square brackets as directed.

abbreviations

ch = chain

sc = single crochet

dc = double crochet

foll = following

RS = right side

ss = slip stitch

st(s) = stitch(es)

[ ] = work instructions in square brackets as directed.

winter tree

This motif starts with a simple strip for the tree trunk surrounded on three sides with blue for the sky and white for the snow below, all worked in single crochet. The branches are in freestyle surface chain and the scattered gold snowflakes are embroidered afterward.

instructions

Colors: Brown (A), pale blue (B), warm white (C), and metallic gold yarn for the embroidery.

Tree trunk Using A, make 5ch.

1st row (WS) 1sc in 2nd ch from hook, 1sc in each of next 3ch. 4 sts.

2nd row 1ch, [1sc in each sc] to end.

2nd row forms sc. Work 9 more rows sc. Fasten off.

Sky With RS facing, join B in first row-end at right of trunk.

1st row 1ch, 1sc in same place as join, 1sc in each of next 9 row-ends, [1sc, 2ch, 1sc] in corner sc, 1sc in each of next 2sc, [1sc, 2ch, 1sc] in last sc, 1sc in each of next 10 row-ends, turn.

2nd row 1ch, 1sc in each of next 11sc, [1sc, 2ch, 1sc] in first 2ch sp, 1sc in each of next 4sc, [1sc, 2ch, 1sc] in last 2ch sp, 1sc in each of next 11sc.

3rd row 1ch, 1sc in each of next 12sc, [1sc, 2ch, 1sc] in first 2ch sp, 1sc in each of next 6sc, [1sc, 2ch, 1sc] in last 2ch sp, 1sc in each of next 12sc.

4th row 1ch, 1sc in each of next 13sc, [1sc, 2ch, 1sc] in first 2ch sp, 1sc in each of next 8sc, [1sc, 2ch, 1sc] in last 2ch sp, 1sc in each of next 13sc.

5th row 1ch, 1sc in each of next 14sc, [1sc, 2ch, 1sc] in first 2ch sp, 1sc in each of next 10sc, [1sc, 2ch, 1sc] in last 2ch sp, 1sc in each of next 14sc.

6th row 1ch, 1sc in each of next 15sc, [1sc, 2ch, 1sc] in first 2ch sp, 1sc in each of next 12sc, [1sc, 2ch, 1sc] in last 2ch sp, 1sc in each of next 15sc.

7th row 1ch, 1sc in each of next 16sc, [1sc, 2ch, 1sc] in first 2ch sp, 1sc in each of next 14sc, [1sc, 2ch, 1sc] in last 2ch sp, 1sc in each of next 16sc.

8th row 1ch, 1sc in each of next 17sc, [1sc, 2ch, 1sc] in first 2ch sp, 1sc in each of next 16 sc, [1sc, 2ch, 1sc] in last 2ch sp, 1sc in each of next 17sc. Fasten off.

Ground With RS facing and tree trunk upside down, join C in first row-end of sky.

1st row 1ch, 1sc in same place as join, 1sc in each of next 7 row-ends, 4sc in sts across base of trunk, 1sc in each of next 8 row-ends. 20 sts.

Work 5 more rows sc, do not fasten off.

Edging Continue in C.

1st round 1ch, [1sc, 2ch, 1sc] in first sc of lower edge, 1sc in each of next 18sc, [1sc, 2ch, 1sc] in last sc of lower edge, 1sc in each of next 6 row-ends, * 1sc in each of next 18sc, [1sc, 2ch, 1sc] in next 2ch sp, rep from * once more, 1sc in each of next 18sc, 1sc in each of next 6 row-ends, ss in first sc, turn.

2nd round 1ch, * 1sc in each of next 26sc, [1sc, 2ch, 1sc] in next 2ch sp, 1sc in each of next 20sc, [1sc, 2ch, 1sc] in foll 2ch sp, rep from * once more, ss in first sc. Fasten off.

Branches Holding A below work, insert hook at top right of tree trunk, catch A and pull loop through to RS, insert hook one st to the right and pull loop through fabric and loop on hook. Continue making surface chain moving hook to make a curved branch shape. At the tip of the branch there's no need to fasten off, just remove hook, insert from back of work, catch loop and pull through, then turn and inserting hook farther down branch, pull chain loops through to RS again to work extra branch tips and to work closely spaced chain for thicker branches.

To complete Using metallic gold yarn embroider scattered snowflakes by working a cross stitch, then an extra vertical stitch over the cross stitch to make a six-pointed cross.

abbreviations

ch = chain

sc = single crochet

foll = following

rep = repeat

RS = right side

sp = space

ss = slip stitch

st(s) = stitch(es)

WS = wrong side

[ ] = work instructions in square brackets as directed.

geometric

This wonderful array of fascinating-to-work shapes—from the classic square to hexagons, diamonds, triangles, and circles—is enhanced with textured patterns, such as popcorn stitches, loops, and bobbles, that make them even more fun to create.

daisy stitch block

This pretty, textured block has a center square in a stitch pattern that has loops pulled through to make rows of daisy-like flowers. For a larger or smaller block, work a multiple of two plus five for the starting chain. The edging is just rounds of single crochet and chain loops.

instructions

Make 25ch.

1st row (RS) Insert hook in 2nd ch from hook, yo and pull through, [insert hook in next ch, yo and pull through] 4 times, yo and pull through 6 loops on hook, 1ch, * insert hook in hole at top of daisy just made, yo and pull loop through, insert hook in back of last loop of same daisy, yo and pull loop through, insert hook in same ch as last loop of same daisy, yo and pull loop through, [insert hook in next ch, yo and pull loop through] twice, yo and pull through 6 loops on hook, 1ch, rep from * 8 more times, 1sc in last ch.

2nd row 2ch, 1sc in center hole of first daisy, [1ch, 1sc in hole of next daisy] 9 times, 1sc in end ch.

3rd row 3ch, miss first ch, [insert hook in next ch, yo and pull loop through] twice, [insert hook in next sc, yo and pull loop through] twice, insert hook in next 1ch sp, yo and pull loop through, yo and pull through 6 loops on hook, 1ch, * insert hook in hole at top of daisy just made, yo and pull loop through, insert hook in back of last loop of same daisy, yo and pull loop through, insert hook in same 1ch sp as before, yo and pull loop through, insert hook in next sc, yo and pull loop through, insert hook in next ch, yo and pull loop through, yo and pull through 6 loops on hook, 1ch, rep from * 8 more times, 1sc in end ch.

Work 2nd and 3rd rows 6 more times, then work 2nd row again.

Edging. 1st round (RS) 2sc in corner st, 19sc along top edge, 3sc in corner st, 19sc in row-ends down left edge, 3sc in corner st, 19sc in base of ch along lower edge, 3sc in corner st, 19sc in row-ends up right edge, 1sc in first corner st, ss in first sc, turn.

2nd round 1ch, 2sc in same place as ss, [1sc in each of next 21sc, 3sc in foll sc] 3 times, 1sc in each of next 21sc, 1sc in same place as first 2sc, ss in first sc, turn.

3rd round 1ch, 1sc in same place as ss, 4ch, 1sc in same place as first sc, miss 1sc, *[1sc, 4ch, 1sc] in next sc, miss 1sc, rep from * 46 more times, ss in first sc. Fasten off.

abbreviations

ch = chain

sc = single crochet

foll = following

rep = repeat

sp = space

ss = slip stitch

yo = yarn over hook

[ ] = work instructions in square brackets as directed.

popcorn square

Although double crochet is the basic stitch for this square, bunching double crochet to make popcorns alternates with sections worked around the stem to create ridges. These techniques give this simple square a lot of texture.

instructions

Wind yarn around finger to form a ring.

1st round 1ch, 1sc in ring, [4ch, 2sc in ring] 3 times, 4ch, 1sc in ring, ss in first sc.

2nd round Ss in first 4ch sp, * 1ch, 1sc in same sp, 2ch, 3dc in same sp, remove hook, insert in 2nd ch, catch loop and pull through to make first pc, 5ch, 4dcpc in same sp *, ** 2ch, [4dcpc, 5ch, 4dcpc] in next 4ch sp, rep from ** two more times, 2ch, ss in top of first pc.

3rd round Ss in first 5ch sp, work from * to * of 2nd round, [2ch, 3dc in next 2ch sp, 2ch, 4dcpc in next 5ch sp, 5ch, 4dcpc in same 5ch sp] 3 times, 2ch, 3dc in last 2ch sp, 2ch, ss in top of first pc.

abbreviations and key

○ **ch** = chain

✛ **sc** = single crochet

foll = following

pc = popcorn

sp = space

● **ss** = slip stitch

┃ **dc** = double crochet

4dcpc = work 4dc, remove hook and insert in top of first dc, catch loop and pull through to close top of popcorn

[ ] = work instructions in square brackets as directed.

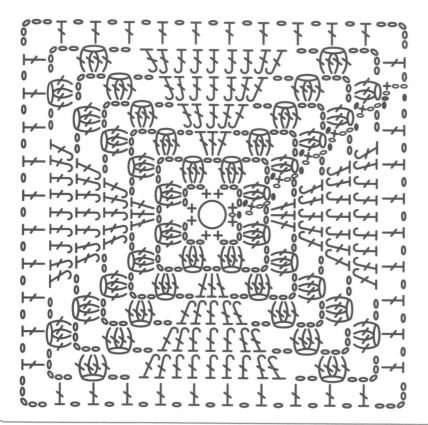

4th round Ss in first 5ch sp, work from * to * of 2nd round, [** 2ch, inserting hook from back, work 2dc around stem of next dc, 1dc around stem of foll dc, 2dc around stem of next dc, 2ch **, 4dcpc in next 5ch sp, 5ch, 4dcpc in same 5ch sp] 3 times, rep from ** to **, ss in top of first pc.

5th round Ss in first 5ch sp, work from * to * of 2nd round, [** 2ch, 2dc around stem of next dc, 1dc around stem of each of foll 3dc, 2dc around stem of next dc, 2ch **, 4dcpc in next 5ch sp, 5ch, 4dcpc in same 5ch sp] 3 times, rep from ** to **, ss in top of first pc.

6th round Ss in first 5ch sp, work from * to * of 2nd round, [** 2ch, 2dc around stem of next dc, 1dc around stem of each of foll 5dc, 2dc around stem of next dc, 2ch **, 4dcpc in next 5ch sp, 5ch, 4dcpc in same 5ch sp] 3 times, rep from ** to **, ss in top of first pc.

7th round Ss in first 5ch sp, 1ch, 1sc in same sp, 3ch, 1dc in same sp, 5ch, [1dc, 1ch] twice in same sp, * 1dc in next 2ch sp, 1ch, [miss 1dc, 1dc in next dc, 1ch] 4 times, miss 1dc, 1dc in next 2ch sp **, [1ch, 1dc] twice in next 5ch sp, 5ch, [1dc, 1ch] twice in same 5ch sp, rep from * two more times, then rep from * to **, 1ch, ss in 2nd ch.

Fasten off.

popcorn diamond

The center of this motif is subtly shaped to coax the initial circle into a diamond. The popcorns emphasize the Aran-style effect and working the final rounds around the stem of the previous stitches gives the appearance of a knitted edging.

instructions

Make 8ch, ss in first ch to form a ring.

1st round 1ch, 16sc in ring, ss in first sc.

2nd round 1ch, [1sc, 2ch, 3dc] in same place as ss, remove hook, insert in 2nd ch, catch loop and pull through to close first popcorn, [1ch, 1sc in each of next 3sc, 1ch, 4dcpc in next sc] 3 times, 1ch, 1sc in each of last 3sc, 1ch, ss in first popcorn.

3rd round 1ch, 1sc in 1ch sp before ss, 5ch, [2dc in next 1ch sp, 1dc in each of next 3sc, 2dc in foll 1ch sp, 3ch] 3 times, 2dc in next 1ch sp, 1dc in each of next 3sc, 1dc in first 1ch sp, ss in 2nd ch.

4th round 1ch, [1sc, 2ch, 3dc] in same place as ss, remove hook, insert in 2nd ch, catch loop and pull through to make first popcorn, * [1dc, 3ch, 1dc] in next 3ch sp, [4dcpc in next dc, 1dc in each of foll 2dc] twice, 4dcpc in next dc, rep from * two more times, [1dc, 3ch, 1dc] in last 3ch sp, [4dcpc in next dc, 1dc in each of foll 2dc] twice, ss in first popcorn.

5th round Ss in first 3ch sp, 1ch, [1sc, 5ch, 2dc] in same 3ch sp, * 1dc in each of next 9 sts, [2dc, 3ch, 2dc] in next 3ch sp, rep from * two more times, 1dc in each of next 9 sts, 1dc in first 3ch sp, ss in 2nd ch.

6th round 1ch, 1sc in back loop of next ch, 3ch, miss 1ch, 1sc in strand behind foll ch, * taking hook behind, work 1sc around the stem of each of next 13dc, 1sc in strand behind next ch, 3ch, miss 1ch, 1sc in strand behind of foll ch, rep from * two more times, 1sc around the stem of each of last 13dc, ss around the stem of first sc.

7th round 1ch, 1sc around the stem of same sc as ss, [1sc in strand behind next ch, 3ch, miss 1ch, 1sc in strand behind foll ch, taking hook behind, work 1sc around the stem of each of next 15sc] 4 times omitting last sc, remove hook, insert from back in first sc, catch loop and pull through. Fasten off.

abbreviations

ch = chain

sc = single crochet

foll = following

rep = repeat

sp = space

ss = slip stitch

st(s) = stitch(es)

dc = double crochet

4dcpc = work 4dc, remove hook, insert in first dc, catch loop and pull through to close popcorn

[ ] = work instructions in square brackets as directed.

nine-patch square

The classic nine-patch quilt block inspires this square. Longer stitches at the corners give these little one-round patches a really square shape. The patches are joined as they're made, then finished with a decorative edging that has chain spaces to make it easy to join the squares to make a pillow cover or an afghan.

instructions

Colors: Pale blue (A), bright blue (B), and navy (C).

1st patch (RS) Using A, wind yarn around finger to form a ring,

1ch, 1sc in ring, 4ch, [1tr, 1dc, 1ch, 1dc, 1tr, 2ch] 3 times in ring, [1tr, 1dc, 1ch, 1dc] in ring, ss in 3rd ch. Fasten off.

2nd patch Using B, work as first patch joining in along one edge by working 1ch, 1sc in corner sp of first patch, 1ch instead of 2ch at each of two corners and 1sc in 1ch sp of first patch instead of 1ch at center of same side.

3rd patch Using A, work as first patch joining in along opposite edge of 2nd patch to first join in same way as 2nd patch.

4th, 5th, 6th, 7th, 8th, and 9th patches Using A for odd numbered patches and B for even numbered patches, work in same way, joining 4th patch to lower edge of 3rd patch, 5th patch to left edge of 4th patch and lower edge of 2nd patch, 6th patch to left edge of 5th patch and lower edge of 1st patch, 7th patch to lower edge of 6th patch, 8th patch to lower edge of 5th patch and right edge of 7th patch, and 9th patch to lower edge of 4th patch and right edge of 8th patch.

With RS facing, join C in top right-hand corner sp.

Edging round 1ch, 1sc and [3ch, 1sc] twice in same corner sp, * [1sc, 3ch, 1sc] in each of next 7 sps, 1sc and [3ch, 1sc] twice in next corner sp, rep from * two more times, [1sc, 3ch, 1sc] in each of next 7 sps, ss in first sc. Fasten off.

abbreviations

ch = chain
sc = single crochet
tr = treble
RS = right side
sp(s) = space(s)
ss = slip stitch

dc = double crochet
[ ] = work instructions in square brackets as directed.

simple circle medallion

Even the most simple combination of stitches can be very satisfying. This motif is just easy-to-work rounds of single crochet, chain, and double crochet.

instructions
Wind yarn around finger to form a ring.

1st round 1ch, 1sc in ring, 2ch, 19dc in ring, ss in 2nd ch.

2nd round 1ch, 1sc in same place as ss, 3ch, [1dc in next dc, 1ch] 19 times, ss in 2nd ch.

3rd round Ss in next 1ch sp, [1ch, 1sc, 2ch, 1dc] in same sp, 2dc in each of next 19 sps, ss in 2nd ch.

4th round 1ch, 1sc in same place as ss, [4ch, miss 1dc, 1sc in next dc] 19 times, 4ch, ss in first sc.

5th round Ss in first 4ch sp, [1ch, 1sc, 2ch, 1dc] in same 4ch sp, 1ch, [3dc in next 4ch sp, 1ch] 19 times, 1dc in first 4ch sp, ss in 2nd ch. Fasten off.

abbreviations and key
○ ch = chain
✛ sc = single crochet
sp = space
● ss = slip stitch
ⵜ dc = double crochet
[ ] = work instructions in square brackets as directed.

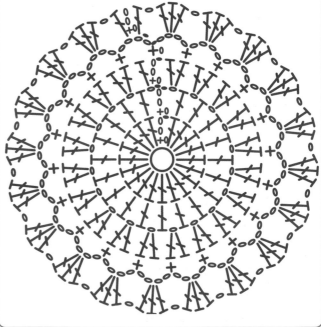

four square

This pattern is arranged in quarters and uses chain, single crochet, and double crochet stitches to create a pretty openwork design.

instructions

Wind yarn around finger to form a ring.

1st round 1ch, 8sc in ring, ss in first sc.

2nd round 1ch, 1sc in same place as ss, 5ch, [miss 1sc, 1sc in next sc, 5ch] 3 times, ss in first sc.

3rd round Ss in first 5ch sp, 1ch, [1sc, 2ch, 4dc] in same 5ch sp, 3ch, [5dc in next sp, 3ch] 3 times, ss in 2nd ch.

4th round 1ch, 1sc in same place as ss, [5ch, miss 3dc, 1sc in next dc, 3ch, 1sc in 3ch sp, 3ch, 1sc in next dc] 4 times omitting last sc, ss in first sc.

5th round Ss in first 5ch sp, 1ch, [1sc, 2ch, 6dc] in same 5ch sp, [1sc in next 3ch sp, 3ch, 1sc in foll 3ch sp, 7dc in next 5ch sp] 3 times, 1sc in next 3ch sp, 3ch, 1sc in foll 3ch sp, ss in 2nd ch.

6th round 1ch, 1sc in same place as ss, [3ch, miss 1dc, 1sc in next dc, 5ch, miss 1dc, 1sc in foll dc, 3ch, miss 1dc, 1sc in next dc, 3ch, 1sc in next 3ch sp, 3ch, 1sc in next dc] 4 times omitting last sc, ss in first sc. Fasten off.

abbreviations and key

o ch – chain
+ sc = single crochet
foll = following
sp = space

● ss = slip stitch
T dc = double crochet
[ ] = work instructions in square brackets as directed.

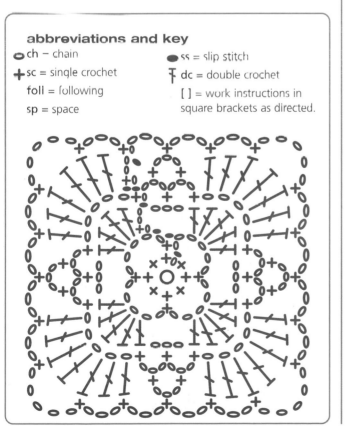

bullseye

This round motif is inspired by the thrift quilts made from circles of fabric edged with blanket stitch. Although there are eight increases on each round, a regular octagon is avoided because the increases move along in a swirling pattern to give a more rounded edge. Change color for each round for a shaded target effect and use up even tiny scraps of left-over yarn or, if you prefer, ignore the color changes and work each motif in a single color.

instructions

Colors: Navy (A), pale pink (B), pink (C), pale lilac (D), and lilac (E).

Using A, wind yarn around finger to form a ring.

1st round 1ch, 8sc in ring, ss in first sc. 8 sts. Fasten off.

Join B in same place as ss.

2nd round 1ch, 2sc in each sc, ss in first sc. 16 sts. Fasten off.

Join C in same place as ss.

3rd round 1ch, 1sc in same place as join, [2sc in next sc, 1sc in foll sc] 7 times, 2sc in last sc, ss in first sc. 24 sts. Fasten off.

Join D in same place as ss.

4th round 1ch, 1sc in same place as ss, 1sc in next sc, [2sc in foll sc, 1sc in each of next 2sc] 7 times, 2sc in last sc, ss in first sc. 32 sts. Fasten off.

Join E in same place as ss.

5th round 1ch, 1sc in same place as ss, 1sc in each of next 2sc, [2sc in foll sc, 1sc in each of next 3sc] 7 times, 2sc in last sc, ss in first sc. 40 sts. Fasten off.

Join A in same place as ss.

6th round 1ch, 1sc in same place as ss, 2ch, [miss 1sc, 1sc in next sc, 2ch] 19 times, ss in first sc. Fasten off.

abbreviations

ch = chain
sc = single crochet
foll = following
ss = slip stitch
[ ] work instructions in square brackets as directed.

mesh octagon

This octagon is made using the basic filet mesh of one double crochet and one chain, but arranged in the round instead of in rows. The pattern of increases is very simple, so after a few rounds it's easy to see how to extend the octagon.

instructions

Wind yarn around finger to form a ring.

1st round 1ch, 1sc in ring, 3ch, [1dc in ring, 1ch] 7 times, ss in 2nd ch.

2nd round 1ch, 1sc in same place as ss, 3ch, 1dc in same place as sc, 1ch, * [1dc, 1ch] twice in each of next 7dc, ss in 2nd ch.

3rd round 1ch, 1sc in same place as ss, 3ch, 1dc in same place as sc, 1ch, 1dc in foll dc, 1ch, * [1dc, 1ch] twice in next dc, 1dc in foll dc, 1ch, rep from * 6 more times, ss in 2nd ch.

4th round 1ch, 1sc in same place as ss, 3ch, 1dc in same place as sc, 1ch, [1dc, 1ch] in each of foll 2dc, * [1dc, 1ch] twice in next dc, [1dc, 1ch] in each of foll 2dc, rep from * 6 more times, ss in 2nd ch.

5th round 1ch, 1sc in same place as ss, 3ch, 1dc in same place as sc, 1ch, [1dc, 1ch] in each of foll 3dc, * [1dc, 1ch] twice in next dc, [1dc, 1ch] in each of foll 3dc, rep from * 6 more times, ss in 2nd ch.

Fasten off.

double crochet square

This square grows quickly as there are just three double crochet rounds. Although it's simple to make, the corner join and increases worked in corner spaces give an elegant overall effect.

instructions

Make 5ch, ss in first ch to form a ring.

1st round 5ch, [4dc in ring, 2ch] 3 times, 3dc in ring, ss in 3rd ch.

2nd round Ss in corner sp, 5ch, 2dc in same corner sp, * 1dc in each of next 4dc, [2dc, 2ch, 2dc] in next 2ch sp, rep from * two more times, 1dc in each of next 4 sts, 1dc in first corner sp, ss in 3rd ch.

3rd round Ss in corner sp, 5ch, 2dc in same corner sp, * 1dc in each of next 8dc, [2dc, 2ch, 2dc] in next 2ch sp, rep from * two more times, 1dc in each of next 8 sts, 1dc in first corner sp, ss in 3rd ch.

Fasten off.

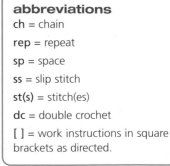

abbreviations and key

- **ch** = chain
- **sc** = single crochet
- **foll** = following
- **rep** = repeat
- **ss** = slip stitch
- **dc** = double crochet
- **[ ]** = work instructions in square brackets as directed.

abbreviations

ch = chain

rep = repeat

sp = space

ss = slip stitch

st(s) = stitch(es)

dc = double crochet

[ ] = work instructions in square brackets as directed.

bobble diamonds square

Take away the bobbles and this block is just a double crochet square with two-chain corners. Because the trebles are longer and four stitches are worked together, the bobbles stand up firmly from the background.

instructions

Make 8ch, ss in first ch to form a ring.

1st round 1ch, 20sc in ring, ss in first sc.

2nd round 1ch, 1sc in same place as ss, 4ch, [*1dc in each of next 2sc, 4trtog in foll sc *, 1dc in each of next 2sc, 2ch] 3 times, rep from * to *, 1dc in last sc, ss in 2nd ch.

3rd round Ss in first sp, 1ch, 1sc in same sp, 4ch, * 1dc in same sp, [1dc in next st, 4trtog in foll dc] twice **, 1dc in next dc, 1dc in next sp, 2ch, rep from * two more times, then rep from * to **, 1dc in 2nd ch of 2nd round, ss in 2nd ch.

4th round Ss in first sp, 1ch, 1sc in same sp, 4ch, * 1dc in same sp, [1dc in next st, 4trtog in foll dc] 3 times **, 1dc in next dc, 1dc in next sp, 2ch, rep from * two more times, then rep from * to **, 1dc in 2nd ch of 3rd round, ss in 2nd ch.

abbreviations and key

- **o** ch = chain
- **+** sc = single crochet
- **4trtog** – leaving last loop of each st on hook, work 4tr, yarn over hook and pull through 5 loops on hook.
- **foll** = following
- **rep** = repeat
- ss = slip st
- **●** st(s) = stitch(es)
- dc = double crochet
- **[ ]** = work instructions in square brackets as directed.

5th round Ss in first sp, 1ch, 1sc in same sp, 4ch, * 1dc in same sp, 1dc in each of next 3 sts, 4trtog in foll dc, 1dc in 4trtog, 4trtog in next dc **, 1dc in each of next 3 sts, 1dc in next sp, 2ch, rep from * two more times, then rep from * to **, 1dc in each of next 2 sts, 1dc in 2nd ch of 4th round, ss in 2nd ch.

6th round Ss in first sp, 1ch, 1sc in same sp, 4ch, * 1dc in same sp, 1dc in each of next 5 sts, 4trtog in foll dc **, 1dc in each of next 5 sts, 1dc in next sp, 2ch, rep from * two more times, then rep from * to **, 1dc in each of next 4 sts, 1dc in 2nd ch of 5th round, ss in 2nd ch.

7th round Ss in first sp, 1ch, 1sc in same sp, 4ch, * 1dc in same sp, 1dc in each of next 13 sts, 1dc in next sp, 2ch, rep from * two more times, 1dc in same sp, 1dc in each of next 12 sts, 1dc in 2nd ch of 6th round, ss in 2nd ch.

8th round Ss in first sp, 1ch, 1sc in same sp, 4ch, * 1dc in same sp, [2ch, miss 1dc, 1dc in next dc] 7 times, 2ch, 1dc in next sp, 2ch, rep from * two more times, 1dc in same sp, [2ch, miss 1dc, 1dc in next dc] 7 times, 2ch, ss in 2nd ch.

Fasten off.

granny triangle

Working groups of double crochet into chain spaces is the basic unit for making a granny square. This motif takes a fresh look at the traditional stitch groups, arranging them to make a triangle and giving a modern look to an old favorite.

instructions

Wind yarn around finger to form a ring.

1st round 1ch, 1sc in ring, 5ch, [3dc in ring, 3ch] twice, 2dc in ring, ss in 2nd ch.

2nd round Ss in first sp, 1ch, [1sc, 5ch, 3dc] in same sp as ss, * 2ch, [3dc, 3ch, 3dc] in next 3ch sp, rep from * once more, 2ch, 2dc in first sp, ss in 2nd ch.

3rd round Ss in first sp, 1ch, [1sc, 5ch, 3dc] in same sp as ss, * 2ch, 3dc in next 2ch sp, 2ch, [3dc, 3ch, 3dc] in foll 3ch sp, rep from * once more, 2ch, 3dc in next 2ch sp, 2ch, 2dc in first sp, ss in 2nd ch.

4th round Ss in first sp, 1ch, [1sc, 5ch, 3dc] in same sp as ss, * [2ch, 3dc in next 2ch sp] twice, 2ch, [3dc, 3ch, 3dc] in foll 3ch sp, rep from * once more, [2ch, 3dc in next 2ch sp] twice, 2ch, 2dc in first sp, ss in 2nd ch.

Fasten off.

oblong

Working alternate sections of single and double crochet gives two short and two long sides to each round, making an oblong with rounded corners. Just five rounds are given here, but it's easy to see the rhythm of increases and change of stitch height if you want to make a larger oblong.

instructions

Wind yarn around finger to make a ring.

1st round 1ch, 10sc in ring, ss in first sc. 10 sts.

2nd round 1ch, 1sc in same place as ss, 2ch, 1dc in same place as sc, 2dc in next sc, * 2sc in foll sc, 1sc in next sc, 2sc in foll sc *, 2dc in each of next 2sc, rep from * to *, ss in 2nd ch. 18 sts.

3rd round 1ch, 1sc in same place as ss, 2ch, 1dc in same place as sc, * 1dc in each of next 2dc, 2dc in foll dc, 2sc in next sc, 1sc in each of next 3sc, 2sc in foll sc *, 2dc in next dc, rep from * to *, ss in 2nd ch. 26 sts.

4th round 1ch, 1sc in same place as ss, 2ch, 1dc in same place as sc, * 1dc in each of next 4dc, 2dc in foll dc, 2sc in

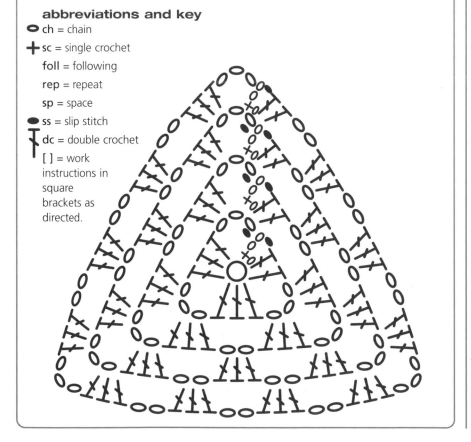

abbreviations and key

- **ch** = chain
- **sc** = single crochet
- **foll** = following
- **rep** = repeat
- **sp** = space
- **ss** = slip stitch
- **dc** = double crochet
- **[ ]** = work instructions in square brackets as directed.

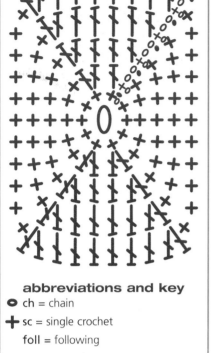

abbreviations and key

● ch = chain

✛ sc = single crochet

   foll = following

   rep = repeat

● ss = slip st

   st(s) = stitch(es)

Ŧ dc = double crochet

swirl hexagon

This hexagon motif is worked in a spiral so there's no need to start with a chain stitch or to join each round, simply work on. The rounds follow smoothly into each other but it's easy to check which round you're on by counting the number of rows in each section, or by marking the beginning of the rounds with a safety pin.

instructions

Wind yarn around finger to form a ring.

1st round 6sc in ring.

2nd round 1sc in first sc, 3ch, [1sc in next sc, 3ch] 5 times.

3rd round 1sc in first sc, 1sc in first sp, 3ch, [1sc in next sc, 1sc in next sp, 3ch] 5 times.

4th round [Miss 1sc, 2sc in next sc, 1sc in sp, 3ch] 6 times.

5th round [Miss 1sc, 2sc in next sc, 1sc in foll sc, 1sc in sp, 3ch] 6 times.

6th round [Miss 1sc, 2sc in next sc, 1sc in each of foll 2sc, 1sc in sp, 3ch] 6 times.

7th round [Miss 1sc, 2sc in next sc, 1sc in each of foll 3sc, 1sc in sp, 3ch] 6 times.

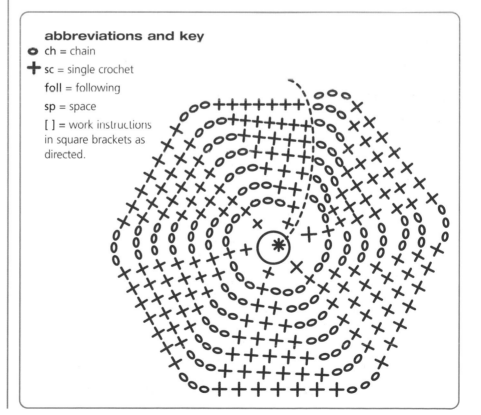

8th round [Miss 1sc, 2sc in next sc, 1sc in each of foll 4sc, 1sc in sp, 3ch] 6 times.

Fasten off and take end under first sc of 8th round and back through last ch to make a smooth join.

next sc, 1sc in each of next 5sc, 2sc in foll sc *, 2dc in next dc, rep from * to *, ss in 2nd ch. 34 sts.

5th round 1ch, 1sc in same place as ss, 2ch, 1dc in same place as sc, * 1dc in each of next 6dc, 2dc in foll dc, 2sc in next sc, 1sc in each of next 7sc, 2sc in foll sc *, 2dc in next dc, rep from * to *, ss in 2nd ch. 42 sts.

abbreviations and key

● ch = chain

✛ sc = single crochet

   foll = following

   sp = space

   [ ] = work instructions in square brackets as directed.

diagonal square

This square is worked in rows from the corner to create two sides with row-ends and two sides with stitches. The sample is worked in four-row stripes with a border, but you could omit the border and use it square-on for a right angle, or tip it to make a chevron, then join blocks to form zigzags, waves, or a Greek key pattern.

instructions

Colors: Cream (A), pale blue (B), and mid-blue (C).

1st row Using A, 2ch, 3sc in first ch.

2nd row 1ch, 1sc in first sc, 3sc in next sc, 1sc in last sc.

3rd row 1ch, 1sc in each of first 2sc, 3sc in next sc, 1sc in each of last 2sc.

4th row 1ch, 1sc in each of first 3sc, 3sc in next sc, 1sc in each of last 3sc.

5th row 1ch, 1sc in each of first 4sc, 3sc in next sc, 1sc in each of last 4sc.

Continue in this way working 1ch at beginning then 1sc in each sc and 3sc in sc at corner on each row, work 4 rows B, 4 rows C, 4 rows B, and 4 rows A. Fasten off.

If wished, finish square with 2 rounds of sc.

abbreviations

ch = chain

sc = single crochet.

granny hexagon

The granny design unit is reduced to two double crochet and one chain to accommodate the extra stitches needed for a six-sided shape while at the same time creating a flat motif.

instructions

Wind yarn around finger to form a ring.

1st round 1ch, 1sc in ring, 4ch, [2dc in ring, 2ch] 5 times, 1dc in ring, ss in 2nd ch.

2nd round Ss in first sp, 1ch, [1sc, 4ch, 2dc] in same sp as ss, 1ch, * [2dc, 2ch, 2dc] in next 2ch sp, 1ch, rep from * 4 times, 1dc in first sp, ss in 2nd ch.

3rd round Ss in first sp, 1ch, [1sc, 4ch, 2dc] in same sp as ss, * 1ch, 2dc in next 1ch sp, 1ch, [2dc, 2ch, 2dc] in foll 2ch sp, rep from * 4 more times, 1ch, 2dc in last 1ch sp, 1ch, 1dc in first sp, ss in 2nd ch.

4th round Ss in first sp, 1ch, [1sc, 4ch, 2dc] in same sp as ss, * [1ch, 2dc in next 1ch sp] twice, 1ch **, [2dc, 2ch, 2dc] in foll 2ch sp, rep from * 4 more times, then rep from * to **, 1dc in first sp, ss in 2nd ch.

5th round Ss in first sp, 1ch, [1sc, 4ch, 2dc] in same sp as ss, * [1ch, 2dc in next 1ch sp] 3 times, 1ch **, [2dc, 2ch, 2dc] in foll 2ch sp, rep from * 4 more times, then rep from * to **, 1dc in first sp, ss in 2nd ch.

Fasten off.

abbreviations and key

- **ch** = chain
- **sc** = single crochet
- **foll** = following
- **rep** = repeat
- **sp** = space
- **ss** = slip stitch
- **dc** = double crochet
- **[ ]** = work instructions in square brackets as directed.

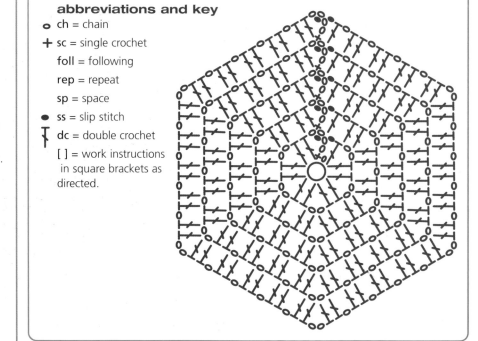

filet heart square

The silhouette heart is made by working groups of double crochet to fill in the shape on a grid of double crochet and chain mesh. Filet designs are often charted as black squares on a white grid, but the method of charting used here shows exactly where to place each stitch.

instructions

Make 34ch.

1st row 1dc in 6th ch from hook, [1ch, miss 1ch, 1dc in next ch] 14 times.

2nd row 1sc in first dc, 3ch, [1dc in next dc, 1ch] 14 times, 1dc in 2nd ch.

3rd row 1sc in first dc, 3ch, [1dc in next dc, 1ch] 6 times, 1dc in foll dc, 1dc in ch, 1dc in foll dc, 1ch, [1dc in next dc, 1ch] 6 times, 1dc in 2nd ch.

4th row 1sc in first dc, 3ch, [1dc in next dc, 1ch] 5 times, 1dc in foll dc, 1dc in next ch, 1dc in each of foll 3dc, 1dc in next ch, [1dc in next dc, 1ch] 6 times, 1dc in 2nd ch.

5th row 1sc in first dc, 3ch, [1dc in next dc, 1ch] 4 times, 1dc in foll dc, 1dc in next ch, 1dc in each of foll 7dc, 1dc in next ch, [1dc in next dc, 1ch] 5 times, 1dc in 2nd ch.

6th row 1sc in first dc, 3ch, [1dc in next dc, 1ch] 3 times, 1dc in foll dc, 1dc in next ch, 1dc in each of foll 11dc, 1dc in next ch, [1dc in next dc, 1ch] 4 times, 1dc in 2nd ch.

7th row 1sc in first dc, 3ch, [1dc in next dc, 1ch] twice, 1dc in foll dc, 1dc in next ch, 1dc in each of foll 15dc, 1dc in next ch, [1dc in next dc, 1ch] 3 times, 1dc in 2nd ch.

8th row 1sc in first dc, 3ch, [1dc in next dc, 1ch] twice, 1dc in each of foll 19dc, 1ch, [1dc in next dc, 1ch] twice, 1dc in 2nd ch.

9th and 10th rows As 8th.

11th row 1sc in first dc, 3ch, [1dc in next dc, 1ch] twice, 1dc in each of foll 9dc, 1ch, miss 1dc, 1dc in each of next 9dc, 1ch, [1dc in next dc, 1ch] twice, 1dc in 2nd ch.

12th row 1sc in first dc, 3ch, [1dc in next dc, 1ch] 3 times, miss 1dc, 1dc in each of next 5dc, 1ch, miss 1dc, 1dc in next dc, 1ch, 1dc in next dc, 1ch, miss 1dc, 1dc in each of next 5dc, 1ch, [1dc in next dc, 1ch] 3 times, 1dc in 2nd ch.

13th row 1sc in first dc, 3ch, [1dc in next dc, 1ch] 4 times, [miss 1dc, 1dc in next dc, 1ch] twice, [1dc in next dc, 1ch] 3 times, [miss 1dc, 1dc in next dc, 1ch] twice, [1dc in next dc, 1ch] 3 times, 1dc in 2nd ch.

14th row As 2nd.

Fasten off.

If wished finish square with 2 rounds of sc.

abbreviations and key

O ch = chain

+ sc = single crochet

foll = following

T dc = double crochet

[ ] = work instructions in square brackets as directed.

popcorn hexagon

Six popcorns at the center are outlined with ridges of single crochet. Another round of popcorns is worked around the stem ridge round. A finishing round of double crochet and spaces adds more texture.

instructions

Wind yarn around finger to form a ring.

1st round 1ch, 1sc in ring, 2ch, [2sc in ring, 2ch] 5 times, 1sc in ring, ss in first sc.

2nd round Ss in first 2ch sp, 1ch, [1sc, 2ch, 3dc] in same 2ch sp, remove hook, insert hook in 2nd ch, catch loop and pull through to close first pc, 1dc in same 2ch sp, 2ch, * [1dc, 4dcpc, 1dc] in next 2ch sp, 2ch, rep from * 4 more times, 1dc in first 2ch sp, ss in first pc.

3rd round 1ch, 1sc in same place as ss, 1sc in next dc, [1sc, 2ch, 1sc] in next 2ch sp, * 1sc in each of next 3 sts, [1sc, 2ch, 1sc] in next 2ch sp, rep from * 4 more times, 1sc in next dc, remove hook, insert hook from back in first sc and pull loop through to join round.

4th round 1ch, 1sc around the stem of each of first 3sc, 2ch, [1sc around the stem of each of next 5sc, 2ch] 5 times, 1sc around the stem of each of last 2sc, ss in first sc.

5th round 1ch, 1sc in same place as ss, 1sc in each of next 2sc, [1sc, 2ch, 1sc] in next 2ch sp, * 1sc in each of next 5sc, [1sc, 2ch, 1sc] in next 2ch sp, rep from * 4 more times, 1sc in each of last 2sc, remove hook, insert hook from back in first sc and pull loop through to join round.

6th round 1ch, 1sc around the stem of each of first 4sc, 2ch, [1sc around the stem of each of next 7sc, 2ch] 5 times, 1sc around the stem of each of last 3sc, ss in first sc.

7th round 1ch, [1sc, 2ch, 3dc] in same place as ss, remove hook, insert hook in 2nd ch, catch loop and pull through to close first pc, 1dc in each of next 2sc, 4dcpc in foll sc, [1dc, 2ch, 1dc] in next 2ch sp, * [4dcpc in next sc, 1dc in each of foll 2sc] twice, 4dcpc in next sc, [1dc, 2ch, 1dc] in next 2ch sp, rep from * 4 more times, 4dcpc in next sc, 1dc in each of last 2sc, ss in first pc.

8th round 1ch, 1sc in same place as ss, 1sc in each of next 4 sts, [1sc, 2ch, 1sc] in next 2ch sp, * 1sc in each of next 9 sts, [1sc, 2ch, 1sc] in next 2ch sp, rep from * 4 more times, 1sc in each of last 4 sts, ss in first sc.

9th round 1ch, 1sc around the stem of each of first 6sc, 2ch, [1sc around the stem of each of next 11sc, 2ch] 5 times, 1sc around the stem of each of last 5sc, remove hook, insert hook from back in first sc and pull loop through to join round.

10th round 1ch, 1sc in same place as join, 3ch, [miss next sc, 1dc in foll sc, 1ch] twice, [1dc, 2ch, 1dc] in next 2ch sp, * [1ch, miss next sc, 1dc in foll sc] 5 times, 1ch, [1dc, 2ch, 1dc] in next 2ch sp, rep from * 4 more times, [1ch, miss next sc, 1dc in foll sc] twice, 1ch, ss in 2nd ch. Fasten off.

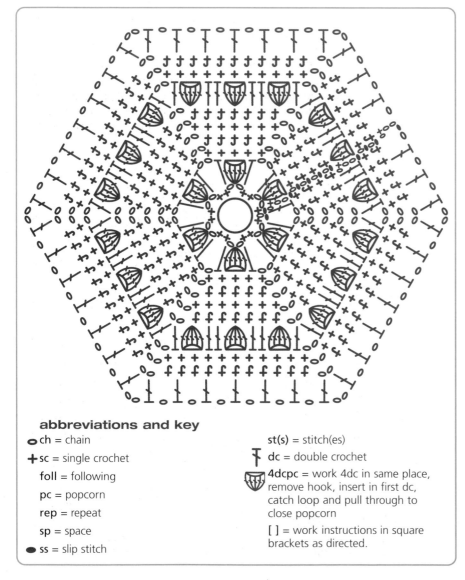

abbreviations and key

○ ch = chain

✚ sc = single crochet

foll = following

pc = popcorn

rep = repeat

sp = space

● ss = slip stitch

st(s) = stitch(es)

┬ dc = double crochet

4dcpc = work 4dc in same place, remove hook, insert in first dc, catch loop and pull through to close popcorn

[ ] = work instructions in square brackets as directed.

victorian bedspread square

This handsome square is in the style of a traditional bedspread square and although it's richly textured, it's very easy to work. The bold popcorns make a cross on the single square shown here, but when squares are joined the popcorns make a diamond pattern.

instructions

Wind yarn around finger to form a ring.

1st round 1ch, 1sc in ring, [3ch, 3sc in ring] 3 times, 3ch, 2sc in ring, ss in first sc.

2nd round Ss in first 3ch sp, 1ch, [1sc, 5ch, 2dc] in same 3ch sp, * 1ch, miss next sc, 5dcpc in foll sc, 1ch, miss next sc, [2dc, 3ch, 2dc] in next 3ch sp, rep from * two more times, 1ch, miss next sc, 5dcpc in foll sc, 1ch, miss next sc, 1dc in first 3ch sp, ss in 2nd ch.

3rd round Ss in first 3ch sp, 1ch, [1sc, 5ch, 2dc] in same 3ch sp, * 1ch, 5dcpc in next 1ch sp, 1dc in next st, 5dcpc in foll 1ch sp, 1ch, [2dc, 3ch, 2dc] in next 3ch sp, rep from * two more times, 1ch, 5dcpc in next 1ch sp, 1dc in next st, 5dcpc in foll 1ch sp, 1ch, 1dc in first 3ch sp, ss in 2nd ch.

4th round Ss in first 3ch sp, 1ch, [1sc, 5ch, 2dc] in same 3ch sp, * 1ch, 5dcpc in next 1ch sp, 1dc in each of next 3 sts, 5dcpc in foll 1ch sp, 1ch, [2dc, 3ch, 2dc] in next 3ch sp, rep from * two more times, 1ch, 5dcpc in next 1ch sp, 1dc in each of next 3 sts, 5dcpc in foll 1ch sp, 1ch, 1dc in first 3ch sp, ss in 2nd ch.

5th round Ss in first 3ch sp, 1ch, [1sc, 5ch, 2dc] in same 3ch sp, * 1ch, 5dcpc in next 1ch sp, 1dc in each of next 5 sts, 5dcpc in foll 1ch sp, 1ch, [2dc, 3ch, 2dc] in next 3ch sp, rep from * two

more times, 1ch, 5dcpc in next 1ch sp, 1dc in each of next 5 sts, 5dcpc in foll 1ch sp, 1ch, 1dc in first 3ch sp, ss in 2nd ch.

6th round Ss in first 3ch sp, 1ch, [1sc, 5ch, 2dc] in same 3ch sp, * 1ch, 5dcpc in next 1ch sp, 1dc in each of next 7 sts, 5dcpc in foll 1ch sp, 1ch, [2dc, 3ch, 2dc] in next 3ch sp, rep from * two more times, 1ch, 5dcpc in next 1ch sp, 1dc in each of next 7 sts, 5dcpc in foll 1ch sp, 1ch, 1dc in first 3ch sp, ss in 2nd ch.

7th round Ss in first 3ch sp, 1ch, [1sc, 5ch, 2dc] in same 3ch sp, * 1ch, 5dcpc in next 1ch sp, 1dc in each of next 9 sts, 5dcpc in foll 1ch sp, 1ch, [2dc, 3ch, 2dc] in next 3ch sp, rep from * two more times, 1ch, 5dcpc in next 1ch sp, 1dc in each of next 9 sts, 5dcpc in foll 1ch sp, 1ch, 1dc in first 3ch sp, ss in 2nd ch. Fasten off.

abbreviations and key

○ **ch** = chain

✛ **sc** = single crochet

foll = following

rep = repeat

sp = space

● **ss** = slip stitch

st(s) = stitch(es)

╀ **dc** = double crochet

5dcpc = work 5dc in same place, remove hook, insert hook in first of the 5dc, catch loop and pull through to close popcorn

[ ] = work instructions in square brackets as directed.

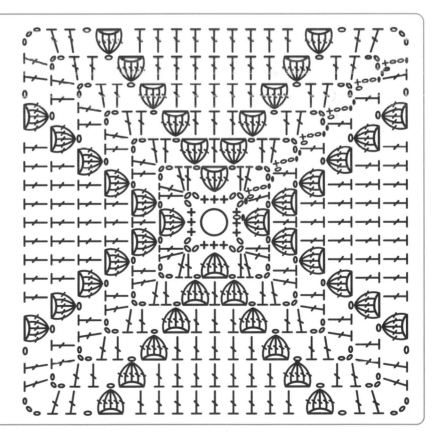

off-center hexagon

Working two of each of the six sides in different-height stitches moves the starting ring away from the center to give an unusual hexagon motif. Changing colors on every round emphasizes the off-center effect.

instructions

Colors: Lime green (A) and bright green (B).

Using A, wind yarn around finger to form a ring.

1st round 1ch, 1sc in ring, 2ch, 2sc in ring, 2ch, 2hdc in ring, [2ch, 2dc in ring] twice, 2ch, 2hdc in ring, 2ch, 1sc in ring, ss in first sc.

Change to B.

2nd round Ss in first sp, 1ch, [1sc, 2ch, 1sc] in same sp, 1sc in each of next 2sc, [1sc, 2ch, 1hdc] in next 2ch sp, 1hdc in each of next 2hdc, [1hdc, 2ch, 1dc] in next 2ch sp, 1dc in each of next 2dc, [1dc, 2ch, 1dc] in next 2ch sp, 1dc in each of next 2dc, [1dc, 2ch, 1hdc] in next 2ch sp, 1hdc in each of next 2hdc, [1hdc, 2ch, 1sc] in next 2ch sp, 1sc in each of next 2sc, ss in first sc.

Change to A.

3rd round Ss in first sp, 1ch, [1sc, 2ch, 1sc] in same sp, 1sc in each of next 4sc, [1sc, 2ch, 1hdc] in next 2ch sp, 1hdc in each of next 4hdc, [1hdc, 2ch, 1dc] in next 2ch sp, 1dc in each of next 4dc, [1dc, 2ch, 1dc] in next 2ch sp, 1dc in each of next 4dc, [1dc, 2ch, 1hdc] in next 2ch sp, 1hdc in each of next 4hdc, [1hdc, 2ch, 1sc] in next 2ch sp, 1sc in each of next 4sc, ss in first sc.

Change to B.

4th round Ss in first sp, 1ch, [1sc, 2ch, 1sc] in same sp, 1sc in each of next 6sc, [1sc, 2ch, 1hdc] in next 2ch sp, 1hdc in each of next 6hdc, [1hdc, 2ch, 1dc] in next 2ch sp, 1dc in each of next 6dc, [1dc, 2ch, 1dc] in next 2ch sp, 1dc in each of next 6dc, [1dc, 2ch, 1hdc] in next 2ch sp, 1hdc in each of next 6hdc, [1hdc, 2ch, 1sc] in next 2ch sp, 1sc in each of next 6sc, ss in first sc.

Fasten off.

abbreviations and key

- **o** ch = chain
- **+** sc = single crochet
- **T** hdc = half double crochet
- sp = space
- **●** ss = slip stitch
- **T** dc = double crochet
- [ ] = work instructions in square brackets as directed.

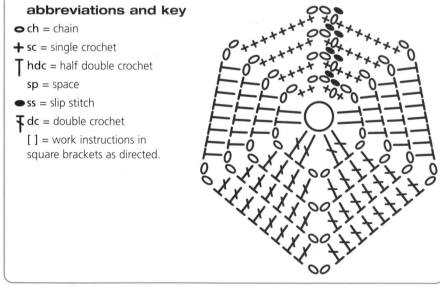

log cabin square

Stripes of single crochet imitate the classic log cabin patchwork block. Use up scraps of yarn to make a jazzy thrift blanket or plan a more sophisticated scheme. Work alternate sections in light and dark tones.

instructions

Colors: Cream (A), four shades of pink (B), and four shades of lilac (C).

Center Using A, make 5ch.

1st row 1sc in 2nd ch from hook, [1sc in each ch] to end. 4 sts.

2nd row (RS) 1ch, [1sc in each sc] to end.

2nd row forms sc. Work 2 more rows sc. Fasten off.

1st round Each round is worked in four overlapping sections.

1st section. 1st row Using 1st shade of B, make 3ch, 1sc in 2nd ch from hook, 1sc in next ch, with RS facing, work 1sc in each sc of last row of center. 6 sts. Work 1 more row sc. Fasten off.

With RS facing, turn work so that row-ends of 1st section are at top right and join 1st shade of C in 1st row-end of first section.

2nd section. 1st row 1ch, 1sc in same place as join, 1sc in each of next 5 row-ends. 6 sts. Work 1 more row sc. Fasten off.

With RS facing, turn work so that row-ends of 2nd section are at top right and join 2nd shade of C in first row-end of 2nd section.

3rd section 1ch, 1sc in same place as join, 1sc in next row-end, 1sc in each of next 4 sts. 6 sts. Work 1 more row sc. Fasten off.

With RS facing, turn work so that row-ends of 3rd section are at top right and join 2nd shade of B in first row-end of 3rd section.

4th section Work as given for 2nd section.

Use yarn end to sew row-ends of 4th section to base of 2ch at start of 1st section.

2nd round. 1st section. 1st row Using 3rd shade of B, make 3ch, 1sc in 2nd ch from hook, 1sc in next ch, with RS facing, work 1sc in each sc of 2nd row of 1st section of 1st round, 1sc in each of next 2 row-ends. 10 sts. Work 1 more row sc. Fasten off.

2nd, 3rd, and 4th sections Using 3rd and 4th shades of C and 4th shade of B, and noting that there will be 10 sts each time, complete in same way as 1st round.

3rd round. 1st section. 1st row Using 1st shade of B, make 3ch, 1sc in 2nd ch from hook, 1sc in next ch, with RS facing, work 1sc in each sc of 2nd row of 1st section of 2nd round, 1sc in each of next 2 row-ends. 14 sts. Work 1 more row sc. Fasten off.

2nd, 3rd, and 4th sections Using 1st and 2nd shades of C and 2nd shade of B, and noting that there will be 14 sts each time, complete in same way as 1st round.

4th round. 1st section. 1st row Using 3rd shade of B, make 3ch, 1sc in 2nd ch from hook, 1sc in next ch, with RS facing, work 1sc in each sc of 2nd row of 1st section of 3rd round, 1sc in each of next 2 row-ends. 18 sts. Work 1 more row sc. Fasten off.

2nd, 3rd, and 4th sections Using 3rd and 4th shades of C and 4th shade of B, and noting that there will be 18 sts each time, complete in same way as 1st round.

abbreviations

ch = chain
sc = single crochet
RS = right side
[ ] = work instructions in square brackets as directed.

treble bobble square

The raised texture of this simple square is made by working treble bobbles on double crochet rounds, thus making the bobbles stand out from the surface. The motif is shown in one color but if you want a flowerlike effect, change yarn colors for the bobble rounds.

instructions

Wrap yarn around finger to form a ring.

1st round 1ch, [1sc in ring, 2ch] 12 times, ss in first sc.

2nd round Ss in first 2ch sp, 1ch, [1sc, 3ch, 3trtog] in same 1ch sp, [2dc in each of next 2 sps, 4trtog in foll sp] 3 times, 2dc in each of last 2 sps, ss in 3trtog.

3rd round 1ch, [1sc, 2ch, 1sc] in same place as ss, * [2ch, 1sc in next dc] 4 times, 2ch, [1sc, 2ch, 1sc] in next 4trtog, rep from * two more times, [2ch, 1sc in next dc] 4 times, 2ch, ss in first sc.

4th round Ss in first 2ch sp, 1ch, [1sc, 3ch, 3trtog] in same

abbreviations and key

○ ch = chain

+ sc = single crochet

3trtog = leaving last loop of each st on hook work 3tr, yarn over hook and pull through 4 loops on hook

4trtog = leaving last loop of each st on hook work 4tr, yarn over hook and pull through 5 loops on hook

foll = following

rep = repeat

sp = space

● ss = slip stitch

st(s) = stitch(es)

dc = double crochet

[ ] = work instructions in square brackets as directed.

1ch sp, [2dc in next 2ch sp, 4trtog in foll 2ch sp] 11 times, 2dc in last 2ch sp, ss in 3trtog,

5th round 1ch, [1sc, 2ch, 1sc] in same place as ss, * 1sc in each of next 8 sts, [1sc, 2ch, 1sc] in next 4trtog, rep from * two more times, 1sc in each of next 8 sts, ss in first sc, turn.

6th round 1ch, 1sc in same place as ss, 1sc in each of next 9sc, * [1sc, 2ch, 1sc] in next 2ch sp, 1sc in each of next 10sc, rep from * two more times, [1sc, 2ch, 1sc] in last 2ch sp, ss in first sc. Fasten off.

single crochet square

This example has six rounds but you can work more or less rounds as required. The sample swatch is worked in the round without turning; if you want your square to look like single crochet worked in rows, simply turn the work after each round.

instructions
Wind yarn around finger to form a ring.

1st round 1ch, 8sc in ring, ss in first sc. 8 sts.

2nd round 1ch, 2sc in same place as ss, [1sc in next sc, 3sc in foll sc] 3 times, 1sc in next sc, 1sc in same place as first sc, ss in first sc. 16 sts.

3rd round 1ch, 2sc in same place as ss, [1sc in each of next 3sc, 3sc in foll sc] 3 times, 1sc in each of next 3sc, 1sc in same place as first sc, ss in first sc. 24 sts.

4th round 1ch, 2sc in same place as ss, [1sc in each of next 5sc, 3sc in foll sc] 3 times, 1sc in each of next 5sc, 1sc in same place as first sc, ss in first sc. 32 sts.

5th round 1ch, 2sc in same place as ss, [1sc in each of next 7sc, 3sc in foll sc] 3 times, 1sc in each of next 7sc, 1sc in same place as first sc, ss in first sc. 40 sts.

6th round 1ch, 2sc in same place as ss, [1sc in each of next 9sc, 3sc in foll sc] 3 times, 1sc in each of next 9sc, 1sc in same place as first sc, ss in first sc. 48 sts. Fasten off.

single crochet triangle

Six rounds are given for this triangle but you can work more or less rounds as required for a larger or smaller motif. The sample swatch is worked in the round without turning, if you want your triangle to look like single crochet worked in rows, simply turn the work after each round.

instructions
Wind yarn around finger to form a ring.

1st round 1ch, 6sc in ring, ss in first sc. 6 sts.

2nd round 1ch, 2sc in same place as ss, [1sc in next sc, 3sc in foll sc] twice, 1sc in next sc, 1sc in same place as first sc, ss in first sc. 12 sts.

3rd round 1ch, 2sc in same place as ss, [1sc in each of next 3sc, 3sc in foll sc] twice, 1sc in each of next 3sc, 1sc in same place as first sc, ss in first sc. 18 sts.

4th round 1ch, 2sc in same place as ss, [1sc in each of next 5sc, 3sc in foll sc] twice, 1sc in each of next 5sc, 1sc in same place as first sc, ss in first sc. 24 sts.

5th round 1ch, 2sc in same place as ss, [1sc in each of next 7sc, 3sc in foll sc] twice, 1sc in each of next 7sc, 1sc in same place as first sc, ss in first sc. 30 sts.

6th round 1ch, 2sc in same place as ss, [1sc in each of next 9sc, 3sc in foll sc] twice, 1sc in each of next 9sc, 1sc in same place as first sc, ss in first sc. 36 sts. Fasten off.

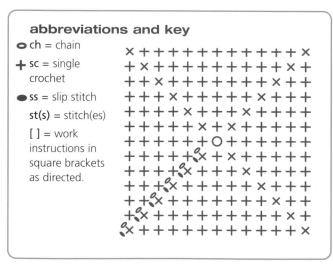

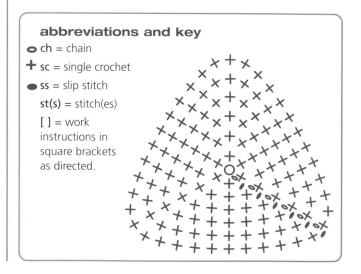

abbreviations and key
- **o** ch = chain
- **+** sc = single crochet
- **●** ss = slip stitch
- st(s) = stitch(es)
- [ ] = work instructions in square brackets as directed.

abbreviations and key
- **o** ch = chain
- **+** sc = single crochet
- **●** ss = slip stitch
- st(s) = stitch(es)
- [ ] = work instructions in square brackets as directed.

sunshine and shadow square

This interpretation of a traditional log cabin patchwork square has overlapping chevrons alternating around opposite sides of a central square. Whatever colors you choose for your motif, make sure that the tones are grouped in the same way as here for the best effect.

instructions

Colors: Dark orange (A), cream (B), pale blue (C), pale yellow (D), bright blue (E), bright yellow (F), and navy (G).

Center Using A, make 11ch.

1st row 1sc in 2nd ch from hook, [1sc in each ch] to end. 10 sts.

2nd row (RS) 1ch, [1sc in each sc] to end.

2nd row forms sc. Work 8 more rows sc. Fasten off.

1st section With RS facing, join B in first sc at top right.

1st row 1ch, 1sc in same place as join, 1sc in each of next 8sc, 3sc in foll sc, 1sc in each of next 9 row-ends, turn.

2nd row 1ch, 1sc in each of next 10sc, 3sc in foll sc, 1sc in each of last 10sc.

3rd row 1ch, 1sc in each of next 11sc, 3sc in foll sc, 1sc in each of last 11sc.

4th row 1ch, 1sc in each of next 12sc, 3sc in foll sc, 1sc in each of last 12sc.

Fasten off.

2nd section With RS facing and 1st section at lower right, join C in first row-end.

1st row 1ch, 1sc in same place as join, 1sc in each of next 3 row-ends, 1sc in base of each of next 9ch, 3sc in base of last ch, 1sc in each of next 13 row-ends, turn.

2nd row 1ch, 1sc in each of first 14sc, 3sc in next sc, 1sc in each of last 14sc.

3rd row 1ch, 1sc in each of first 15sc, 3sc in next sc, 1sc in each of last 15sc.

4th row 1ch, 1sc in each of first 16sc, 3sc in next sc, 1sc in each of last 16sc.

Fasten off.

3rd section With RS facing and 2nd section at lower right, join D in first row-end.

1st row 1ch, 1sc in same place as join, 1sc in each of next 3 row-ends, 1sc in each of next 13sc, 3sc in next sc, 1sc in each of next 13sc, 1sc in each of next 4 row ends, turn.

2nd row 1ch, 1sc in each of first 18sc, 3sc in next sc, 1sc in each of last 18sc.

3rd row 1ch, 1sc in each of first 19sc, 3sc in next sc, 1sc in each of last 19sc.

4th row 1ch, 1sc in each of first 20sc, 3sc in next sc, 1sc in each of last 20sc.

Fasten off.

4th section With RS facing and 3rd section at lower right, join E in first row-end.

1st row 1ch, 1sc in same place as join, 1sc in each of next 3 row-ends, 1sc in each of next 17sc, 3sc in next sc, 1sc in each of next 17sc, 1sc in each of next 4 row-ends, turn.

2nd row 1ch, 1sc in each of first 22sc, 3sc in next sc, 1sc in each of last 22sc.

3rd row 1ch, 1sc in each of first 23sc, 3sc in next sc, 1sc in each of last 23sc.

4th row 1ch, 1sc in each of first 24sc, 3sc in next sc, 1sc in each of last 24sc.

Fasten off.

5th section With RS facing and 4th section at lower right, join F in first row-end.

1st row 1ch, 1sc in same place as join, 1sc in each of next 3 row-ends, 1sc in each of next 21sc, 3sc in next sc, 1sc in each of next 21sc, 1sc in each of next 4 row-ends, turn.

2nd row 1ch, 1sc in each of first 26sc, 3sc in next sc, 1sc in each of last 26sc.

3rd row 1ch, 1sc in each of first 27sc, 3sc in next sc, 1sc in each of last 27sc.

4th row 1ch, 1sc in each of first 28sc, 3sc in next sc, 1sc in each of last 28sc.

Fasten off.

6th section With RS facing and 5th section at lower right, join G in first row-end.

1st row 1ch, 1sc in same place as join, 1sc in each of next 3 row-ends, 1sc in each of next 25sc, 3sc in next sc, 1sc in each of next 25sc, 1sc in each of next 4 row-ends, turn.

2nd row 1ch, 1sc in each of first 30sc, 3sc in next sc, 1sc in each of last 30sc.

3rd row 1ch, 1sc in each of first 31sc, 3sc in next sc, 1sc in each of last 31sc.

4th row 1ch, 1sc in each of first 32sc, 3sc in next sc, 1sc in each of last 32sc.

Fasten off.

abbreviations

ch = chain

sc = single crochet

[ ] = work instructions in square brackets as directed.

basketweave block

The woven effect is made by taking the hook alternately to the front and the back when working around the stem of groups of double crochet. This makes the fabric dense, so you may need to use a larger hook than usual for the weight of yarn you choose.

instructions

Make 19ch.

1st row 1dc in 4th ch from hook, 1dc in each of next 15ch. 17 sts.

2nd row 2ch, take hook to front, 1dc around the stem of each of next 3dc, [take hook to back, 1dc around the stem of each of foll 3dc, take hook to front, 1dc around the stem of each of next 3dc] twice, 1dc in next ch.

3rd row 2ch, take hook to back, 1dc around the stem of each of next 3dc, [take hook to front, 1dc around the stem of each of foll 3dc, take hook to back, 1dc around the stem of each of next 3dc] twice, 1dc in next ch.

4th row As 3rd row.

5th row As 2nd row.

Work 2nd to 5th rows once more, then work 2nd, 3rd, and 2nd rows again, do not fasten off.

Edging [1ch, 1sc] in corner, [15sc along edge, 3sc in corner] 4 times omitting last sc, ss in first sc. Fasten off.

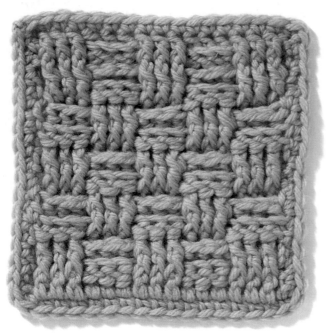

abbreviations

ch = chain

sc = single crochet

foll = following

ss = slip stitch

dc = double crochet

[ ] = work instructions in square brackets as directed.

pentagon

Just four rounds of this five-sided shape are given here; for a larger motif continue working two more stitches on each side between increase groups on every round. Pentagon shapes used alone will join to make a ball, so mix them with other motifs if you want a flat piece of work.

instructions

Wind yarn around finger to form a ring.

1st round 1ch, 1sc in ring, 1ch, 9hdc in ring, ss in top ch. 10 sts.

2nd round 1ch, 1sc in same place as ss, 1ch, 1hdc in same place as ss, [1hdc in next hdc, 3hdc in foll hdc] 4 times, 1hdc in last hdc, 1hdc in same place as first sc, ss in top ch. 20 sts.

3rd round 1ch, [1sc, 1ch, 1hdc] in same place as ss, [1hdc in each of next 3hdc, 3hdc in foll hdc] 4 times, 1hdc in each of next 3hdc, 1hdc in same place as first sc, ss in top ch. 30 sts.

4th round 1ch, [1sc, 1ch, 1hdc] in same place as ss, [1hdc in each of next 5hdc, 3hdc in foll hdc] 4 times, 1hdc in each of next 5hdc, 1hdc in same place as first sc, ss in top ch. 40 sts. Fasten off.

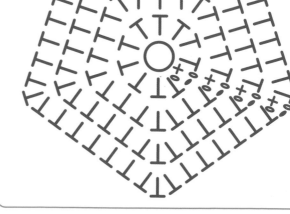

abbreviations and key

● ch = chain

✚ sc = single crochet

foll = following

T hdc = half double crochet

● ss = slip stitch

st(s) = stitch(es)

[ ] = work instructions in square brackets as directed.

double crochet hexagon

A six-sided shape is one of the most useful and versatile patchwork motifs. It takes just three rounds to establish the increases. Work more rounds in the same way for a larger motif, or choose a shorter stitch for a smaller motif.

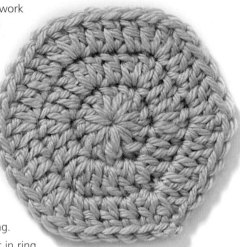

instructions

Wind yarn around finger to form a ring.

1st round 1ch, 1sc in ring, 2ch, 11dc in ring, ss in 2nd ch. 12 sts.

2nd round 1ch, [1sc, 2ch, 1dc] in same place as ss, [1dc in next dc, 3dc in foll dc] 5 times, 1dc in next dc, 1dc in same place as first sc, ss in 2nd ch. 24 sts.

3rd round 1ch, [1sc, 2ch, 1dc] in same place as ss, [1dc in each of next 3dc, 3dc in foll dc] 5 times, 1dc in each of next 3dc, 1dc in same place as first sc, ss in 2nd ch. 36 sts. Fasten off.

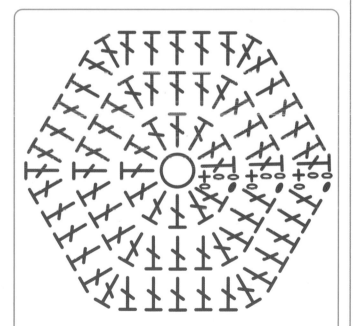

abbreviations and key

o ch = chain

+ sc = single crochet

• ss = slip stitch

st(s) = stitch(es)

⊤ dc = double crochet

[ ] = work instructions in square brackets as directed.

two-color square

This is just a single crochet square worked in rows, but diagonally divided into two colors. The squares may be simple but they can be joined patchwork fashion to create different designs, such as wild goose chase, pinwheel, or pieced star.

instructions

Colors: Cream (A) and turquoise (B).

Using A, make 13ch.

1st row (WS) 1sc in 2nd ch from hook, 1sc in each of next 10ch, change to B, 1sc in last ch. 12 sts.

2nd row 1ch, 1sc in each of first 2sc, change to A, 1sc in each of last 10sc.

3rd row 1ch, 1sc in each of first 9sc, change to B, 1sc in each of last 3sc.

4th row 1ch, 1sc in each of first 4sc, change to A, 1sc in each of last 8sc.

5th row 1ch, 1sc in each of first 7sc, change to B, 1sc in each of last 5sc.

6th row 1ch, 1sc in each of first 6sc, change to A, 1sc in each of last 6sc.

7th row 1ch, 1sc in each of first 5sc, change to B, 1sc in each of last 7sc.

8th row 1ch, 1sc in each of first 8sc, change to A, 1sc in each of last 4sc.

9th row 1ch, 1sc in each of first 3sc, change to B, 1sc in each of last 9sc.

10th row 1ch, 1sc in each of first 10sc, change to A, 1sc in each of last 2sc.

11th row 1ch, 1sc first sc, change to B, 1sc in each of last 11sc.

12th row 1ch, 1sc in each of 12sc. Do not fasten off, turn.

First half edging Using B, 1ch, 1sc in each of first 11sc, 3sc in last sc, 1sc in each of next 10 row-ends, 2sc in last row-end. Fasten off.

2nd half edging With RS facing, pull a loop of A through first sc in B at top left, 2sc in same sc as sc in B, 1sc in each of next 10 row-ends, 3sc in corner sc, 1sc between each of next 10sc, 1sc in same sc as 2sc in B.

Fasten off and thread end under top loops of next sc in B and back down through last sc in A before darning in end.

abbreviations

ch = chain

sc = single crochet

RS = right side

WS = wrong side.

the projects

Incorporate the motif blocks in a range of fun, easy-to-complete garments and accessories. The projects include cute baby bootees, throws, hats, and cushions.

granny flower square jacket

Have fun playing with a wild mix of colors when you make the squares, then join them and work the sleeves and edgings all in one color to unify the color scheme.

size
To fit: age 2 to 3 years.
Chest: 26in (66cm)
Length: 14⅛in (36cm)
Sleeve: (without turning back cuff)10⅝in (27cm)

materials
• 200g wool or wool-mix DK weight yarn in dark green (A)

• 80g same in shades of light green (B)

• 30g same in each of shades of yellow (C), shades of orange (D), and shades of pink (E)

• E/4 (3.50mm) crochet hook

• 4 buttons

gauge
Each square measures 3⅛ x 3⅛in, 17 sts and 10 rows to 4in over double crochet both using DK yarn and E4 (3.50mm) hook. Change hook size, if necessary, to obtain this size square and this gauge.

abbreviations
ch = chain; **sc** = single crochet; **dc** = double crochet; **2dctog** = leaving last loop of each st on the hook work 2dc, yarn over hook and pull through 3 loops on hook; **3dctog** = leaving last loop of each st on the hook work 3dc, yarn over hook and pull through 4 loops on hook; **dec** = decrease; **rep** = repeat; **RS** = right side; **sp** = space; **st(s)** = stitches; **WS** = wrong side; **[ ]** = work instructions in square brackets as directed.

note
• Yarn amounts are approximate as this is a scrap yarn project and different brands of DK yarn will vary in thickness slightly.

BACK AND FRONTS
Make 36 Granny Flower Squares as given on page 11 of Flowers section, using colors for center, petals, and surround at random as wished but working last round of 18 squares with A and last round of 18 squares with B.

Neck shaping For clarity, these part motifs have colors designated but you may vary them according to your color scheme.

Left front neck motif Using C, wind yarn around finger to form a ring.

1st row (RS) 1ch, 2sc in ring, [3ch, 3sc in ring] twice, 3ch, 1sc in ring.

Fasten off.

With WS facing, join B in first sc.

2nd row 1ch, 1sc in first sc, 3ch, [1sc in 2nd of next 3sc, 5ch] twice, 1sc in last sc, turn.

3dctog] twice in next 5ch sp, 3ch, [3dctog, 2ch] twice in same 5ch sp, [3dctog, 2ch, 3dctog, 3ch] twice in last 5ch sp, ss in last sc. Fasten off.

With RS facing, join A in 2nd ch at start of 3rd row.

4th row 1ch, 1sc in 2nd ch, 3ch, * [2dc in next 2ch sp, 1ch] 3 times, [2dc, 3ch, 2dc, 1ch] in next 3ch sp *, rep from * to *, 2dc in next 2ch sp, 1ch, 1dc in last 3ch sp. Fasten off.

Alternating A and B squares, join 16 squares for the back and 7 squares and one neck square for each front, then join shoulders. Join squares with RS together, working 1sc in adjacent spaces of two squares together and 2ch between each sc along seam, the neck squares are a dc group short at the shoulder edge, so work 2ch, 1sc in last corner sp to complete these seams.

SLEEVES

With WS facing, join A in first corner sp of 3rd square on left back edge for left sleeve and on right front for right sleeve.

1st row 1ch, 1sc in same sp as join, [2ch, 1sc in next sp] 23 times, turn.

2nd row 1sc in first sc, 2ch, 2dc in each of next 23 sps, 1dc in last sc. 48 sts.

3rd row 1sc in first dc, 2ch, [1dc in each st] to end.

3rd row forms dc.

Dec row 1sc in first dc, 2ch, 2dctog, [1dc in each dc] to last 3 sts, 2dctog, 1dc in 2nd ch. 46 sts.

Cont in dc, dec in this way at each end of next 3 rows, then on 5 foll 3rd rows. 30 sts. Work 6 more rows dc. Fasten off.

COLLAR

Alternating A and B squares join remaining 6 squares in strip.

Neck edging With RS facing, join A in first st at right front neck.

1st row (RS) 1ch, work 22sc around right front neck to shoulder, 1sc in corner 3ch sp of first back neck square, [2ch, 1sc in next sp] 11 times across back neck, work 22sc down left front neck to front edge.

2nd row 1ch, 1sc in each of first 22sc, 2sc in each of next eleven 2ch sps, 1sc in each of next 22sc. 66 sts.

3rd row 1ch, 1sc in each sc.

Place RS of collar to WS of jacket, work with WS of jacket facing.

Join collar 1sc in corner sp of first square of collar together with first sc of neck

edging, * [1ch, miss 1sc of neck edging, 1sc in next sp and sc together] 5 times across square **, 1sc in first sp of next square and next sc together, rep from * 4 more times, then rep from * to **. Fasten off.

LOWER EDGING

Join side and sleeve seams in the same way as the squares.

With WS facing, join A in first corner sp of right front.

1st row 1ch, 1sc in same sp as join, [2ch, 1sc in next sp] 47 times.

2nd row (RS) 1sc in first sc, 2ch, 3dc in each 2ch sp, 1dc in last sc. 143 sts.

Work 2 more rows dc and 1 row sc.

Fasten off.

BANDS

Left front With WS facing, join A in first sc row-end at lower edge.

1st row 1ch, 1sc in sc row-end, [2ch, 1sc in next dc row-end] twice, 2ch, 1sc in next sc row-end, [2ch, 1sc in next sp] 21 times, 1sc in each of last 3 sc row-ends.

2nd row 1ch, 1sc in each of first 4sc, 2sc in each 2ch sp, 1sc in last sc. 53 sts.

3rd row 1ch, 1sc in each sc **.

Work 4 more rows sc. Fasten off.

Right front With WS facing, join A in first sc row-end at neck edge, starting 1st row, 1ch, 1sc in each of first 3 row-ends, 1sc in next sp, work to match left front band to **.

Buttonhole row (RS) 1ch, 1sc in each of first 19sc, [2ch, miss 2sc, 1sc in each of next 8sc] 3 times, 2ch, miss 2sc, 1sc in each of last 2sc.

Working 2sc in each 2ch sp on next row, work 3 more rows sc. Fasten off.

COLLAR EDGING

With WS facing, join A in first corner sp at neck edge of collar. Working 1sc, 2ch, 1sc in each corner sp, on 1st row, 2sc, 2ch, 2sc in each corner sp on 2nd row and 2sc in each corner sp on 3rd row, work 3 rows in same way as bands.

Fasten off.

TO COMPLETE

Press according to ball band of most delicate yarn. Sew row-ends of collar edging to bands. Darn in ends. Sew on buttons.

3rd row 1ch, 1sc in first sc, 2ch, [3dctog, 2ch, 3dctog, 3ch, 3dctog, 2ch, 3dctog] in first 5ch sp, [2ch, 3dctog] twice in next 5ch sp, 3ch, [3dctog, 2ch] twice in same 5ch sp, [3dctog, 2ch, 3dctog] in next 3ch sp, 3ch, ss in last sc. Fasten off.

With RS facing, join another shade of B in 2nd ch at start of 3rd row.

4th row 1ch, 1sc in 2nd ch, 3ch, 2dc in next 2ch sp, * 1ch, [2dc, 3ch, 2dc] in next 3ch sp, [1ch, 2dc in next 2ch sp] 3 times, rep from * once more, 1ch, 1dc in last 3ch sp. Fasten off.

Right neck square Using C, wind yarn around finger to form a ring.

1st row (RS) 1ch, 1sc in ring, [3ch, 3sc in ring] twice, 3ch, 2sc in ring.

Fasten off. With WS facing, join B in first sc.

2nd row 1ch, 1sc in first sc, [5ch, 1sc in 2nd of next 3sc] twice, 3ch, 1sc in last sc, turn.

3rd row Ss in 3ch sp, 1ch, [1sc, 2ch, 3dctog, 2ch, 3dctog] in first 3ch sp, [2ch,

filet flower top & sweater

Join four Filet Flower motifs to make a block for the front and another four for the back, then incorporate the blocks into a gently shaped double crochet fabric to make a cropped top, or add more rows and three-quarter length sleeves for a fitted sweater.

sizes

To fit bust:
32(**34**:36:**38**:40)in/81(**86**:91:**97**:102)cm

Black top

Bust: 32½(**34½**:36½:**39**:41)in/
82.5(**88**:93.5:**99**:104.5)cm;
length: 17(**17¾**:18:**18¼**:18¾)in/
44(**45**:46:**46.5**:47.5)cm

Cream sweater

Bust: as top;
length: 20(**20¼**:20½:**21**:21¼)in/
51(**51.5**:52.5:**53.5**:54)cm;
sleeve: 13in (33cm)

Figures in round brackets refer to larger sizes; one figure refers to all sizes.

materials

For the black top:

• 2(**2**:3:**3**:3) x 100g balls of 4ply cotton in black

For the cream sweater:

• 4(**4**:4:**5**:5) x 100g balls of 4ply cotton in cream

For both:

• C/2 (2.50mm) crochet hook

gauge

22 sts and 12 rows to 4in over double crochet, each mesh and flower motif measures 3½in square, four motifs joined and edged measure 9in all using C/2 (2.50mm) hook. Change hook size, if necessary, to obtain these gauges.

abbreviations

beg = beginning; **ch** = chain; **cont** = continue; **dec** = decrease; **sc** = single crochet; **dc** = double crochet; **foll** = following; **inc** = increase; **rep** = repeat; **RS** = right side; **sp(s)** = space(s); **ss** = slip stitch; **st(s)** = stitch(es); **tog** = together; **tr** = treble; **2trtog** = leaving last loop of each st on hook, work 2tr, yo and pull through all 3 loops on hook; **3trtog** = leaving last loop of each st on hook, work 3tr, yo and pull through all 4 loops on hook; **WS** = wrong side; **yo** = yarn over; **[ ]** = work instructions in square brackets as directed.

note

• Yarn amounts may vary depending on the brand used. The cotton used for the garments in the pictures has approximately 361 yards to a 100g ball.

black top

FILET FLOWER BLOCK

Four Filet Flower motifs are joined then little infill flowers and an edging are added to complete each block.

1st Filet Flower motif Work Filet Flower as given on page 22 in the Flowers section.

2nd Filet Flower motif Work as 1st motif to 5th round.

5th round * [7ch, 1sc in next 9ch sp] twice, 9ch, 1sc in next 9ch sp, rep from * twice, [7ch, 1sc in next 9ch sp] twice, 4ch, 1sc in corner 9ch sp of 1st motif, 4ch, ss in 5th ss. Fasten off.

3rd Filet Flower motif Work as 1st motif to 5th round. Work 5th round as 2nd motif, joining into next 9ch sp of 1st motif.

4th Filet Flower motif Work as 1st motif to 5th round. Working in same way as 2nd motif, join into corner 9ch sps of 2nd and 3rd motifs, so making a large block with a hole at the center. Fasten off.

Center joining flower Wind yarn twice around finger to form a ring, insert hook in ring, yo, and pull through.

1st round 1ch, 8sc in ring, ss in 1st sc.

2nd round 2ch, [1sc in next sc, 1ch] 7 times, ss in first ch.

3rd round 4ch, 2trtog in first 1ch sp, 2ch, with WS tog work 1sc in first 7ch sp of 1st Filet Flower motif, 2ch, * 3trtog in next 1ch sp, 2ch, with WS tog work 1sc in next 7ch sp of 1st motif, 2ch, working into 7ch sps of 2nd, then 3rd and 4th motifs, rep from * 6 more times, ss in 4th ch. Fasten off.

Side joining flowers

Joining into two 7ch sps of each motif at the sides, work as center flower until 5 petals have been completed. Fasten off.

Corner joining flowers Joining into the two 7ch sps at each corner, work as center flower until 3 petals have been completed. Fasten off.

1st block edging round With RS facing, join yarn with a sc in center 1ch sp of a side flower, 1sc in next 1ch sp, * 5ch, 1tr in top of petal, 5ch, 1dc in next 9ch sp, 5ch, 1tr in top of petal, 7ch, 1sc in corner 1ch sp, 7ch, 1tr in top of petal, 5ch, 1dc in 9ch sp, 5ch, 1tr in top of petal, 5ch, 1sc in each of next three 1ch sps, rep from *, ending 1sc in next 1ch sp, ss in first sc.

2nd block edging round 5ch, * 1dc in next 5ch sp, 1ch, 1dc in same 5ch sp, 1ch *, 1dc in tr, 1ch, rep from * to *, 1dc in dc, 1ch, rep from * to *, 1dc in tr, 1ch, ** 1dc in next 7ch sp, 1ch, [1dc in same 7ch sp, 1ch] twice **, 1dc in corner sc, 1ch, rep from ** to **, 1dc in tr, 1ch, rep from * to *, 1dc in dc, 1ch, rep from * to *, 1dc in tr, 1ch, rep from * to *, miss 1sc, 1dc in next sc, 1ch, rep from first * to end, omitting last dc, ss in 3rd ch.

Fasten off.

Make a 2nd block in the same way.

BACK

1st row (RS) 3ch, 1sc in 3rd ch from hook, [4ch, 1sc in 3rd ch from hook] 41(**44**:47:**50**:53) times. 42(**45**:48:**51**:54) picots.

2nd row Ss in 1st picot, 5ch, miss 1ch, [1dc in next picot, 2ch, miss 1ch] 40(**43**:46:**49**:52) times, 1dc in last picot.

3rd row 3ch, [1dc in 2ch sp, 1dc in next dc] to end, working last dc in 3rd ch. 83(**89**:95:**101**:107) sts.

4th row 3ch, miss 1st dc, 1dc in each dc to last st, 1dc in 3rd ch.

4th row forms double crochet patt **. Cont in dc, work 2 more rows.

Joining row (RS) 3ch, miss first dc, 1dc in each of next 14(**17**:20:**23**:26) dc, with WS of filet flower block and back tog, ss in center dc at corner, [2ch, miss 1dc of back, ss in next dc of back, 2ch, ss in next dc of block] 26 times, so ending at center dc at next corner of block, miss next dc of back, 1dc in each of next 14(**17**:20:**23**:26) dc of back, 1dc in 3rd ch.

Left side. 1st row (WS) 3ch, miss 1st dc, 1dc in each of next 13(**16**:19:**22**:25) dc, miss next dc, ss in first 1ch sp at side of block, ss in next 1ch sp of block, turn.

2nd row 1dc in each dc to last st, 1dc in 3rd ch. 14(**17**:20:**23**:26) sts.

Cont in dc joining to next two 1ch sps at side of block on every WS row, work 4 more rows. Cont in dc joining to block, inc by working in dc usually missed at beg of next row and on 4 foll 4th rows. 19(**22**:25:**28**:31) sts. Work 2 more rows.

Shape armhole. Next row (RS) Work to last 5 sts, turn. 14(**17**:20:**23**:26) sts.

Next row 2ch, miss 1st dc, 1dc in each of next 13(**16**:19:**22**:25) dc, ss to center dc corner of block. 13(**16**:19:**22**:25) sts. Fasten off.

Right side With WS facing, join yarn to first 1ch sp at side of block, miss 1dc of back, 1dc in each of next 13(**16**:19:**22**:25)

dc, 1dc in 3rd ch. 14(**17**:20:**23**:26) sts.

Cont in dc joining to spaces of block on RS rows in same way as left side, work 5 more rows, then inc one st by working 2dc in 3rd ch at end of next row and on 4 foll 4th rows. 19(**22**:25:**28**:31) sts. Work 2 more rows.

Shape armhole. Next row (RS) Ss in each of first 6dc, 3ch, miss dc with last ss, 1dc in each dc to end, ss in ch sp of block. 14(**17**:20:**23**:26) sts.

Next row Ss in center dc at corner of block, 1dc in each of next 12(**15**:18:**21**:24) dc, work 2dctog in next 2 sts. 13(**16**:19:**22**:25) sts.

Yoke. Next row (RS) 2ch, miss first st, 1dc in each of next 12(**15**:18:**21**:24) dc of right side, 1dc in center dc at corner of block, [1dc in next sp, 1dc in next dc] 26 times, 1dc in each of next 11(**14**:17:**20**:23) dc of left side, 2dctog. 77(**83**:89:**95**:101) sts.

Cont in dc, dec at set at each end of next 5(**6**:7:**8**:9) rows. 67(**71**:75:**79**:83) sts ***. Work 8 more rows dc.

Shape neck. Next row 3ch, miss first dc, 1dc in each of next 11(**13**:15:**17**:19) dc, turn. 12(**14**:16:**18**:20) sts. Cont in dc,

work 5 rows. Fasten off. With RS facing, leave center 43 dc, join yarn in next dc, 3ch, 1dc in each dc to last st, 1dc in 3rd ch. 12(**14**:16:**18**:20) sts. Work 5 more rows dc.

Fasten off.

FRONT

Work as given for back to ***.

Work 2 more rows dc.

Shape neck As given for back, working 11 more rows instead of 5, at each side.

EDGINGS

Matching sts, join shoulders.

Armholes With RS facing, join yarn in first st at underarm. Spacing sts evenly around edge, work 1ch, [1sc in edge, 3ch, ss in side of last sc, 1sc in edge] to end, ss in first sc. Fasten off.

Neck Join yarn with 1ch in right shoulder seam, work in same way as armhole edging around neck. Ss in first sc. Fasten off.

TO COMPLETE

Press according to ball band. Join side seams. Darn in ends.

cream sweater

BACK

Work as given for top to **. Cont in dc, work 10 more rows.

Complete as given for top from joining row.

FRONT

Work as given for top back to **. Cont in dc, work 10 more rows.

Cont as given for top from joining row to ***. Work 2 more rows dc.

Work neck shaping as given for top front.

SLEEVES

Working in same way as given for first row of lower edge of back, make 30(**31**:32:**33**:34) picots.

2nd row Ss in 1st picot, 5ch, miss 1ch, [1dc in next picot, 2ch, miss 1ch] 28(**29**:30:**31**:32) times, 1dc in last picot.

3rd row 3ch, [1dc in 2ch sp, 1dc in next dc] to end, working last dc in 3rd ch. 59(**61**:63:**65**:67) sts.

4th row 3ch, miss 1st dc, 1dc in each dc to last st, 1dc in 3rd ch.

4th row forms dc **. Cont in dc, work 2 more rows.

Inc row 3ch, 1dc in first dc usually missed, 1dc in each dc to last st, 2dc in 3rd ch. 61(**63**:65:**67**:69) sts.

Cont in dc, inc in this way at each end of 7 foll 4th rows. 75(**77**:79:**81**:83) sts. Work 6 rows.

Shape top Ss in each of next 6 dc, 3ch, miss dc with last ss, 1dc in each dc to last 5 sts, turn. 65(**67**:69:**71**:73) sts. Dec in same way as back armholes at each end of next 7(**8**:9:**10**:11) rows. 51 sts. Fasten off.

TO COMPLETE

Matching sts, join shoulders. Work neck edging as given for top. Set in sleeves. Press according to ball band. Join side and sleeve seams. Darn in ends.

silhouette flower hat

Work the Silhouette Flower Medallion on page 27 for the top of the hat, then continue in rounds of double crochet and finish with a pretty edging for a sweet little welcome-to-the-world present.

size

To fit: age 0 to 3 months

Actual measurement: 12¾in (32.5cm) around head

materials

• 1 x 50g ball of 4ply wool

• C/2 (2.50mm) crochet hook

gauge

The Silhouette Flower Medallion measures 4¾in (12cm) across, 22 sts and 14 rows to 4in (10cm) over double crochet worked in rounds both using 4ply wool and C/2 (2.50mm) hook. Change hook size, if necessary, to obtain this size motif and this gauge.

abbreviations

ch = chain; **sc** = single crochet; **dc** = double crochet; **sp** = space; **ss** = slip stitch; **[ ]** = work instructions in square brackets as directed.

note

• The pure wool 4ply used for this hat has approximately 200 yards to a 50g ball.

Crown Make a Silhouette Flower Medallion as given on page 27 in the Lace section, do not fasten off.

Brim. 1st round Ss in first 3ch sp, 1ch, 1sc in same 3ch sp, 3ch, [1sc in next 3ch sp, 3ch] 23 times, ss in first sc.

2nd round Ss in first 3ch sp, 1ch, [1sc, 2ch, 2dc] in same 3ch sp, 3dc in each of next 23 sps, ss in 2nd ch. 72 sts.

clematis coverlet

Alternate little Clematis squares from page 19 of the Flowers section, with plain green Double Crochet Squares from page 92 of the Geometrics section for a pretty, flowery crib cover or afghan.

3rd round 1ch, 1sc in same place as ss, 2ch, [1dc in each dc] to end, ss in 2nd ch.

3rd round forms dc. Work 12 more rounds dc.

Edging. 1st round 1ch, 1sc in same dc as ss, [3ch, miss 1dc, 1sc in next dc] 35 times, 3ch, miss last dc, ss in first sc, turn.

2nd round Ss in first 3ch sp, 1ch, [1sc, 1dc, 4ch, ss in 4th ch from hook, 1dc, 1sc] in each 3ch sp, ss in first sc.

Fasten off. Darn in ends. Fold front of brim back.

victorian aster baby's bootees

These bootees are worked mainly in half double crochet so they're quick to do. The Victorian Aster motifs on page 10 of the Flowers section make a delicate, lacy decoration when scaled down in fine yarn and worked all in one color to match the bootees.

size
To fit: age 0 to 3 months

Actual measurements: 3½in (9cm) along sole

materials
• 1 x 50g ball of 4ply wool
• C/2 (2.50mm) crochet hook

gauge
22 sts and 20 rows to 4in (10cm) over half double crochet using 4ply wool and C/2 (2.50mm) hook. Change hook size, if necessary, to obtain this gauge.

abbreviations
ch = chain; **cont** = continue; **sc** = single crochet; **dc** = double crochet; **dec** = decrease; **hdc** = half double crochet; **2hdctog** = yo, insert hook in first st, yo and pull through, yo, insert hook in 2nd st, yo and pull through, yo and pull through 5 loops on hook; **RS** = right side; **sp** = space; **ss** = slip stitch; **st(s)** = stitch(es); **yo** = yarn over; **[ ]** = work instructions in square brackets as directed.

notes
• The pure wool 4ply used for the bootees has approximately 200 yards to a 50g ball.

• Do not count the 2ch at the start of each row of hdc as a stitch.

TOP

1st row 5ch, 1dc in 5th ch from hook, [4ch, 1dc in previous dc] 17 times, do not turn, work next row along straight edge.

2nd row (RS) 1ch, [2sc in each dc sp] to end. 36 sts.

3rd row 2ch, [1hdc in each sc] to end.

4th row 2ch, [1hdc in each hdc] to end.

4th row forms hdc. Cont in hdc, work 13 more rows.

Fasten off.

INSTEP

Turn and join yarn in 11th hdc.

1st row (RS) 2ch, 1hdc in same place as join, 1hdc in each of next 15hdc, turn and complete instep on these 16 sts.

Cont in hdc, work 5 rows.

Dec row 2ch, 2hdctog, [1hdc in each hdc] to last 2hdc, 2hdctog.

Cont in hdc, dec in this way at each end of next 3 rows. 8 sts.

Fasten off.

SOLE

Join yarn in first hdc at right of last row of top.

1st row (RS) 2ch, 1hdc in each of 10hdc along first side of last row of top, 10hdc in row-ends along first side of instep, 8hdc across toe, 10hdc in row-ends down 2nd side of instep, 1hdc in each of 10hdc along 2nd side of last row of top. 48 sts.

Work 1 row.

1st dec row 2ch, 1hdc in first hdc, 2hdctog, 1hdc in each of next 15hdc, [2hdctog] twice, 1hdc in each of next 4hdc, [2hdctog] twice, 1hdc in each of next 15hdc, 2hdctog, 1hdc in last hdc. 42 sts.

Work 1 row.

2nd dec row 2ch, 1hdc in first hdc, 2hdctog, 1hdc in each of next 11hdc, [2hdctog] 3 times, 1hdc in each of next 2hdc, [2hdctog] 3 times, 1hdc in each of next 11hdc, 2hdctog, 1hdc in last hdc. 34 sts.

Work 1 row.

3rd dec row 2ch, 1hdc in first hdc, 2hdctog, 1hdc in each of next 8hdc, [2hdctog] 6 times, 1hdc in each of next 8hdc, 2hdctog, 1hdc in last hdc. 26 sts.

Fasten off.

With WS facing, join yarn in first sp at top of bootee.

Edging row 1ch, [1sc, 1dc, 4ch, ss in 4th ch from hook, 1dc, 1sc] in each sp.

Fasten off.

DECORATIONS

Make two Victorian Aster motifs as given in the Flowers section on page 10. To work the motifs in one color, where appropriate slip stitch into spaces at start of rounds instead of breaking off and rejoining yarn. To give more definition in the center, on the 2nd and 3rd rounds, work around the stem of the stitches in the previous round instead of into the back loop. Fasten off at the end of the 8th round.

TO COMPLETE

Join sole and back seams, reversing seam for turn down tops. Sew on flowers.

rosette hexagon top

Joining flower hexagons in a half-drop arrangement makes a lovely, lacy top that can be layered over a sweater in winter or a camisole in the summer.

sizes

To fit: bust 32 to 34(**36 to 38**)in./ 81 to 86(**91 to 97**)cm

Actual measurements: bust 37¾(**40**)in/96(**102**)cm; **length** (to center back neck) 23(**24¼**)in/58(**61.5**)cm; **sleeve** 12½(**13½**)in/32(**34**)cm

Figures in round brackets refer to larger size; one figure refers to both sizes.

materials

• 8(**9**) x 50g balls of Debbie Bliss Cashmerino DK in magenta
• E/4 (3.50mm) (F/5 [4.00mm]) crochet hook

gauge

Using E/4 (3.50mm) hook, each motif measures 3⅛in (8cm), using F/5 (4.00mm) hook each motif measures 3⅜in (8.5cm). Change hook sizes, if necessary, to obtain these motif sizes.

abbreviations

ch = chain; **cont** = continue; **sc** = single crochet; **dc** = double crochet; **rep** = repeat; **sp(s)** = space(s); **ss** = slip stitch; **st(s)** = stitch(es); [ ] = work instructions in square brackets as directed.

notes

• The motifs are joined in rounds working from the top down with spaces left for the sleeves, which are worked later.

• To join motifs, work 2ch, 1sc in sp of adjacent motif, 2ch instead of 4ch, where appropriate on 3rd round.

• Darn in ends as you work and there's no making up to do!

YOKE

1st round of motifs Working Rosette Hexagon from page 32 in the Lace section, make the first motif. Make and join 2nd motif to 2 sps at one side of 1st motif. Leaving 4 sps free above and below each time, make and join 11 more motifs. Make 14th motif, joining to 2 sps of 13th motif and 2 sps of 1st motif to form a ring.

2nd round of motifs Make and join 1st motif to 2 sps of each of 2 adjacent motifs of first round. Join the next 12 motifs to the previous motif and to the two motifs above, then join 14th motif to 13th motif, 2 above and 1st motif.

Shape armholes Mark 1st, 2nd, 8th and

9th motifs of 2nd round.

3rd round of motifs Omitting marked motifs, join 12 motifs to each other and to the unmarked motifs of the 2nd round.

Cont in rounds of 12 motifs, work 4 more rounds.

SLEEVES

1st round of motifs Join first motif at center of sleeve top between the 2 marked motifs of the 2nd round. Join 2nd motif at the underarm between 2 motifs of 3rd round. Join first 2 chain groups of 3rd motif to 2 sps at right edge of 1st motif, work 4 more chain groups, then join next 2 chain groups to 2 sps at side of 2nd motif, foll chain group to next sp of next motif of 3rd round, miss next sp of same motif and join foll 2 chain groups to 2 sps of next motif of 2nd round, miss first sp of foll motif and join last chain group to last sp. Starting with underarm motif,

join 4th motif in the same way.

Cont in rounds of 4 motifs, work 3 more rounds.

NECK EDGING

With RS facing, join yarn in 2nd sp of right shoulder motif.

1st round 1ch, 1sc in same sp as join, [4ch, 1sc in next sp of same motif] twice, * 4ch, 1sc over sc join between motifs, [4ch, 1sc in next sp] 4 times, rep from * 12 more times, 4ch, 1sc over sc join, 4ch, 1sc in last sp, 4ch, ss in first sc.

2nd round Ss in first 4ch sp, 1ch, [1sc, 3ch, 1dc, 1ch] in same 4ch sp, [1dc, 1ch] twice in next 4ch sp, * [1dc, 1ch] in each of next two 4ch sps, [1dc, 1ch] twice in each of next three 4ch sps, rep from * 12 more times, [1dc, 1ch] in each of next two 4ch sps, [1dc, 1ch] twice in last 4ch sp, ss in 2nd ch.

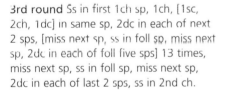

3rd round Ss in first 1ch sp, 1ch, [1sc, 2ch, 1dc] in same sp, 2dc in each of next 2 sps, [miss next sp, ss in foll sp, miss next sp, 2dc in each of foll five sps] 13 times, miss next sp, ss in foll sp, miss next sp, 2dc in each of last 2 sps, ss in 2nd ch.

4th round 1ch, 1sc in same place as ss, 3ch, [1dc in next dc, 1ch] 3 times, * miss next 5 sts, [1dc in next dc, 1ch] 6 times, rep from * 12 more times, miss next 5 sts, [1dc in next dc, 1ch] twice, ss in 2nd ch.

5th round Ss in first 1ch sp, 1ch, [1sc, 2ch, 1dc] in same sp, 2dc in foll sp, * miss next sp, ss in foll sp, miss next sp, 2dc in foll sp, 3dc in next sp, 2dc in foll sp, rep from *12 more times, miss next sp, ss in foll sp, miss next sp, 2dc in last sp, 1dc in first sp, ss in 2nd ch.

Fasten off.

double crochet amish afghan

This afghan is inspired by the exquisite interplay of dark and bright colors of Amish patchwork. It uses the Double Crochet Square from page 92 in the Geometric section.

size
Approximately 32¼ x 51in (82 x 130cm)

materials
• approximately 500g wool DK weight yarn, in dark or dull shades of purple, green, and brown (A)

• 250g same in light or bright pink, lilac, orange, and green (B)

• 100g same in dark purple (C)

• E/4 (3.50mm) crochet hook

gauge
Each Double Crochet Square measures 3⅛in (8cm) using wool DK weight yarn and E/4 (3.50mm) hook. Change hook size, if necessary, to obtain this size square.

CENTER
Using A, make 107 Double Crochet Squares. Using B, make 53 squares. Arranging the squares in an oblong 10 squares wide and 16 squares high, start with one A square in the top left corner, then alternating one B and two A squares, continue in diagonal left slanting rows of two lines of A and one line of B squares, ending with two A at the lower right corner. Using C, join squares with flat seams over-sewn on the right side.

BORDER
Using C, work two rounds of single crochet, working into each double crochet and space on the first round with 3 stitches into the corner spaces and working 3 stitches in each corner stitch on the 2nd round.

TO COMPLETE
Press. Darn in ends.

christmas tree slipper socks

These simple socks are worked in sturdy single crochet. Make just one sock, decorate it with a tree motif, and fill it with presents in the traditional way, or make a pair and you have a present to keep feet cozy on Christmas day.

sizes

To fit: small(**medium**:large) feet

Height (with top folded down): 9(9½:9½)in/23(**24**:24)cm

Sole: 7(8½:10¼)in/18(**22**:26)cm

Figures in round brackets refer to larger sizes; one figure refers to all sizes.

materials

For the pair of socks:

• 2(**2**:3) x 100g balls of wool or wool mix Aran weight yarn in red (A)

• 1 x 100g ball of same in cream (B)

• H/8 (5.00mm) crochet hook

For the decoration:

• approximately 10g in total of wool or wool mix DK weight yarn in red, green, and cream

• E/4 (3.50mm) crochet hook

• 20 gold beads and 2 sew-on shiny stars

gauge

14 sts and 18 rows to 4in (10cm) over single crochet using Aran weight yarn and H/8 (5.00mm) hook. Motif height 4¼in (11cm), width at base of tree 3½in (9cm) using DK weight yarn and E/4 (3.50mm) hook. Change hook sizes, if necessary, to obtain this gauge and this size motif.

abbreviations

ch = chain; **sc** = single crochet; **2sctog** = insert hook in first st and pull loop through, insert hook in 2nd st and pull loop through, yarn around hook and pull through 3 loops on hook; **dec** = decrease; **rep** = repeat; **RS** = right side; **ss** = slip stitch; **st(s)** = stitch(es); **[ ]** = work instructions in square brackets as directed.

notes

• If you're making just one sock, you'll need half the amount of A and about 20g of B.

• The Aran weight yarn used for the socks in the picture is a mix of wool, nylon, and acrylic and has approximately 180 yards to a 100g ball.

LEG

Using A, make 37(**41**:45) ch loosely, ss in first ch to form a ring.

1st round (RS) 1ch, 1sc in same ch as ss, 1sc in each of 36(**40**:44) ch, ss in first sc, turn. 37(**41**:45) sts.

2nd round 1ch, [1sc in each sc] to end, ss in first sc, turn.

2nd round forms sc.

Turning each time, work 22 more rounds sc.

Dec round 1ch, 1sc in each of first 2sc, 2sctog, [1sc in each sc] to last 4sc, 2sctog, 1sc in each of last 2sc, ss in first sc, turn. 35(**39**:43) sts.

Turning each time, work 7 more rounds sc, then work dec round again. 33(**37**:41) sts.

Work 1 round sc, turn.

Instep. 1st row (RS) 1ch, 1sc in each of next 22(**24**:26)sc, mark next sc with contrast thread, turn.

2nd row 1ch, 1sc in each of first 11sc, turn. 11 sts.

Turning each time, work 10(**14**:18) rows sc on these 11 sts.

Dec row 1ch, 1sc in first sc, [1sc in next sc, 2sctog] 3 times, 1sc in last sc. 8 sts. Fasten off.

With RS facing, join A in marked sc of first row of instep, 1ch, 1sc in same sc as join, 1sc in each of next 10(**12**:14)sc, ss in first sc of first row, turn.

Next round 1ch, 1sc in each of next 11(**13**:15)sc, 1sc in each of next 10(**14**:18) row-ends, 1sc in each of next 8sc, 1sc in each of next 10(**14**:18) row-ends, 1sc in each of last 11(**13**:15)sc, ss in first sc, turn. 50(**62**:74) sts.

Turning each time, work 5(**7**:7) rounds sc.

Using B, work 1 round sc.

Using A, work 1 round sc.

SOLE

Cont in A, do not turn at ends of rounds.

1st round 1ch, 1sc in same sc as ss, * [2sctog] twice, 1sc in each of next 15(**21**:26)sc, [2sctog] twice *, 1sc in each of next 2(**2**:4)sc, rep from * to *, 1sc in last sc, ss in first sc. 42(**54**:66) sts.

Work 1 round sc.

3rd round 1ch, 1sc in same sc as ss, * [2sctog] twice, 1sc in each of next 11(**17**:22)sc, [2sctog] twice *, 1sc in each of next 2(**2**:4)sc, rep from * to *, ss in first sc. 34(**46**:58) sts.

4th round 1ch, 1sc in same sc as ss, * [2sctog] twice, 1sc in each of next 7(**13**:18)sc, [2sctog] twice *, 1sc in each of next 2(2:4)sc, rep from * to *, ss in first sc. 26(38:50) sts.

5th round 1ch, 1sc in same sc as ss, * [2sctog] twice, 1sc in each of next 3(9:14)sc, [2sctog] twice *, 1sc in each of next 2(2:4)sc, rep from * to *, ss in first sc. 18(30:42) sts.

Fasten off leaving a long end. Using end, join foot seam.

CUFF

With RS facing, join A to first ch of 1st round at top of leg. Working 1st round in base of chain and turning each time, work

7 rounds sc. Change to B. Work 2 rounds sc. Fasten off. Darn in ends. Fold cuff down.

Make 2nd sock in the same way.

DECORATION

Using DK yarn, make two Christmas Tree motifs as given on page 85 in the Pictures section. Sew 10 gold beads scattered at random and one star on each Christmas Tree, sew one motif on each sock.

geometric blocks house picture

This design puts triangle and square geometric shapes together with simple areas of single crochet to create a traditional house-on-a-hill picture block. Make one to hang on the wall as a housewarming present or to use as a little coverlet. Piece blocks together before adding an edging for a bigger blanket.

size
Center block: 9½ x 11in (24 x 28cm); with border: 17¼ x 20½in (44 x 52cm)

materials
• 1 x 50g ball of Debbie Bliss Cashmerino DK in each of cream (A), red (B), pale blue (C), camel (D), blue (E), and green (F)
• 2 x 50g balls same in yellow (G)
• E/4 (3.50mm) crochet hook

gauge
18 sts and 25 rows to 4in (10cm) over sc using E/4 (3.50mm) hook. Change hook size, if necessary, to obtain this gauge

abbreviations
beg = beginning; **ch** = chain; **cont** = continue; **sc** = single crochet; **dc** = double crochet; **foll** = following; **inc** = increase; **RS** = right side; **sp** = space; **st(s)** = stitch(es); **WS** = wrong side; [ ] = work instructions in square brackets as directed.

HOUSE BLOCK

End gable (Make 1 in A) Work a Single Crochet Triangle from page 102 of the Geometric section but turning after the 2nd and every foll round and continuing to inc as set until 8 rounds have been completed. Fasten off.

Door and window (Make 2 in B, 1 in C, and 1 in D) Work a Single Crochet Square from page 102 of the Geometric section, turning after the 2nd round and fastening off at the end of 3rd round.

Narrow oblong (Make 2 in A) Make 8ch.

1st row (WS) 1sc in 2nd ch from hook, [1sc in each ch] to end.

2nd row 1ch, [1sc in each sc] to end.

This row forms sc. Work 12 more rows sc. Fasten off.

Wide oblong (Make 2 in D) Make 10 ch. Work 1st row as given for narrow oblong.

9 sts. Complete as given for narrow oblong.

Roof (Make 1 in B) Make 24ch.

1st row As 1st row of narrow oblong. 23 sts

2nd row 1ch, miss first sc, [1sc in each sc] to last sc, 2sc in last sc.

3rd row 1ch, [1sc in each sc] to end.

Work 2nd and 3rd rows 6 more times, then work 2nd row again. Fasten off.

Assemble house Using appropriate colors and working in sc on RS to join pieces

edge to edge, join one side of each of the two squares in B to make the door. Join narrow oblongs in A at each side of door, then join house end to one edge of triangle. Join squares in C and D in same way as door, then join wide oblongs in D at each side. Join front of house to end of house, then set in roof.

Sky. Left wedge (Make 1 in E)

Make 2ch.

1st row (RS) 1sc in 2nd ch from hook. One st.

2nd row 1ch, 2sc in sc. 2 sts.

3rd row 1ch, 2sc in first sc, 1sc in last sc. 3 sts.

4th row 1ch, [1sc in each sc] to end.

5th row 1ch, 2sc in first sc, [1sc in each sc] to end. 4 sts.

Cont in sc, inc in this way at beg of next 6 RS rows. 10 sts. Fasten off.

Right wedge (Make 1 in E) Make 2ch.

1st row (RS) 1sc in 2nd ch from hook. One st.

2nd row 1ch, 2sc in sc. 2 sts.

3rd row 1ch, 1sc in first sc, 2sc in last sc. 3 sts.

4th row 1ch, [1sc in each sc] to end.

5th row 1ch, [1sc in each sc] to last sc, 2sc in last sc. 4 sts.

Cont in sc, inc in this way at end of next 6 RS rows. 10 sts.

Using B and placing wedges behind edges of roof and gable end, join house to sky with surface sc.

Sky and chimney pots. 1st row (WS) Using E, 1ch, 1sc in each of 10 sc of left wedge, 1sc in point of triangle, 1sc in each of next 7sc of roof, change to D, 1sc in each of next 7sc of roof, change to E, 1sc in each of last 9 sc of roof, 1sc in each of 10sc of right wedge. 44 sts.

2nd row Using E, 1ch, 1sc in each of first 19sc, change to D, 1sc in each of next 7 sc, change to E, 1sc in each of last 18sc.

Work 1 more row sc in colors as set.

4th row Using E, 1ch, 1sc in each of next 20sc, change to B, 1sc in each of next 2sc, change to E, 1sc in next sc, change to B, 1sc

in each of next 2sc, change to E, 1sc in each of next 19sc.

Work 2 more rows sc in colors as set.

Cont in E, work 5 more rows sc. Fasten off.

Ground With RS facing, join F to first ch at lower edge.

1st row 1ch, taking hook between sts, work 44sc along lower edge.

Cont in sc, work 14 rows. Fasten off.

Using A and B for detached chain petals and G for small straight stitches at centers, embroider lazy daisies on area in F.

EDGING

With RS facing, join F in top row-end in F along left edge.

1st round 1ch, 1sc in same place as join, 1sc in each of next 13 row-ends down left edge, 2ch, 1sc in each of 44sc along lower edge, 2ch, 1sc in each of 14 row-ends up right edge, change to E, 1sc in each of next 42 row-ends up right edge, 2ch, 1sc in each of next 44sc along top edge, 2ch, 1sc each of next 42 row-ends down left edge, ss in first sc, turn.

Cont in sc for 3 more rounds, working 1sc, 2ch, 1sc in each corner 2ch sp and changing colors as set. Fasten off.

Border With RS facing join G in a corner 2ch sp, starting 5ch, 1dc in first corner sp and 1dc, 2ch, 1dc in the other corner sps on 1st round and continuing to inc at corners on foll rounds, work 4 rounds double crochet in G, 2 rounds double crochet in F and 2 rounds double crochet in G.

Fasten off.

simple lace block pillow

Many of the motifs in this book are repetitive and can easily be made larger. This design shows how the Simple Lace Block on page 40 of the Lace section, can be extended to make a sleek, modern pillow cover.

size

Finished pillow: 13¾ x 13¾in (35 x 35cm)

materials

• 1 x 100g ball of firm, smooth 4ply cotton

• C/2 (2.50mm) crochet hook

• 13¾ x 13¾in (35 x 35cm) pillow pad and cover

gauge

The first 4 rounds of the Simple Lace Block measure 2¾ x 2¾in (7 x 7cm), when pressed, using 4ply cotton and C/2 (2.50mm) hook. Change hook size, if necessary, to obtain this size square.

1st to 4th rounds Work 1st to 4th rounds of the Simple Lace Block.

5th round Continue in the same way but introduce another panel of double crochet by working 2 chain, 1double crochet in the first 2 chain space, 1 chain, 7 double crochet,

1chain, 1double crochet in the last 2 chain space, 2 chain, on each side between corner double crochet groups.

6th to 11th rounds Work one more double crochet at each end of each side of the square, so ending with 3 panels of 7 double crochet on the 11th round.

12th round Introduce another double crochet panel by starting and ending each side of the square in the same way as the 5th round.

13th to 18th rounds Work as 6th to 11th rounds to complete 5 panels of double crochet stitches.

19th round Work in same way as 18th round but without introducing more panels.

Edging Return to the instructions for the Simple Lace Block and work in the same way as the two edging rounds to finish the square.

To complete Spray the back of the work lightly with starch and press to set the stitches. Sew the square on the front of the pillow pad.

irish rose lace pillow

This exquisite round pillow front has a complete Irish rose motif in the center, surrounded by rings of smaller roses, linked with a picot mesh. The fine yarn gives a delicate effect but because of the open spaces, it's surprisingly fast to finish.

size
To fit: round pillow 15in (38cm) diameter

materials
• 1 x 100g ball of 4ply cotton in cream
• C/2 (2.50mm) crochet hook
• 15in (38cm) round pillow pad with white cover

gauge
Center motif measures 4in (10cm) across, finished pillow front measures 15in (38cm) across using C/2 (2.50mm) hook. Change hook size, if necessary, to obtain this size motif.

abbreviations
ch = chain; sc = single crochet; dc = double crochet; foll = following; hdc = half double crochet; rep = repeat; sp(s) = space(s); ss = slip stitch; st(s) = stitch(es); [ ] = work instructions in square brackets as directed.

notes
• The 4ply cotton used for the pillow has 370 yards (338 metres) to a 100g ball.

• Because the motifs are worked in one color, there's no need to fasten off, simply slip stitch into the next space each time.

Center Make an Irish Rose motif as given on page 7 in the Flowers section.

1st ring of roses. 1st flower Work 6 rounds of Irish Rose motif.

Next round 1ch, 1sc around stem of first sc of 5th round, [9ch, 1sc around stem of next sc of 5th round] 6 times, * 4ch, 1sc between picot and dc of center motif, 4ch *, 1sc around stem of next sc of 5th round, rep from * to *, ss in first sc. Fasten off.

Work 2nd flower in the same way, joining in next 2 sps of center motif and 2 sps of 1st flower. Make and join 5 more flowers in the same way, then 8th flower to 1st flower, center and 7th flower.

1st ring edging With RS facing, join yarn in a sp on the right of two joined sps between flowers.

1st round 1ch, 1sc in same sp as join, * 2ch, 1sc in next sp, [6ch, ss in 4th ch from hook, 7ch, ss in 4th ch from hook, 2ch, 1sc in next sp] 3 times, rep from * 7 times omitting last sc and ending ss in first sc, turn, ss in each st to center between picots, turn.

2nd round 1ch, 1sc between picots in sp, [6ch, ss in 4th ch, 7ch, ss in 4th ch, 2ch, 1sc between picots in next sp] 24 times, omitting last sc, ss in first sc. Fasten off.

2nd ring of roses. 1st motif Work 4 rounds of Irish Rose motif.

Next round 1ch, 1sc around stem of first sc of 3rd round, 4ch, 1sc between picots in first of two sps above a 1st ring flower in 2nd round of edging, 4ch, 1sc around stem of next sc of 3rd round, 4ch, 1sc between picots in next sp of edging, 4 ch, [1sc around stem of next sc of 3rd round, 9ch] 6 times, ss in first sc. Fasten off.

Work 2nd flower in the same way, joining it to two sps of the 1st flower and twice in next sp of edging. Alternating between joining once in each of next two sps of edging and twice in foll sp of edging, make and join 13 more flowers. Join 14th flower to 13th and 1st flowers.

2nd ring edging. 1st round Work as given for 1st round of 1st ring edging but repeat from * 15 times.

2nd round 1ch, 1sc between picots in first sp, 5ch, [1sc between picots in next sp, 5ch] to end, ss in first sc.

3rd round Ss in first sp, 1ch, [1sc, 1hdc, 3dc, 1hdc, 1sc in each sp] to end, ss in first sc. Fasten off.

To complete Darn in ends. Spray starch on back of work and press, turn over and press between petals to raise flowers. Sew on front of pillow cover and insert pillow pad.

popcorn flower octagon block

If you want to make a blanket using the Popcorn Flower Octagons as given on page 19 of the Flowers section, you'll need to fill in the gaps between the eight-sided shapes with Double Crochet Squares on page 92.

size
Joined block: 10in (25cm) across

materials
To make one block as shown:

• approximately 35g of wool DK weight yarn in yellow (A), orange (B), purple (C), and green (D).

• 20g same in light orange (E)

• E/4 (3.50mm) crochet hook

gauge
Each Popcorn Flower Octagon measures 4in (10cm) across, each double crochet square measures 2in (5cm) across both using wool DK weight yarn and E/4 (3.50mm) hook. Change hook size, if necessary, to obtain these sizes.

note

These motifs can be joined because both the octagon and the square have a space, 8 double crochets, and a space on each side.

Octagons Using A, B, C, and D, make four Popcorn Flower Octagons.

Squares Fastening off at the end of the 2nd round, work 5 Double Crochet Squares.

Joining the block Arranging the motifs as in the picture, Join the squares and octagons with single crochet worked on the wrong side to give a neat over-sew effect.

forget-me-not square pillow cover

This pillow cover combines a lively center of four-petal flowers worked in the same way as the Forget-me-not Square on page 9 of the Flowers section, with a frame of simple Double Crochet Squares on page 92 of the Geometric section.

size
Pillow front: 12½ x 12½in (32 x 32 cm)

materials
• 50g of wool or wool mix DK weight yarn in an assortment of at least 12 different shades of pink (A)

• 60g same in deep pink (B)

• 15g in magenta (C)

• E/4 (3.50mm) crochet hook

• 13¾ x 13¾in (35 x 35 cm) pillow pad and cover

gauge
3 joined flowers measure 3⅛in (8cm), each double crochet square measures 3⅛in (8cm) both using wool DK and E/4 (3.50mm) hook. Change hook size, if necessary, to obtain these sizes.

Center Changing shades of A as wished, work in the same way as the center of the Forget-me-not Square but continue to make and join flowers until you have 36 flowers arranged in a 6 x 6 square. Using the lightest shade of A, work a chain and single crochet round in the same way as the 1st round of the border of the Forget me-not Square, then placing 4 stitches in each space, work a round of single crochet.

Frame Using B, make 12 Double Crochet Squares. Join the squares with single crochet on the wrong side to make a frame, then matching the 28 stitches along each side, join the frame to the center with a round of single crochet on the wrong side.

Edging Using C, placing 3 stitches in each corner and one stitch in each double crochet, space and seam along each edge, work a round of single crochet. Work 5 double crochet shells along each edge and finish off with a round of slip stitches over the single crochet round.

To complete Sew front on pillow.

snowflake gloves

Spark up a pair of woolly gloves with winter white Snowflakes on page 24 of the Lace section.

materials
- a small amount of wool 4ply in white
- No. 5 steel (1.75mm) crochet hook
- a pair of woolly gloves

gauge
Each Snowflake measures 2¾in (7cm) across using wool 4ply and No. 5 steel (1.75mm) hook. Change hook size, if necessary, to obtain this size motif.

Motifs Fastening off after the first 4 rounds have been completed, make two Snowflake motifs.

To complete Using white sewing thread, a sharp needle, and tiny stitches, sew the motifs on the back of the gloves. Using white wool and a blunt-pointed needle, embroider short straight stitches radiating out from each motif.

squared circle skinny scarf

Make a long, skinny, lightweight scarf using the Squared Circle motifs on page 30 of the Lace section.

size
4 x 59in (10 x 150cm), excluding fringes

materials
- 1 x 100g ball of smooth 4ply cotton in lilac
- C/2 (2.50mm) crochet hook

gauge
Each Squared Circle motif measures 3½ x 3½in (9 x 9cm) using 4ply cotton and C/2 (2.50mm) hook. Change hook size, if necessary, to obtain this size motif.

Motifs Make 15 Squared Circle motifs. Join motifs in a strip with a single crochet and 2-chain zigzag.

Edging Placing 2 double crochet stitches in each join, one double crochet in each space and one double crochet, 3 chain, one double crochet in each corner space, work around edge of scarf in the same way as the 6th round of the motif.

Fringe Cut four 12in (30 cm) lengths of yarn for each space along the short edges of the scarf, fold in half and loop through a space for each tassel.

To complete Darn in ends. Press scarf and trim fringes level.

filet hearts tablecloth

Work Filet Heart Square motifs on page 97 of the Geometric section in fine cotton and join them in rows to use as a lacy insertion for a special teatime tablecloth. If you're joining motifs in square, work a plain filet mesh motif for each corner.

sunflower square potted plant

This evergreen plant is a bigger, 3D version of the center motif of the Sunflower Square (page 15).

size
Height: Around 9½in (24cm)

materials
- small amounts of wool DK weight yarn in brown (A), yellow (B), and ocher (C)
- small amounts of olive green (D), bright green (E), red (F), black (G)
- E/4 (3.50mm) crochet hook
- 32in (80cm) plastic coated wire
- 6in (15cm) fine wire
- dark stuffing
- a small plant pot and florist's foam

gauge
The flower center measures 2⅛in (5.5cm) across using wool DK weight yarn and E/4 (3.50mm) hook. Change hook size, if necessary, to obtain this size center.

Center Using A, work center of Sunflower Square motif.

1st ring of petals Using B, work in same way as 1st ring of petals on motif but placing one petal in each stitch to make 24 petals.

2nd ring of petals Using C, work petals into the 24 spaces to make 48 petals in all.

Back of flower Using D, work 3 single crochet stitches in each 2 chain space to make 72 stitches in the round. Work another round of single crochet, then reduce the stitches on the next round by missing every third stitch. Work another round on these 48 stitches, then halve the amount of stitches on the next round and on following alternate round. 12 stitches.

Stem Make a loop in the plastic coated wire, insert into back of flower and stretch it to fill the center, fold remaining wire in half and hide end in loop. Stuff the back of the flower, then to close aperture work another round of single crochet on the 12 stitches, reduce to 6 stitches on the next round, then work in single crochet over the stem, covering the end of the wire with a few over-sew stitches after fastening off.

Leaf Using E, F, and G, make the Ladybug on a Leaf as given on page 81 in the Pictures section. Loop fine wire around stem of the sunflower, then thread through leaf to attach leaf to stem.

To complete Leaving a hole for the stem, work a sunflower center for the earth. Insert stem and wedge in pot with florist's foam.

siamese cat mini bag

Turn the Siamese Cat motif on page 76 of the Pictures section into a sweet little bag.

size
6 x 4½in (15 x 11.5cm), excluding handle

materials
- approximately 30g of DK weight pure wool yarn in each of cream (A), blue (B), and soft brown (C)
- embroidery wool in black, bright blue, and pink
- E/4 (3.50mm) crochet hook
- one button

gauge
Siamese Cat motif measures 6 x 4½in (15 x 11cm), 20 stitches to 4in (10cm) over single crochet both using wool DK weight yarn and E/4 (3.50mm) hook. Change hook size, if necessary, to obtain this size motif and this tension.

Front Using colors as given, work the Siamese Cat motif.

Back Using A, make 24 chain for 23 stitches, then work in single crochet until the back measures 6in (15cm).

Edging Work single crochet along the row-ends of one edge of the back, then join the motif to the back by working in single crochet down the left edge, along the lower edge and up the right edge, inserting the hook into the spaces and the edge of the back together, making a chain between each stitch and working an extra single crochet and chain in each corner to keep the edges flat, then work along the top edge of the front.

Handle Using three 48-in (1.2m) lengths of cream and three 48-in (1.2m) lengths of blue, make a two-color twisted cord approximately 39½in (100cm) long. Knot and trim the ends to make tassels. Sew cord on sides of bag. Sew on a button.

121

butterfly blanket

Capture a flock of butterflies on a pretty stroller blanket by working the Butterfly motif on page 68, in a variety of colors.

size
26½ x 32¾in (67 x 83cm)

materials
• 30g of wool or wool-mix DK weight yarn in black (A)

• a total of 150g same in assorted shades of yellow, orange, blue (B), and cream (C)

• 200g same in lime green (D)

• 40g same in dark green (E)

• E/4 (3.50mm) crochet hook

gauge
Each motif measures 7⅞ x 7½in (20 x 19cm) when pressed using wool or wool mix DK weight yarn and E/4 (3.50mm) hook. Change hook size, if necessary, to obtain this size motif.

Motifs Changing B and C as wished but using A for the body and D for the background each time, make 12 Butterfly motifs.

Joining Using E, join the squares with a single crochet and 2-chain zigzag.

Edging Working in the same way as the last round of the background finish the blanket with an edging of one round E and two rounds D.

To complete Press according to the ball band on the most delicate yarn used. Darn in ends.

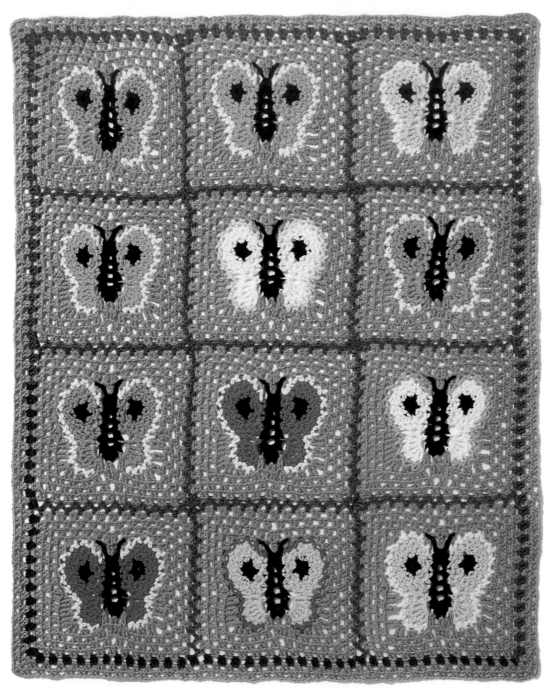

shell-edged flower medallion mohair cape

For a special occasion, make this light and lacy cape by joining Shell-Edged Flower Medallion motifs from page 39 of the Lace section.

size
42in (105cm) around lower edge

materials
- 5 x 25g balls of Sublime Kid Mohair in Vellum, shade 29
- F/5 (4.00mm) crochet hook

gauge
Each medallion measures 6in (15cm) across using Kid Mohair and F/5 (4.00mm) hook. Change hook size, if necessary, to obtain this size motif.

note
The fabric created when joining these motifs is very flexible so the cape will easily adjust to fit bust 32 to 40in (81 x 102cm).

1st line of motifs Joining motifs by working 1chain, a single crochet stitch in adjacent space, 1chain, in place of a 3-chain group of the last round. Starting at the center back lower edge, make 1st motif, then make 2nd motif joining it to 2 spaces of the 1st motif, join the 3rd, 4th, and 5th motifs to the opposite 2 spaces each time so the 5th motif is at the center back neck.

2nd line of motifs The 2nd line of motifs is to the left of the 1st line. Join the 1st motif to next 2 spaces of the 1st motif and next 2 spaces the 2nd motif of the 1st line. Join 2nd, 3rd, and 4th motifs to 2 spaces of the previous motif of 2nd line and next 2 motifs of 1st line. Join 5th motif to 4th motif of 2nd line and 5th motif of 1st line.

3rd line of motifs Working in the same way as 2nd line of motifs, join the 3rd line of motifs to the right of the 1st line.

4th and 5th lines of motifs Working in the same way, join 4 more motifs at each side.

6th and 7th lines of motifs Working in the same way, join 3 more motifs at each side.

Tie Make 4 chain. Work 3 double crochet stitches into the first chain. Continue in double crochet on these 4 stitches until tie measures 35½in (90cm), take 4 double crochet together and fasten off.

To complete Allowing top motifs of 2nd and 3rd lines to fold back for the collar, wrap cape over shoulders, slip tie through the next two free spaces, and fasten the front with a bow.

buttercup square

If you'd like to make a Buttercup blanket, use this way of combining the five-petal flowers to make a neat square with an easy-to-join openwork edging. You could also adapt this method of making a composite block to other motifs, such as the Daisy or the Pansy.

size
4¾ x 4¾in (12 x 12cm)

materials
For each square:
- small amounts of wool or wool-mix DK weight yarn in green (A) and yellow (B)
- E/4 (3.50mm) crochet hook

abbreviations
ch = chain; sc = single crochet; dc = double crochet; rep = repeat; RS = right side; ss = slip stitch; sp = space, [ ] = work instructions in square brackets as directed.

Buttercups Using colors as given, make 4 Buttercup motifs as given on page 12 in the Flowers section.

Leaving 3 petals free at outer edge, sew two petals of adjacent flowers together, as shown in the picture.

Center Using A, make 4ch, ss in first ch to form a ring.

1st round (RS) 1ch, 1sc in ring, 3ch, taking hook behind ss around the stem of center free dc of one petal, 3ch, [1sc in ring, 3ch, taking hook behind ss around the stem of center free dc of next petal, 3ch] 7 times, ss in first sc.

Fasten off.

Edging Taking hook behind join A around the stem of center dc of one corner petal

1st round (RS) 1ch, 1sc in same place as join, 7ch, taking hook behind 1sc around the stem of center dc of next petal] 11 times, 7ch, ss in first sc.

2nd round 7ch, 1dc in same place as ss, * [2ch, 1dc in 7ch sp] twice, 2ch, 1dc in next sc, rep from * twice **, 4ch, 1dc in same sc as last dc, ***, rep from * to *** 2 more times, then rep from * to ** omitting last dc, ss in 3rd ch.

Fasten off.

two-color spirals belt

This dramatic belt uses the Two-color Spiral on page 56 of the Shapes section, to make a Celtic-style design.

size
35½in (90cm) excluding ties

materials
• 1 x 50g ball of matt cotton DK in each of cream (A) and black (B)

• E/4 (3.50mm) crochet hook.

gauge
Each spiral motif measures 3⅛in (8cm) across using cotton DK weight yarn and 3.50mm hook. Change hook size, if necessary, to obtain this tension.

note
• Although each motif should measure 3⅛in (8cm) across, overlapping the 12 motifs gives a belt that measures 35½in (90cm), not including the ties. You can try the belt on as you make it and if you want a larger or a smaller belt, make more or less motifs. If your belt has an odd number of motifs, you'll find that you need to make one motif with a tie in A and one in B.

Belt Leaving ends about 6in (15cm) long each time you fasten off, make 10 Two-color Spiral motifs.

Ties On the 11th motif work as given but do not fasten off the B yarn. Work a double crochet chain by placing the hook under the two strands at the side of the previous double crochet in B each time to work a chain of 30 double crochet. Fasten off.

Work 12th motif in the same way.

To complete Matching colors and placing motifs with ties at each end, overlap the row-ends of the spirals. Using the ends left when fastening off, over-sew two stitches together at each side of the join.

hexagon hat

This six-sided hat is based on the Double Crochet Hexagon motif on page 105 of the Geometric section. In chunky yarn with a big hook, it took just a couple of hours to complete.

size
22in (56cm) around brim

materials
• 1 x 100g ball of pure wool chunky yarn

• M/13 (9.00mm) crochet hook

gauge
7 stitches and 4 rounds to 4in (10cm) over double crochet, 7½ stitches to 4in (10cm) over single crochet both using chunky wool and 9.00mm hook. Change hook size, if necessary, to obtain these tensions.

Crown Work the three-round Double Crochet Hexagon. Increasing as set, work another round to give a total of 48 stitches. Work 3 rounds straight.

Brim Continue in single crochet, decrease to 42 sts by missing every 8th stitch on the next round. Work 3 more rounds straight. Fasten off.

To complete Darn in ends. Roll up brim.

flower and lace motifs t-shirt

Choose your favorite openwork motifs and work them on fine thread to give a designer touch to a simple Tee. For smaller motifs, work just the first couple of rounds before fastening off.

daisy cardigan

Give a designer touch to a hand-knit cardigan by scattering Daisy motifs as given on page 16 of the Flowers section, on a spring green background.

materials

• a hand knit or ready-made cardigan

• approximately 5g smooth 4ply cotton in yellow (A)

• approximately 15g same in warm white (B)

• No. 5 steel (1.75mm) crochet hook

gauge

Each Daisy measures 1¾in (4.5cm) across using 4ply cotton and No. 5 steel (1.75mm) hook. Change hook size, if necessary, to obtain this size motif.

note

• The cardigan used in the sample is from the *Debbie Bliss Pure Silk Pattern Book*.

Motifs Using A and B, make a dozen Daisy motifs.

To complete For a random design, scatter the daisies on the fronts of the cardigan, pin in place, then sew on using matching sewing thread and a fine, sharp needle.

stars blanket

Joining five-sided motifs can be tricky but if you'd like to make a blanket using the Star motif on page 58 of the Shapes section, all you need to do to make a flat fabric is to fill in the gaps with diamonds and hexagons. Once you've made this piece you'll be able to see how to add more rings of stars and filler motifs to make whatever size blanket you want. To help plan ahead, stick paper stars on graph paper to create your own design.

size
Block: 20½in (52cm) across

materials
For the block as shown:

• 2 x 50g balls of wool mix DK weight yarn in each of cream (A) and duck egg (B)

• E/4 (3.50mm) crochet hook

gauge
Each Star motif measures 3¾in (9.5cm) from the center to the tip of a point using wool mix DK weight yarn and E/4 (3.50mm) hook. Change hook size, if necessary, to obtain this tension.

Stars Using A, make 6 Star motifs.

Diamonds (Make 5) Using B, make 3 chain. Work 2 double crochet stitches in 3rd chain from hook, continue in double crochet on these 3 stitches, increase by working 2 double crochet in first and last stitch of every row until there are 15 stitches, then decrease by taking 2 double crochet together at each end of every row until one stitch is left. Fasten off.

Hexagons (Make 5) Using B, work the 3-round Double Crochet Hexagon as given on page 105 of the Geometric section, don't fasten off after the 3rd round, work 3 more rounds increasing as set, the last round will have 9 double crochet between increases and a total of 72 stitches.

To complete Place the stars flat with the points touching, fill the inner ring spaces with 5 diamonds and the outer ring spaces with 5 hexagons. With right side facing, sew motifs together.

double crochet squares jacket

Here's that useful Double Crochet Square motif from the Geometric section again (see page 92). Tipped at an angle, it makes a more flexible shape for creating a flowing jacket with a pointed edge. Alternating colors, arrange the squares in rows working from cuff to cuff using the diagonal edges to add movement to the underarm and to shape a V neck. Leave the front edges free to flutter or fill them in and add a border.

little flowers card

You can say it with flowers on so many occasions. This pretty card uses the Little Flower motif on page 13 of the Flowers section and is just right for Mother's Day, birthdays, and weddings.

size

4⅛ x 6in (10.5 x 15cm)

materials

• stranded embroidery cotton in pink, orange, peach, and green

• No. 6 steel (1.50mm) crochet hook

• 4⅛ x 6in (10.5cm x 15cm) blank white card

• 8 tiny yellow beads

• 4 little buttons

• 8in (20cm) narrow satin ribbon

• 18in (45cm) narrow lacy trimming

• sharp needle and white sewing thread

note

• Use all six strands of the embroidery thread together.

Large flowers Working both rounds of the Little Flower motif, make 1 orange and 1 peach flower.

Small flowers Working the first round of the Little Flower motif only, make 1 orange, 2 pink, and 3 green flowers.

To complete Open out the card and measuring equally from each corner of front pierce holes, sewing through the card and joining the lacy trimming at one corner, make a frame. Sew buttons on the corners of the frame. Arrange the flowers and stitch through the card to hold them in place with a bead in the center of each flower. Using green, make 3 short straight stitches for the upper stems and 3 longer stitches for the lower stems. Tie the satin ribbon in a bow, trim ends, and sew on card.

bow bag

Make a funky felt boxy bag and decorate the front with the Bow motif on page 84 of the Pictures section.

size

Approximately 10¼ x 8½ x 2¾in (26 x 22 x 7cm), excluding handle

you will need

• 1 x 50g ball of Debbie Bliss Cotton DK in each of light pink, dark pink, and cream

• E/4 (3.50mm) crochet hook

• 1 piece 11x 39½in (28 x 100cm) heavy pink felt for the back and front

• 2 pieces 3⅛ x 19¾in (8 x 50cm) same for the gussets and handle

• sharp needle, pink and cream sewing thread

gauge

Bow motif measures 8 x 7in (20 x 18cm) using Debbie Bliss Cotton DK and E/4 (3.50mm) hook. Change hook size, if necessary, to obtain this tension.

Motif Using light pink for the first 2 rows and dark pink for the last row of the ribbon and cream for the background, work the bow motif.

Bag Using pink thread, seam the short ends of the back and front piece and place seam to inside center so the folds form the top edges of the bag. Mark center of one short end of each gusset and placing markers to line up with seam, set gussets so that back and front of bag each measures approximately 10¼ x 8½in (26 x 22cm). Join the ends of the gusset pieces, then roll and stitch to make the handle.

To complete Using cream thread, stitch the motif on the front of the bag.

trefoil and heart cards

A handmade card is always special. Wish someone Good Luck by adding another leaf to the Trefoil Leaf motif on page 62 to make a four leaf clover design, or show how you feel on St Valentine's day with a Swirling Heart, from page 55 of the Shapes section.

sheep scarf

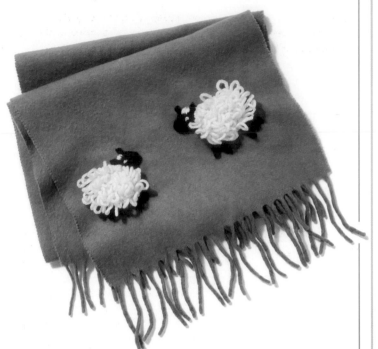

If you're into woolly thinking, decorate a plain lambswool scarf with a pair of Sheep motifs from page 70 of the Pictures section.

size
Scarf: 12 x 55in (30 x 140cm), excluding fringes

materials
- small amounts of wool DK weight yarn in each of cream (A), black (B), and yellow (C)
- E/4 (3.50mm) crochet hook
- green scarf
- sharp needle, cream and black sewing thread

Motifs Using A, make 2 bodies. Using B, make 2 heads.

To complete Using cream thread, sew bodies on scarf. Using black sewing thread and placing heads to center, sew on heads. Using A, B, and C, embroider details as given for motif.

violets posy

Combine Violets from page 6 of the Flowers section with the Leaf motif without the ladybug on page 81 of the Shapes section, to make a pretty posy to pin on your lapel.

waves and sailboats blanket

For a nautical theme, combine the Waves and Sailboat motifs from pages 74 and 82 of the Pictures section. To work out how the squares fit together, first make one of each motif. If they're not the same size, adjust the amount of stitches or rows on the sailboat so it matches the size of the waves.

star decoration

For a pretty decoration to hang on the Christmas tree or in a window, make the Star motif from page 58 of the Shapes section, in metalic thread and stiffen the edges with wire.

size
5½in (14cm) across from point to point

materials
- small amount of metalic gold 4ply yarn
- No. 5 steel (1.75mm) crochet hook
- copper wire
- gold plated bead and jump ring

Motif Make star motif.

To complete
Overlapping ends, bend copper wire to fit around the edge of the star. Work a round of double crochet over the wire and into the edge of the star. Sew bead and jump ring on the top point, then thread a length yarn through the jump ring and knot ends to hang up star.

trees four seasons picture

Adapt the motifs from the Pictures section to make a tree for each season. Work the Apple Tree on page 79 in soft spring colors and embroider flowers instead of apples, use fall shades for the Winter Tree on page 86, and substitute falling leaves for the snowflakes.

millefiore brooch

It takes just a few minutes to crochet the Millefiore flower motifs on page 6 of the Flowers section, so this pretty brooch is very quick to make.

size
Approximately 2⅜in (6cm) across

materials
• small amounts of wool DK weight yarn in pink and blue
• E/4 (3.50mm) crochet hook
• 2 green sequins and 2 tiny beads
• sharp needle and matching thread
• brooch pin
• glue

gauge
Each Millefiore flower measures 1⅜in (3.5cm) using wool DK weight yarn and E/4 (3.50mm) hook. Change hook size, if necessary, to obtain this size flower.

Motifs Working just 5 petals each time, make one Millefiore flower in pink and one in blue.

To complete Sew a sequin in the center of each flower, held in place with a bead. Overlapping the flowers, attach them to the brooch pin with glue.

holly leaves card

Send a personal Christmas greeting with this quick-to-make card. The simple design uses the Holly Leaf motif from page 65 of the Shapes section, with a few red beads to add that festive touch.

size
4⅛ x 6in (10.5 x 15cm)

materials
• metallic 4ply yarn in green
• C/2 (2.50mm) crochet hook
• 4⅛ x 6in (10.5 x 15cm) blank white card
• gold embroidery thread
• sharp needle and red sewing thread
• 3 red beads

gauge
Each Holly Leaf motif measures approximately 2⅜in (6cm) from stalk to tip. Using C/2 (2.50mm) crochet hook and metallic 4ply. Change hook size, if necessary, to obtain this size motif

note
• The leaves lean to the left, so turn one over to make a pair.

Motifs Make 2 Holly Leaf motifs as given on page 65 of the Shapes section.

To complete Open out the card and, measuring equally from each corner of front, pierce holes and stitch a gold thread frame. Arrange the leaves and sew in place with the metallic green yarn. Using red thread, sew on the beads for berries.

victorian bedspread square pillow

This luscious motif joins to give a richly textured diamond pattern. Start by making the pillow front shown here and you could get hooked and keep going until you've made enough squares for a bedcover.

size
16½ x 16½in (42 x 42cm), excluding edging

materials
• 5 x 50g balls of Debbie Bliss Cashmerino Aran in cream, shade 01

• F/5 (4.00mm) crochet hook

• 17¾ x 17¾in (45 x 45cm) pillow pad with cover

gauge
Each motif measures 5½ x 5½in (14 x 14cm) using Cashmerino Aran and F/5 (4.00mm) hook. Change hook size, if necessary, to obtain this size square.

abbreviations
dc = double crochet; ch = chain; rep = repeat; sp = space; ss = slip stitch; [ ] = work instructions in square brackets as directed.

note
• Instructions are for the pillow front only. If you want to make another square for the back, you'll need twice as much yarn.

Front Make 9 Victorian Bedspread Squares as given on page 99 in the Geometric section. Join squares with double crochet worked on the wrong side so the ridges do not spoil the pattern.

Edging Join yarn in a corner 3ch sp, * 4ch, 2dc in 3rd ch from hook, ss in next 1ch sp along motif, [4ch, 2dc in 3rd ch from hook, miss 2 sts, ss in next dc] 3 times, 4ch, 2dc in 3rd ch from hook, ss in next sp, 4ch, 2dc in 3rd ch from hook, ss in seam, rep from * two more times, working last ss in next corner 3ch sp, then rep from * along remaining 3 sides.

Fasten off.

To complete Darn in ends. Sew pillow front on to a ready-made pillow.

little piggies top

Perk up the pockets of a baby's jacket with sugar pink pigs worked from the Little Piggy on page 74 of the Pictures section. Adapt the idea to use other animal motifs to decorate children's garments.

size
To fit: age 3 to 6 months

materials
- a baby's jacket
- approximately 10g of pink pure wool DK weight yarn (A)
- small amounts of black (B), cream (C), and dark pink (D) embroidery wool
- C/2 (2.50mm) crochet hook

gauge
Each pig motif measures 2⅜in (6cm) across using wool DK weight yarn and C/2 (2.50mm) hook. Change hook size, if necessary, to obtain this size motif.

note
If you're decorating a garment for an older child, scale up the motif by using a larger hook.

Motif Using A and the Little Piggy design, make two bodies and two heads. Using A, catch down the ears. Using B and C for the eyes and D for the nostrils, embroider features on each head. This jacket is too fluffy to embroider the legs and tail, so work little strips of single crochet 4 stitches long for each leg and make a chain length for each tail and sew on body.

To complete Placing heads to the center, sew pigs on the pockets.

chick sketch book

Personalize a sketchbook or a notebook with a cute Chick as given on page 85 of the Pictures section.

materials
- small amounts of wool DK weight yarn in yellow (A), blue (B), and deep blue (C)
- embroidery wool in rust and brown
- E/4 (3.50mm) crochet hook
- 6 x 4½in (15 x 11cm) sketchbook
- double-sided sticky tape

gauge
The Chick motif measures 3⅜ x 3⅜in (8.5 x 8.5cm) using wool DK weight yarn and E/4 (3.50mm) hook. Change hook size, if necessary, to obtain this size motif.

Motif Work the chick motif.

To complete Leaving a little border, stick the motif on the front of the sketchbook.

tigers hat

Join Tiger motifs from page 70 of the Pictures section in a band to fit around the head, then work around the top edge for the crown of the hat and add earflaps and an edging. Finish the top with a pompom.

poppies on hat

Make a bunch of flowers to add a finishing touch to a felt hat. All these flowers are based on the Poppy Medallion on page 16 of the Flowers section.

size
The large poppy measures approximately 4in (10cm) across

materials
• a felt hat
• small amounts of wool DK weight yarn in dark brown (A), mid-brown (B), and cream (C)
• E/4 (3.50mm) crochet hook

Large poppy Using the colors as given, work the first 5 rounds and the petals as given for the Poppy motif.

Small poppies Varying the order of the colors, make two smaller flowers by fastening off after the 5th round.

To complete Arrange the poppies with the larger flower in the center and the smaller flowers each side, and pin or sew on the side of the hat.

trefoil square dreamcatcher

Cleanse and energize your home with a dreamcatcher hanging at a window to catch and reflect the light. This design uses some of the rounds from the Trefoil Square on page 41 of the Lace section.

size
Approximately 4¾in (12cm) across

mateials
• thin metal ring 2½in (6.5cm) across
• 1 x 5 meter spool of DMC Desire memory thread in each of cream (A) and turquoise (B)
• No. 5 steel (1.75mm) crochet hook
• 12 silvery beads and 7 glass beads in assorted shapes and sizes
• a silver jump ring and a length of silver thread

note
• Pull the stitches and chain tight, as there is just enough thread in the two spools of thread to make the dreamcatcher.

1st round Using A, make 64 single crochet stitches over the wire ring.

2nd round Using B, work the 4th round of the Trefoil square motif but working each group of chain loops on every 8th single crochet stitch instead of every 4th.

3rd round Join A in a 4 chain space and work the 5th round of the Trefoil square but with 5 chain between each single crochet stitch.

To complete Using strong, fine thread and a sharp needle, sew on a bead and jump ring at the top, a string of beads across the center, and hanging beads around the edges of the design. Slip the silver thread through the jump ring, knot to make a loop, and trim the ends.

goldfish bath mat

For a fun bathmat, scale up the size of the Goldfish motif on page 78 of the Pictures section, by working it in super chunky yarn with a giant hook.

size
Approximately 23 x 28½in (58 x 72cm)

materials
- 2 x 100g balls of Sirdar Bigga in Blue Suede, shade 694 (A)
- 5 x 100g balls same in Cream, shade 685 (B)
- P/16 (12mm) crochet hook

gauge
5½ sts to 4in (10cm) over single crochet in the round using Bigga and 12mm hook. Change hook size, if necessary, to obtain this size motif.

Center Work the goldfish motif as given until the 6th round of the water background has been completed. Continue in single crochet increasing at the corners in the same way as before, work 2 more rounds B.

Border Work 1 round in A and 2 rounds in B, turning for the last round before fastening off.

To complete Embroider eye in A with B for center. Darn in ends.

framed flowers scarf

Scale up the size of the Framed Flower motif from page 23 of the Flowers section, by working it in a soft, chunky wool. Work the squares all in the same color, join them with a double crochet and two chain zigzag, then add an edging and fringe to each end.

baby's blocks diamond illusion boxes

The trick to creating this classic illusion effect of boxes with the little Baby's Blocks Diamond on page 66 of the Shapes section, is to use three distinct tones, in this example, cream, blue and navy.

size
Each 3 diamond box: 4 x 4¾in (10 x 12cm)

materials
• small amounts of wool or wool-mix DK weight yarn in cream (A), blue (B), and navy (C)
• E/4 (3.50mm) crochet hook

gauge
Each diamond measures 2⅜ x 3½in (6 x 9cm) using wool or wool-mix DK weight yarn and E/4 (3.50mm) hook. Change hook size, if necessary, to obtain this size diamond.

First box Make a Baby's Blocks Diamond in each of A, B, and C. With A at the top, B on the left and C on the right, sew the diamonds together, making sure that the chain loops of the edging are on the right side. Make as many boxes as required for your design.

Joining boxes Always assemble the boxes with the colors in the same order and, making sure that the chain loops are on the right side to outline each diamond, continue to assemble boxes and join them together in rows.

buttercups and daisies in a jar

Make a handful of Buttercup and Daisy motifs from pages 12 and 16 of the Flowers section, then fill out the back and add a covered wire stem to each flower. Display the flowers in a jam jar for an authentic country feel.

two-color square designs

The Two-color Square from page 105 of the Geometric section is easy to do but when you put motifs together the results can look very complex. Try these ways of arranging the squares to create patchwork designs. Assemble them in pairs and join in rows to make a Wild Goose Chase, alternate the colors to make a larger Pinwheel square, or join 16 motifs to make a Pieced Star.

baby's blocks diamond blazing star

Join the same little Baby's Blocks Diamonds as those used for Illusion Boxes in a different way to make a grand six-pointed star.

size
Star: 14⅛in (36cm) across

materials
• small amounts of wool DK weight yarn in each of red (A), orange (B), cream (C), and yellow (D)
• E/4 (3.50mm) crochet hook

gauge
Each diamond measures 2⅜ x 3½in (6 x 9cm) using wool DK weight yarn and E/4 (3.50mm) hook. Change hook size, if necessary, to obtain this size diamond.

note
• Continue adding more diamonds to make a larger motif or fill in the spaces around the edges with squares at the corners and triangles at the sides to make a square block.

Diamonds Make 3 in each of A and B, 12 in C, and 6 in D.

Star Sewing the diamonds together with the chain loops of the double crochet edging on the right side, alternate A and B diamonds to make a six-pointed center star, join two C diamonds in each space between the points. Fill the gaps with diamonds in D.

the techniques

Working with the motifs in this book gives you so many choices. You can mix and match them to create your own unique patchwork fabrics for coverlets, cushions, or afghans, assemble motifs to make garments, or use individual motifs to make cards or add a personal touch to a present.

WORKING WITH MOTIFS

These motifs are very adaptable. You can create an effect with just one picture, choose a simple geometric shape and be inspired by the colors and designs of fabric patchwork for a long-term project, scale up the motifs in thick yarn for a speedy result, or go for a lightweight look in fine cotton or mohair. You may combine motifs for a crazy patchwork throw but to make a flat fabric, it's best to choose shapes that fit together exactly. Squares, triangles, diamonds, and hexagons tessellate neatly. Other shapes may need another motif to fill the gaps when joining them.

Motifs are so practical in today's busy lifestyle. A crochet hook and yarn are very light and portable. Many motifs are small or repetitive, so it's easy to remember what to do. The work goes quickly and the feeling of achievement starts early and is renewed with each motif completed.

All the motifs in this book were worked using wool or wool-mix DK weight yarn and a 3.50mm hook. No sizes are given for the individual motifs as they may take on a totally different appearance in other yarns. So when you're creating your own design, it's up to you to get a finished fabric that you feel is right for the way you want to use your chosen motif.

FOLLOWING THE INSTRUCTIONS

working the stitches

If you've never tried crochet before, use a smooth, medium-weight, light-colored yarn and a medium-sized hook to try out the basic stitches given on the following pages before starting a project.

measurements

Where motifs are used to make a design in the projects section, the yarn, hook size, and tension are given. Obtaining the exact tension or size of motif is crucial if making a garment, perhaps less so when working a coverlet or afghan.

For the garments, "to fit" sizes are given as a guide only, but check that you will be happy with the finished actual measurements as the amount of movement room varies according to the design.

If you're working out your own design, make and assemble a few motifs, measure them, and plan how many you'll need on graph paper or work free-style by comparing them to an existing garment.

you will need

For the projects, the yarn amounts given are based on the quantity of yarn used to make the original item. Yarn amounts for the scrap yarn projects are approximate as the same weight yarns in different brands may vary depending on the fiber content. To estimate the amount of yarn you'll need for your own design, see how many motifs you can make from one ball of yarn. Work out how many motifs you need to make in total and divide this by

the amount per ball to give you an idea of the number of balls of yarn to buy.

gauge

The size of the hook used is one factor in controlling the size of your motifs, the other is how you hold the yarn. If your motif is too big, try again using a smaller size hook, or wrap the yarn two or more times around the middle finger when tensioning the yarn to release it more slowly. If your motif is too small, try again using a larger hook and also, perhaps, allow the yarn to slip more freely through the fingers.

brackets

For both the motifs and projects, instructions in square brackets should be repeated as indicated. Square brackets are also used to clarify working a group of stitches. One or more asterisks are used to indicate a repeat or a part of the instructions to work again.

how to read the charts

Wherever it is helpful, the motif instructions are given in charted form as well as written out in full. Work from one or both, as necessary. Charts are a way of showing the stitches as symbols that create a diagram picture of the design. Most of the charted motifs in this book are worked in rounds. These charts start with a linear circle for working into a ring of yarn or a circle of chain stitches in the center, with the symbols arranged in rounds, read anticlockwise, radiating outward. Some motifs are worked in rows. For these, begin with the starting chain at the lower edge, then continue reading the rows upward to the top edge of the chart.

symbols

Each symbol represents a stitch or group of stitches.These are the basic symbols, but because crochet fabric is flexible, sometimes the symbols will vary in size, be stretched, spaced out, or squashed to accommodate the stitches.

Note how the number of diagonal bars across the longer T shapes shows the number of times to wrap the yarn around the hook at the start of the stitch.

o	ch = chain
+	sc = single crochet
T	hdc = half double crochet
⊤	dc = double crochet
⊤	tr = treble crochet
⊤	dtr = double treble
⊤	trtr = triple treble
●	ss = slip stitch

These symbols can be modified. For instance, working around the stem is indicated by a hook on the end of the symbol; longer stitches have an arrow on the end. Where stitches are taken together, the symbols are joined with a single bar. When stitches are joined to make a popcorn, the symbol has an oval at the top as in the following examples:

 3dctog = leaving last loop of each st on hook, work 3dc, yarn over hook and pull through 4 loops on hook

 5dcpc = work 5dc in same place, remove hook, insert hook in first of the 5dc, catch loop and pull through to close popcorn

In the alphabet, and occasionally elsewhere, symbols show where the motif starts and ends, and where to join yarn.

- ↰ start
- ↳ end
- ✳ join yarn

holding the hook

Hold the hook like a pencil with the shaft above your hand, your grip should be light so you can easily extend the hook in a forward and back motion.

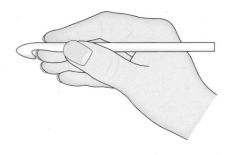

holding the yarn

Make a slip knot on the hook, then catch the yarn that goes to the ball around the little finger of the left hand. Bring the hook toward you to take the yarn over the fingers and hold the tail end of yarn from the slip knot between first finger and thumb. Extend the middle finger to make a space for the hook to catch the yarn. As you make stitches, allow the yarn to ease through the fingers and move the work to keep a grip near the place that a new stitch will be made. If working with fine or slippery yarn, wrap the yarn more times around the middle finger.

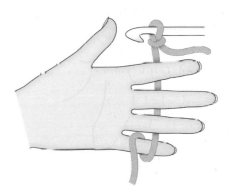

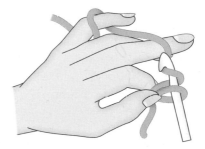

stitch reference

Crochet is a two-handed craft with the left hand tensioning the yarn and holding the work while the right hand uses the hook. Because the left hand does a lot of work, most left-handed people find that they are comfortable working this way but if preferred, left-handers could reverse the actions, reading left for right and right for left, using a mirror if necessary to check the illustrations.

making a slip knot

A slip knot is needed to start some of the motifs and projects. It is not counted as a stitch.

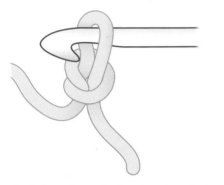

Make a loop in the yarn, insert the hook and catch the back strand of the yarn. Pull a loop through, then gently pull on both ends to tighten the knot and close the loop on the hook.

chain stitch

Chain stitch may be used as a foundation for other stitches, to make spaces, or to reach the height of the other stitches when working in rounds or rows.

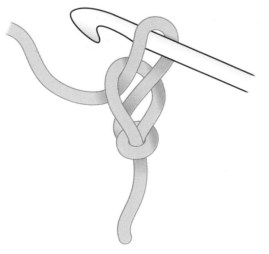

With the hook in front of the yarn, dip the tip to take the yarn over the hook from the back to the front and catch the yarn. This is called yarn over hook and is a basic movement for all crochet stitches. Draw a new loop through the loop on the hook to make a new chain loop.

working into a ring of yarn

This way of starting a motif makes a neat, unobtrusive center. Always darn in the end securely.

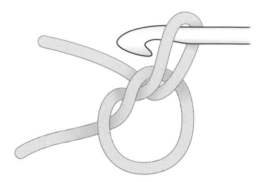

Wind the yarn once around the first finger of left hand. Insert hook in ring, yarn over hook and pull through ring, yarn over hook and pull through to make the first chain. Work stitches into the ring, then pull the end to tighten the ring before joining the round.

joining chain stitches in a round

Chain gives a very firm start. Three or four chains will give a small hole at the center, more chain will give a larger hole.

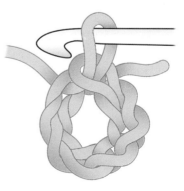

Make the number of chain stitches given in the instructions. Insert hook in first chain, yarn over hook and pull through the first chain and the loop on the hook.

double crochet

Wrapping the yarn around before inserting the hook makes a longer stitch.

1 Yarn over hook, insert hook into chain or stitch indicated in the instructions. Yarn over hook, pull through the stitch to make three loops on the hook. Yarn over hook, pull through the first two loops on the hook, so making two loops on the hook.

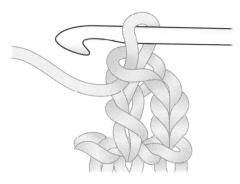

2 Take the yarn over the hook again and pull through the two loops, so ending with one loop on the hook.

half double crochet

This stitch is made in the same way as double crochet, but it is shorter.

Work as given for double crochet until there are three loops on hook. Yarn over hook and draw through three loops on hook, so ending with one loop on the hook.

slip stitch

Slip stitch is the shortest stitch, it's used for joining stitches, to work to a new place in the stitch pattern, or to make a decorative surface crochet chain.

Insert hook into stitch and wrap yarn over hook. Draw a new loop through both the stitch and the loop on the hook, so ending with one loop on the hook.

single crochet

Single crochet is made in the same way as a slip stitch but with an extra step, giving a stitch that is almost square.

1 Insert hook into chain or stitch indicated in the instructions, yarn over hook and draw the yarn through the stitch to make two loops on the hook.

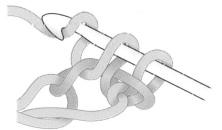

2 Yarn over hook and draw through two loops on hook, so ending with one loop on the hook.

fastening off

The first method is the most usual way of fastening off but it can be hard to hide the join when working in rounds. The second method makes a neat finish, especially when working motifs.

After the last stitch, pull another loop through, cut yarn, and pull end through.

After the last stitch, cut yarn and pull end through, thread the end under the top loops of the first stitch in the round, then back down through the last stitch. Darn in end very securely.

stitch variations

Stitches are usually worked under two strands of the starting chain or under both strands at the top of a stitch but the following give different effects.

insert hook into one strand only

This can be used to work into both sides of a starting chain, to open up a fabric or to make a ridge. Simply take the hook under one strand, either at the front or at the back of the stitch.

insert hook between stitches

This can be used to make a neat edging or it can open up the fabric and make it quicker to work. The hook is placed, as directed, between the stitches of the previous row.

insert hook in the side of a stitch

This is used when closing a picot or to make a single or a double crochet chain. For a single chain, make a slip knot and two chains. Insert hook in first chain and work a single crochet stitch. For each following stitch, insert hook under the threads at the side of the previous stitch. For a double chain, make a slip knot and three chains. Take the yarn over the hook, then insert hook in third chain and complete the double crochet in the usual way. For each following stitch, insert the hook under two strands at the base of the previous stitch. Single and double crochet chains make a more flexible edge than an ordinary starting chain and are easier to count.

working around the stem

Any type of crochet stitch can be worked around the stem of a stitch instead of into the top loops. Taking the hook to the front will make the stitch lie on the surface of the work to give a textured effect. Taking the hook behind will cause the fabric of the previous row to lift forward, as when working the petals of a flower. To work around the stem, take the hook in front or behind and insert it from right to left around the stem of the designated stitch in previous row, then complete the stitch.

working longer stitches

Longer stitches are worked in the same way as a double crochet but with one more wrapping of the yarn around the hook each time, so giving one more step when drawing through two loops at a time.

Here's the number of times to wrap the yarn around the hook when making these longer stitches:

Treble	twice
Double treble	three
Triple treble	four

turning chain

Each row or round needs something at the beginning to take the hook up to the height needed to work the following stitches. In this book, the chain before a single crochet row or round is not counted as a stitch but the chain worked at the beginning of rows or rounds in double or longer stitches is counted as the first stitch. For a neater edge or join, a single crochet stitch is often substituted for the first chain. When working in rounds, always join in the top chain of the first stitch. When working in row, always turn the work in the same direction.

Here's the number of chain or chain and single crochet usually needed at the start of a row or round.

Single crochet (sc)	1 chain
Half double crochet	2 chain or 1sc and 1 chain
Double crochet	3 chain or 1sc and 2 chain
Treble	4 chain or 1sc and 3 chain

grouping stitches

Stitches of any length can be grouped or worked together to increase or decrease the number of stitches in a row or for a decorative effect.

increase, fan, or shell

Working two or more complete stitches into the same stitch can be a method of increasing to shape a fabric, part of a decorative stitch pattern, or an edging. Any stitch can be used and the amount of stitches worked varies. In this example, three double crochet stitches are worked into one stitch in the row below.

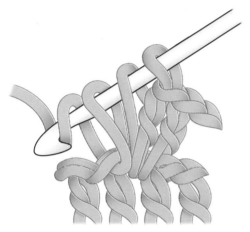

Inserting the hook in the same stitch each time, work three double crochet stitches. Because the stitches are held together at the bottom but not at the top, the extra stitches make a fan shape.

decrease or cluster

Working two or more part stitches and taking them together at the top to make one stitch gives a decrease when working a fabric or a cluster in a stitch pattern. The example shows decreasing by taking three double crochet stitches together.

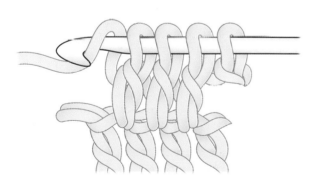

Leaving the last loop of each stitch on the hook, work a double crochet stitch into each of the next three stitches, so making four loops on the hook. Yarn over hook and pull through all four loops to join the stitches together at the top and make one loop on hook.

bobble

When a cluster is worked into one stitch, a bobble is made. The example shows three double crochet stitches worked together but if the stitches used for the bobble are longer than the background stitches, the bobble will stand away from the surface.

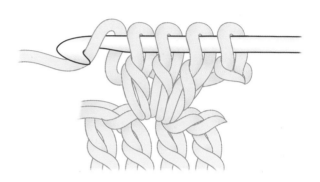

Yarn over hook and insert hook in stitch, yarn over hook and pull through. Do not complete the stitch, leave this last loop on the hook and work two more part double crochet stitches each time leaving one more loop on the hook, so making four loops on the hook. Yarn over the hook and pull through all four loops.

popcorn

This kind of bobble is made from complete stitches. The example shows five double crochet stitches worked in chain space and taken together but a popcorn can be placed in any stitch and be made up of any practical number or combination of stitches.

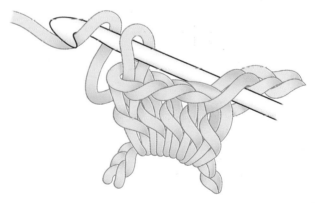

Inserting hook in same place each time, work five complete double crochet stitches. Slip hook out of last loop. Insert hook into the top of the first stitch, then into the last loop, yarn over hook and pull through.

creating a fabric

Although there are an infinite number of variations, basically, there are two ways of making a crochet fabric. Either the stitches can be made on a starting chain, and the work turned at the end of each row, or a series of motifs can be worked in the round and joined together.

working in the round

Many of the motifs shown throughout this book are worked from the center outward. The instructions will tell you if the starting point of the motif in the picture was a ring of chain or a ring made with a loop of yarn around the finger. If you prefer, you may substitute a few chain for the loop of yarn but you should be aware that the center of the motif will be more open.

When a single motif is worked in rounds without turning, the right side of the motif is always facing, so no indication of the right side is given in the instructions. Composite motifs have the right side indicated so that the following sections are joined correctly. It can help if you mark the right side with a loop of contrast yarn so that you can see at a glance which way up to hold the pieces when joining.

In order to create some of the shapes or to match stitch patterns worked in rows, motifs can be turned during or at the end of a round.

The motif instructions will tell you how to join at the end of each round and what stitches to work to match the height of the stitches in the next round.

Usually, rounds are joined with a slip stitch. For a less obtrusive join in some stitch patterns, simply remove the hook after working the last stitch in the round, insert it from the back in the first stitch, catch the loop, and then pull it right through to the back of the work.

working in rows

Rows of stitches can be worked into a foundation chain, or sometimes for a more flexible edge into picot loops. When counting the foundation chain, don't count the loop on the hook. The chain should be made quite loosely; tight chain will be difficult to work into and the edge will pull in. For an even, loose chain, use a hook one or two sizes larger.

When working into a foundation chain, take the hook under two strands of each chain loop unless instructed otherwise. Each row of the instructions will tell you where to place the hook and which stitch to work. Simply turn the work at the end of each row so that the right and the wrong sides face alternately. The instructions will tell you how many turning chain to work or how to cope with the edge stitches. Wherever possible, join in new yarn at the start of a row.

single crochet

A single chain is worked at the start of each round or row to bring the yarn up to the height needed to work in single crochet. This single chain is not worked into the following row, and it is not counted as a stitch.

double crochet

Double crochet rows often start with three chain to bring the yarn up to the height needed, this counts as a stitch and the first stitch of the previous row is missed to compensate. This can leave a gap between the first and second stitches so depending on the design, frequently the first chain is replaced with a single crochet worked directly into the first stitch, then two chain are worked to bring the yarn up to the height needed to work a round or row of double crochet.

finishing

joining motifs

Depending on the effect you want to create, motifs can be worked separately, then joined or they can be joined as the last round of each motif is worked.

sewing seams

The most unobtrusive way of joining is to sew the motifs together, working with the right side facing and taking the needle under a part stitch from each side each time, rather like sewing up knitting with mattress stitch.

More decorative sewing techniques include over-sewing pieces together, perhaps with a contrast color, and blanket-stitching around edges.

single crochet seams

For a firm, solid seam, single crochet makes a quick to work, simple join. Just take the hook through one stitch from each side together each time, tensioning the single crochet stitches so the seam lies flat. This will make a prominent ridge if worked on the right side or gives an effect similar to over-sewing if worked on the wrong side.

decorative joins

For a flexible, decorative zigzag join, work single crochet stitches alternately in stitches or spaces along each edge with one, two or more chain in between.

Lacy motifs with chain intervals in the last round are easily joined as they are worked by substituting a single crochet stitch in the appropriate space of the adjacent motif for the center stitch of a chain group.

Index

Note: Page numbers in **bold** refer to Projects

yarn suppliers

IN THE UNITED STATES

Debbie Bliss and Sirdar
Knitting Fever, Inc.
315 Bayview Avenue
Amityville, NY 11701
tel: 516 546 3600
www.knittingfever.com

IN CANADA

Debbie Bliss and Sirdar
Diamond Yarns
155 Martin Ross Avenue, Unit 3
Toronto, ON M3J 2L9
tel: 416 736 6111
www.diamondyarn.com

IN AUSTRALIA

Debbie Bliss
Prestige Yarns (PTY) Ltd.
P. O .Box 39
Bulli, NSW 2516
tel: 02 4285 6669
website: www.prestigeyarns.com

IN THE UNITED KINGDOM

Debbie Bliss Designer Yarns
Units 8–10
Newbridge Industrial Estate
Pitt Street
Keighley, West Yorkshire BD21 4PQ
tel: 01535 664222
www.designeryarns.uk.com

Sirdar
Sirdar Spinning Ltd
Flanshaw Lane
Alverthorpe
Wakefield
West Yorkshire WF2 9ND
tel: 01924 371501
www.sirdar.co.uk

For more about DMC embroidery
threads, visit www.dmc.com

author's acknowledgments

First of all, a huge thank you to Cindy Richards for seeing the potential of crochet motifs, asking me to do this book, believing that I would get it finished, and for giving me so much creative freedom.

Special thanks to Liz Dean for being so calm, holding it all together, and for the magical words; to Pete Jorgensen for his help, and to Sally Powell, not just an amazing art editor but a miracle worker with space.

Many thanks to everyone else who worked on this book including Geoff Dann for the photographs, Anthony Duke for artworking the charts, Ian Midson for the design, and Kate Haxell for editing, being so supportive and also for keeping track of the number of motifs and projects!

I cannot thank Sue Horan enough, not just for her patience, thoroughness, and professionalism in checking my instructions, but also for her involvement and support.

For creative help when things got tough, many thanks to Betty Speller for the Victorian Bedspread Square Cushion and the Christmas Slipper Socks, and to Lesley Stanfield for the Chick, Scottie Dog, Clematis, and Handbag motifs, the Basketweave Square and the Treble Square Afghan.

Thanks for the lovely yarns to Debbie Bliss and all at Designer Yarns, Caroline Powell and all at Sirdar and Sublime.

Thank you to Lester Hawksby for the plant pot.

Love and thanks to Peter Hawksby for artistic, emotional, and domestic support.